THE GROWNUP'S GUIDE TO
LIVING WITH
KIDS
IN
MANHATTAN

by
Diane Chernoff-Rosen & Lisa Levinson

Resource Marketing Group
New York, New York

Dedicated to
the memory of Janet Eddy Rosenthal

and to
Amanda, Drew, Oliver and Remi
whom we love dearly

◤

Published by Resource Marketing Group LLC
Library of Congress Catalogue Card Number 98-91399
ISBN 0-9663392-0-7

Book and cover design by Chris Hammill Paul
Manufactured in the United States of America

First Edition

10   9   8   7   6   5   4   3   2

Table of Contents

Chapter 1
CITY LIFE

Introduction

Manhattan is an incredible place to raise children. City life is not without its challenges, but once you learn to navigate your way through what this city has to offer to its youngest population and their parents, you begin to see just how manageable, if not terrific, family life in Manhattan can be.

This book was conceived after we, Manhattan parents of four children collectively, found ourselves spending our "free" time researching the things we needed to know as parents, such as selecting a pediatrician, locating parenting classes and hiring a babysitter, applying to nursery schools and then ongoing schools, finding activities for our children, locating children's stores and just generally getting around town. Need we go on?

The truth is that an energetic parent can indeed find

necessary information by tapping a variety of sources: word of mouth, giveaway publications, school bulletin boards, general New York City guides and travel guides and of course the telephone book. Unfortunately, most of the existing resources are narrowly focused, are paid advertiser publications, cover only particular neighborhoods or are too disparate to find without a lot of digging on your part. The problem is that every inquiry requires the use of our most precious and scarce resource—time. So, like the instruction manual you wish your child was born with, we longed for a comprehensive guide to living with kids in Manhattan that would take care of the basics.

Amazingly, with the tremendous resources this city has to offer, there existed no directory that compiled relevant information in a single volume geared toward making our jobs as parents in Manhattan not only somewhat easier but perhaps significantly more enjoyable. So we took to our computers and set about creating such a resource. We share with you the fruits of our labor and present to the harried parents of New York City, *The Grownup's Guide to Living with Kids in Manhattan*.

This is a guide for parents of children ages 0–12. It is not a resource guide for pregnancy and postpartum issues. Once you have your bundle of joy, or if your bundle of joy is becoming a bundle, we will show you how to get the best out of this wonderful city. Regrettably, this book will only take you through the preteen years. Once we have helped you successfully get your children that far, we wish you good luck because from what we hear, that is what you will need plenty of, no matter where you raise your kids.

Here is how to get going. Skim the book and the table of contents to become familiar with the material covered. The book is organized into 12 chapters covering specific topics. Each chapter is followed by a detailed section containing relevant resources. The chapters on children's activities and shopping resources are organized alphabetically for easy reference and followed by indices arranged by category. Certain chapters contain appendices with supplemental information not specifically covered elsewhere.

It is not our intention to serve solely as a telephone book, so if another source already exists that covers a specific subject, you will be directed to it. This is our way of making sure you are equipped for a given project without having to make this book a sequel to *War and Peace*.

Please note that we do not recommend specific individuals, businesses or services (medical practitioners, tutors, schools, agencies, classes, services, etc.). Because Manhattan is full of so many qualified people doing so many different jobs, it would be virtually impossible to check each one's credentials and capabilities or anticipate your goals and expectations in retaining someone's services or purchasing particular products. Our goal is to tell you how to find people, services and organizations and, where appropriate, how to determine whether they are properly credentialed or right for the situation you are seeking to address. Please note that all telephone numbers are 212 area code unless otherwise indicated.

Our hope is that this resource will enable you to draw on the best, most current and thorough information when making decisions. On that note, enjoy.

The Seven Principles of Living with Kids in Manhattan

Whether you are a New York City veteran or a recent arrival, once you become responsible for raising a child here, you quickly learn that city life with a child in tow is a far cry from your pre-child existence. You will discover many wonderful places and things about New York City about which you were previously unaware and find businesses, services and people you never knew existed. However, at the same time that you are delighting in all this city has to offer to its parents and children, you will also unfortunately learn that the Big Apple is not always child-friendly to its core and that living here with children can be hard work.

So how do you organize your life with children in this city to maximize the pleasure and minimize the pain? We have identified seven principles of living with kids in Manhattan that have helped us through many a tough moment. These rules of thumb were distilled from the experiences of many seasoned Manhattanites and are presented with the intention of making your life a little less complicated. Our seven principles are hardly the only coping strategies you will develop or rely on, but we hope that they provide a good starting point. At the very least, they can help you avoid some of the pitfalls and pratfalls of city life.

1 Know what works for you. Life in Manhattan can often feel like a test of your wits, and parents and others caring for children are hardly excused from the exam. In an attempt to be the best parents, aunts, uncles, and so forth we can be, we may seek advice from friends, colleagues, family, parent educators and parenting books. Often, we are more willing to follow the advice of others, who may or may not know us or our children, than to follow our own instincts. In any event, we frequently find ourselves trying to sort out what is the right way, the best way or even just some clue as to how to do something.

OK, so despite what the experts may say about letting your children sleep with you, your family of four somehow finds itself sleeping in the same bed somewhere around 4 a.m. As in all family matters, within the boundaries of basic health and safety, there are no right or wrong ways to parent here or anywhere else. Hence the first principle, **know what works for you.** What works for you may be different from what works for your friend or even all of your friends, but you know better than anyone else what you and your children can handle.

If you do not establish your own personal parenting limits, you will find that it is you, and not your child, who is having the temper tantrum in the middle of the supermarket. Take it from those who have been there, it is not a pretty place to be. Even when you must endure the disapproving looks and rolled-up eyes of others, feeling secure that you are doing what works best for your family will help you get through many a trying moment.

2 **Plan ahead.** So, knowing what works for you, you have determined that you can only handle three hours in the park. You are equipped with a portable potty or a mental map of the area coffee shops, stores or hotels with public rest rooms. You have mastered the art of diversion as you pass every candy store, toy store, fast food stop and ice cream vendor, but you forgot to factor in that it is rush hour and the crosstown bus to Central Park is jammed. The kids are getting antsy and you can tell that they need this outing to get off the ground. You stand at the bus stop, barely holding it together, hoping in vain for a taxi when it starts to rain. This brings us to the second principle, **plan ahead.**

Planning can make all the difference. This does not mean that you have to schedule the spontaneity out of your life, but it does mean that it is worth spending some time anticipating the logistics of your activities and the limitations of your children. The basics: when and where to eat and rest and dealing with boredom. Children inevitably get hungry, thirsty and tired at inopportune times. Depending on where you will be, consider packing snacks (or knowing where to procure one on short notice) or bringing the folding stroller. Many outings can be saved with a surprise treat or rest stop.

Dealing with a fidgety, bored child may be more of a challenge. It is always advisable to have something in your bag for your child to play with: crayons, books, lanyard, a

Walkman or anything else that is self-contained. Many problems can be avoided altogether by being realistic in your planning. Can a two-year-old really sit through a long movie? Will your three-year-old appreciate a guided tour of the Whitney Biennial? Can your five-year-old sit through a four-course dinner? Can your seven-year-old amuse him or herself while you get your passport renewed? Whenever possible, schedule your adult activities solo, but if you must bring your child, bring some entertainment with you.

Remember that children have a short attention span, lose interest in adult outings and do not graciously accept things like traffic, long lines, being closed out of a movie, bad weather, waiting for food in a restaurant or a change in plans. So whenever you can, think ahead, anticipate timing, and be aware of what causes your children to meltdown. With the right diversions, even a trip to the Department of Motor Vehicles can actually be fun . . . well, at least not a total disaster.

3 Never take more than you want to carry. Having observed the second principle, you have meticulously planned ahead. When it began to rain, you ducked into a coffee shop, got everyone a bagel, waited out rush hour and got a taxi. Invoking Plan B, you head to the Metropolitan Museum. You, your two children, the stroller, toys, baseball bat, rollerblades, juice boxes, snacks, hats, visors and sunglasses arrive at the Met. You know better than to schlep up all those lovely steps, so you enter at the street level. The problem is that you are carrying all that stuff. It is one thing to dump it in a pile at the park and quite another to drag it around a museum. You are in luck because you can check your things at the Met, but it does bring us to the third principle, **never take more than you can carry.**

Being prepared is a noble thing, but it is possible to be too prepared. In Manhattan, we walk a lot and when we are not walking, we are taking cabs, busses or riding in a hole in the ground to our destinations. You cannot count on your children to haul any of their gear for too long, and overloaded strollers tend to tip over as soon as your child leaps out. Worse yet, if you do not have a stroller, you will rapidly begin to resemble and feel like a pack mule. What to do? Be realistic about what you need for where you are going, pack accordingly and stick to your guns when the kids drag out more paraphernalia for you to carry.

4 **Make sure that you and anyone caring for your children is equipped to handle an emergency.** Despite the odds, you have a great outing. You return home and leave your children with the caregiver so that you can get that important assignment to Fed Ex before your cover as a freelancer is blown or just so you can have some grown-up time for yourself. You are barely out the door when your nine-year-old jumps off the couch and hits his or her head. While your caregiver is phoning the pediatrician, your three-year-old comes into the room with an empty bottle of cough medicine that he or she seems to have just swallowed. Now what? Fortunately for you, this would never be a problem. The three-year-old did not swallow the cough medicine because your home was properly childproofed and even if he or she had, the poison control number (and every other emergency number) is clearly posted. You have also sent your caregiver to an emergency care course and instructed her on emergency procedures.

Hence the fourth principle, **make sure that you and anyone caring for your children is equipped to handle an emergency.** This principle is not unique to New York parents, but it is especially important here. What is unusual about our city is the diversity of individuals with whom we share this city and in whose care we often leave our children. For that reason, you can never assume that what makes sense to you to do in an emergency will make sense to someone else. It is crucial to instruct caregivers as to how you want them to handle an emergency and give them the tools to do so, such as a list of people to call (and in what order), emergency money (for cab fare), instructions on how to handle themselves in an emergency room and, whenever possible, training in specific emergency procedures (such as CPR).

5 Safety first. Most New York City kids are very savvy, very early. By age six, most children are well versed on social issues such as homelessness and union strikes. It is, however, important to arm our children with the strategies needed to keep themselves safe. And though your child does not need to learn CPR, he or she does need to know age-appropriate safety basics and parents need to invoke the fifth principle, **safety first.**

While there are many specific things you can do to ensure your child's safety, most issues require a cautious, informed approach and a judgment call. For example, once you have checked a prospective babysitter's references, you must still rely on your instincts when deciding to hire. When sending your five-year-old to a new friend's house after school for the first time, you and your child might feel more comfortable if you or your babysitter tag along.

However, by a certain age, you will discover that it is not possible to be with your child at every turn to make those judgment calls and safety assessments. This is why we cannot emphasize enough to all parents, and Manhattan parents in particular, that the seeds you plant early on to help your children to develop judgment and a sense of confidence combined with caution will ultimately allow them to become responsible for themselves and their own safety.

6 Too much of a good thing can be too much. Remember how big your elementary school seemed when you were six years old? Well, imagine how big this city must feel at times to even a 12-year-old. Day in and day out, there is nonstop noise, visual stimulation and the routine of the day to get through. In addition, there are so many options available to fill our children's free time that it is often hard to avoid the temptation to overschedule them. By the age of seven, most city kids will have sampled an incredible number of extracurricular activities, from gymnastics to violin, and some will be deeply engaged in a particular discipline, such as dance, music, chess, or sports, to name only a few.

Whatever you or your child may choose to participate in, we urge you to keep in mind how very important it is to carve out time each day or, at the very least, each week, for your child to reflect and quietly contemplate, without a playdate, television or video game. And even if you believe that your child is destined to be the next Einstein or Martha Graham, remember that a personal balance comes only when there is a genuine desire on the part of the child to make a commitment to an activity or endeavor. With your guidance and sensibility, it is easy to let your children direct you as you help them to discover their own paths.

7 Attitude is everything. As you approach the job of parenting in Manhattan, or anywhere really, it is essential to remember the final principle, **attitude is everything.** Do not be dismayed when even the best laid plans run awry. Life is often 10% what happens to you and 90% how you react to it. Keeping your cool as Murphy's Law wreaks havoc on your day will certainly help you enjoy life's surprises, even if you are the one left picking up the pieces.

▶ **Biting into the Big Apple.** As big and impersonal as this city can seem at times, there is a piece of the Big Apple carved out especially for kids and it is delicious. Manhattan has never lacked the ability to dazzle the eyes of a child, but the place we call home is more than a candied apple. There is no denying that having made the choice to live here with your family, organizing your life in Manhattan with children requires much thought, patience, planning and a sense of humor, if not of the absurd.

To our minds, the price we pay to live in this great metropolis is well worth the value we, and our children, receive from the experience. We hope that our seven principles and the information you find in this book will help you and your family enjoy your New York community and eliminate some of the aggravation that comes with parenting and living in one of the biggest and most exciting cities in the world.

Chapter 2

HOMETOWN NEW YORK

The Big Apple shines for those who call it home. Somehow, despite all that the residents of the city must endure, there is a great sense of satisfaction in being part of a place that is so notoriously dynamic. The familiar refrain "If you can make it here, you can make it anywhere" is a driving force behind many a hard-working New Yorker.

The fast-paced city life to which we have become so accustomed affects how New Yorkers connect to our surroundings. Although Manhattan is packed with people and bustling with activity, there is not the automatic sense of community most often associated, rightly or wrongly, with the suburbs. Time is compressed, and acquaintances outnumber friendships built over time and from mutual support. The idea of the whole of New York as a "community" is, for most, an oxymoron. Yet there are many healthy, if diverse, communities thriving in Manhattan, waiting to be discovered.

▶ **Bringing up baby Manhattan style.** When you first become a parent, a strange metamorphosis begins to take place. Certainly in the first few months, new parents start to see the world with an altered perspective. For some, the air quality they endured for a decade becomes intolerable with the introduction of baby into their lives. For others, the long hours at work, which seemed so normal before, suddenly feel unhealthy.

For almost all new parents, the nesting instinct begins to extend beyond their apartment walls. Most parents quickly realize that without the support of friends, family, other parents and even community organizations, parenting would not only be lonely, but could drive a sane person totally mad. For as much as parenting is an individual experience, it is also very much a collective endeavor. As a result, parents begin looking for a community beyond the dry cleaner, video rental shop and greengrocer. So, while New York has virtually everything to offer, some things cannot be ordered up by phone. Community is one of them.

Each of us must find or develop our own sense of community through our interests, affiliations and, as our families grow, those of our children. However you create a sense of community for your family and however many disparate communities in which you find yourself participating (even in the course of a single day), you will discover over time that you are indeed a full-fledged community member.

Many parents who have decided to raise their families in New York City find themselves at a loss as to how to make the city their hometown. Surprisingly, each of Manhattan's neighborhoods has more of a sense of community than you might imagine. It is however, more or less up to the individual to seek it out. Depending on what stage your family is in, there are different ways to become involved. In this chapter, we will provide you with some suggestions and resources to draw upon to make New York your hometown. The rest is up to you. Remember, the more you put in, the more you get out.

▶ **You have a friend.** The best thing about setting out to become part of a community when you have kids is that you immediately eliminate the first major obstacle to making a connection—finding something in common. You have your children. You will be amazed at the number of people in your building, the park, children's classes, parenting groups, the pediatrician's office and even the gym that you will meet and become friendly with when you have small children. Especially for first-time parents, infant and parenting classes are great for developing friendships and feeling connected, not to mention having people with whom to compare notes on feeding, sleeping and car seats.

Relationships are sometimes forged in the most unlikely situations. When you ask couples how they met, you will hear many funny stories. There are couples who met at Fairway, in the Hamptons, at the gym or while working on the floor of the stock exchange on Black Monday. The same sort of thing occurs among families. Fathers meet at weekend Park Bench classes, nannies meet in the park and introduce the moms, mothers find each other at the Children's Museum.

Sometimes you connect with other parents simply because you are on the same circuit. You take your child to a Little Orchestra Society concert and sit next to a family with a child around the same age. Next you see them at the Museum of Natural History annual family party and maybe on several other occasions over the next few months. Before you know it, you are looking for each other at events and making playdates. If the kids hit it off, you may end up with a friend for life.

Once your children enter school, your family will automatically become part of the school community of families.

Fear not, the PTA is alive and well and always recruiting. Becoming active in the school is a wonderful way to make friends, achieve a sense of belonging and be informed about what goes on at the place where your child spends a huge amount of time. There is the added benefit of sending a message to your child that you care about what goes on at his or her school and are willing to invest your time being a part of it. Parents have many ways to get involved, from volunteering in the classroom to working on fund-raising and parent-faculty committees. Most school administrators recognize that many families have two working parents and make an effort to hold meetings, schedule events and organize volunteer efforts to accommodate working moms and dads.

The Parents League of New York is an all-around excellent resource for families and provides a valuable network for the community. Founded in 1913, the Parents League is a not-for-profit organization of parents and independent schools that offers current information on education, entertainment and enrichment opportunities. The Parents League maintains resource files for activities, babysitters/mother's helpers, family travel information, parenting help and support and tutors. Every year, the Parents League publishes the *New York Independent Schools Directory, Parents League Guide to New York and Calendar, Parents League Review, The Toddler Book* and "The Parents League News." During the course of the year, the Parents League sponsors several workshops and panel discussions on such topics as child safety, homework, independence, learning styles and sibling relationships. You can become a member of the Parents League for a well-worth-it $50 per year by calling 737-7389.

When the time comes to begin your search for nursery and ongoing schools (much more about this in Chapter 8!), the Parents League, and its two indispensable publications, *The Independent Schools Directory* and *The Toddler Book,* can be of enormous assistance. Well-informed parent volunteers can help you navigate your way through the admissions process in New York independent schools and provide information on summer programs for all ages. Advisory services are available to members free of charge. The Parents League also sponsors annual lectures on the application process and Independent School Day.

Beyond classes and schools, there are numerous religious institutions and community centers affiliated with churches and synagogues that work very hard to create a community for members. Although membership in a congregation may not have been very important before becoming parents, once there are children in the picture, religious and cultural traditions, religious school and attending services at a place of worship may become more appealing. Many families experience a sort of religious rebirth when thinking about the moral and ethical education of the children and become reconnected to their faith. Since there are so many and such diverse opportunities in Manhattan, if you are looking for a congregation to join, or if you feel that the congregation with which you are affiliated does not meet your needs, there are many alternatives available.

Manhattan is home to several Y's, a list of which can be found at the end of this chapter. The various Y's offer many types of family programs, classes for all ages, sports facilities and fitness centers, lectures and performances, and some even operate their own preschools and day camps. Your local Y can provide a place to meet other families and become involved in your neighborhood.

For true grass-roots community participation, you can become involved in your local Community Board. There are 12 Community Boards in Manhattan, each of which is comprised of up to 50 unsalaried members. A full-time salaried District Manager and other staff run each district office. The Board members are appointed by the Manhattan Borough President in consultation with the Council members, who represent any part of the district under the jurisdiction of that Community Board. Any person who resides or operates a business in, or has a professional or other significant interest in the community is eligible for appointment to the relevant Community Board.

Community Boards meet once a month to address items of concern to the community. Board meetings are open to the public. Special hearings are conducted as needed on particular issues such as the city budget and local land use. Boards also process block party and street fair permits, coordinate neighborhood cleanup programs, publicize special events, and in some districts organize merchant and tenant associations. To learn more about Community Boards, you can call the office of the Manhattan Borough President at 669-8300.

Local publications are an invaluable resource for city and neighborhood happenings and essentially serve as our community bulletin board. The *New York Times* has a "For Kids" column in its weekend section and *New York* magazine and *Time Out New York* have listings of cultural activities for children. In addition, there are a number of family-oriented publications distributed for free throughout the city at supermarkets, retail establishments, libraries, schools and pediatricians' offices that list numerous activities in the city and metropolitan area for and about children. And, if you want to let your fingers do the walking at your PC, there are many websites devoted to family life. The resource list at the end of this chapter provides a list of local publications to look for.

Neighborhood houses, many of which began as "settlement houses" in the late 19th century, can be another avenue for becoming involved in your community. The neighborhood houses of the 1990s develop programs to meet the changing needs of their constituents and play a role in mobilizing neighborhoods to address complex social issues and provide services for local residents, such as early childhood education and Head Start programs, day care for children and seniors, after-school programs, teen centers, language classes, job training, tutoring, recreation centers, counseling services and art, music and drama classes.

The United Neighborhood Houses of New York, Inc. (481-5570) is the umbrella organization for the 37 neighborhood houses in New York City, 21 of which are in Manhattan (and listed at the end of this chapter). It is certainly worth finding out whether your local neighborhood house offers any classes, programs or projects of interest to you or opportunities to volunteer in, or get involved with issues relevant to, the community.

▶ **Sharing your piece of the Apple.** Community is more than just meeting people and participating in programs. An often overlooked aspect of being a member of a community is the notion of giving something back to the other members. This is for many people a complicated part of connecting to the communities in which we function. With our spare time so tightly scheduled and limited by the reality of attending to the needs of our own families, most of us just do not have the time to give to ourselves, let alone someone we do not know.

On the other hand, there is a wonderful spirit of community experienced when we donate even the least bit of time or expertise to an organization that exists solely to assist other people, to promote an important cause or to enhance the cultural life of our city. While it is easy to feel you are doing your part by writing a check to this or that charity, getting out there yourself and helping to affect the life of even one person in your community can be personally gratifying.

It is less important to what charity or institution you give your time or how much time you can donate than the fact that you are making the effort. A little bit of your time or talent can mean a lot to most people and that is really what community is all about. Keep in mind too, children learn by example, and your volunteering is a wonderful way to teach them how people work together to make the world a better place.

There are many organizations to become involved with if

you want to volunteer your time or talent. The best way to start is by focusing on an issue of interest to you and volunteering with an organization involved in that issue. If you do not know where to begin, you can contact the Mayor's Voluntary Action Center at 788-7550 or the Volunteer Referral Center at 745-8249. The Yorkville Civic Council can provide you with a list of over 150 not-for-profit organizations in New York City. Simply send your request together with a stamped, self-addressed envelope to the Yorkville Civic Council at 110 East 59th Street, New York, NY 10022.

▶ **Next stop Bedford Falls.** After a somewhat rocky transition into parenthood, it has been our experience that as we grew into our roles as parents, our feeling of belonging to a community has grown exponentially. As we have taken the time to get to know the community that surrounds us and to see the people around us as neighbors and fellow parents all trying to do the best for our children, New York City continues to inspire and charm us. And, if all of us, regardless of ethnicity, finances and religion, treat others as we would like to be treated ourselves, our daily travels might prove more fulfilling.

This city is a special place to raise our children. There is no right way to do the job or ready-made community to simply join, but New York is diverse and full of options. We hope that you too are able to discover the hometown within the Big Apple.

Resources

Parents League of New York, Inc.
(open only during the school year)
115 East 82nd Street
New York, NY 10028
737-7385

Community Boards

Community Board Services
Coordinator 788-7426
Office of the Manhattan Borough
President 669-8300

Board No. 1
49-51 Chambers Street
Room 712
New York, NY 10007
442-5050

Board No. 2
3 Washington Square Village
Apt. 1A
New York, NY 10012
979-2272

Board No. 3
59 East Fourth Street
New York, NY 10003
533-5300

Board No. 4
330 West 42nd Street
Suite 2618
New York, NY 10036
736-4536/7

Board No. 5
450 Seventh Avenue
New York, NY 10123
465-0907

Board No. 6
330 East 26th Street
New York, NY 10010
679-0907

Board No. 7
250 West 87th Street
2nd Floor
New York, NY 10024
362-4008

Board No. 8
309 East 94th Street
New York, NY 10128
427-4840

Board No. 9
565 West 125th Street
New York, NY 10027
864-6200

Board No. 10
215 West 128th Street
3rd Floor
New York, NY 10027
749-3105

Board No. 11
55 East 115th Street
New York, NY 10029
831-8929/30

Board No. 12
711 West 168th Street
Ground Floor
New York, NY 10032
568-8500

Neighborhood Houses

United Neighborhood Houses of
New York, Inc. (UNH)
475 Park Avenue South
6th Floor
New York, NY 10016
481-5570

UNH Member Houses in
Manhattan (provide services and
provide volunteer opportunities):
Boys Harbor, Inc. (The Harbor for
Girls and Boys)
1 East 104th Street
New York, NY 10029
427-2244

Chinese-American Planning
Council, Inc.
65-69 Lispenard Street
New York, NY 10013
941-0920

Educational Alliance
197 East Broadway
New York, NY 10002
475-6200

Goddard-Riverside Community
Center
593 Columbus Avenue
New York, NY 10024
873-6600

Grand Street Settlement
80 Pitt Street
New York, NY 10002
674-1740

Greenwich House, Inc.
27 Barrow Street
New York, NY 10014
242-4140

Grosvenor Neighborhood House
176 West 105th Street
New York, NY 10025
749-8500

Hamilton-Madison House
50 Madison Street
New York, NY 10038
349-3724

Hartley House
413 West 46th Street
New York, NY 10036
246-9885

Henry Street Settlement
265 Henry Street
New York, NY 10002
766-9200

Hudson Guild
441 West 26th Street
New York, NY 10001
760-9800

Stanley M. Isaacs Neighborhood
Center, Inc.
415 East 93rd Street
New York, NY 10128
360-7620

James Weldon Johnson
Community Centers, Inc.
2201 First Avenue
New York, NY 10029
860-7250

LaGuardia Memorial House
307 East 116th Street
New York, NY 10029
534-7800

Lenox Hill Neighborhood House
331 East 70th Street
New York, NY 10021

Lincoln Square Neighborhood
Center, Inc.
250 East 65th Street
New York, NY 10023
874-0860

Rena Coa Multi-Service Center,
Inc.
1920 Amsterdam Avenue
New York, NY 10032
368-3295/6

St. Matthew's and St. Timothy's
Neighborhood Center, Inc.
26 West 84th Street
New York, NY 10024
362-6750

Third Street Music School
Settlement
235 East 11th Street
New York, NY 10003
777-3240

Union Settlement Association
237 East 104th Street
New York, NY 10029
360-8800

University Settlement Society
184 Eldridge Street
New York, NY 10002
674-9120

Publications

The Baby Guide. 914 381-7474.
Biannual. Free. Available at pediatricians' offices, libraries and stores.

Big Apple Parent. 533-2277.
Monthly. Free. Widely distributed
throughout the city. Produces an
annual Parents' Source Book.
Subscriptions available.
www.bigappleparents.com

Downtown Kid. 718 349-9850.
Monthly. Free. Available at family
facilities and stores in lower
Manhattan. Subscriptions available.

Expectant Mother's Guide. 787-3789.
Three issues per year (fall, winter,
spring). Free. Available at obstetri-
cians' offices and childbirth class
facilities. To receive an issue, send
your request for the *Expectant
Mother's Guide,* a self-addressed
manila envelope and $4.00 to
Family Publications, 37 West 72nd
Street, New York, NY 10023.

Family Entertainment Guide. 787-
3789. Five issues per year (seasonal
plus holiday). Free. Available at
schools, libraries and family facilities. To receive an issue, send your

request for the *Family
Entertainment Guide,* a self-
addressed manila envelope and
$4.00 to Family Publications, 37
West 72nd Street, New York, NY
10023.

Jewish Parenting Today. Monthly.
Free. Available at synagogues,
Jewish Community Centers and
selected stores.

New York Family. 914 381-7474.
Monthly. Free. Available at pediatricians' offices, schools, libraries
and stores. Subscriptions available.
Produces an annual Family
Resource Guide.
www.nyfamily.com

PARENTGUIDE. 213-8840.
Monthly. Free. Available at pediatricians' offices, schools, libraries
and stores. Subscriptions available.

Working Parents Guide. 787-3789.
Three issues per year (fall, winter
and spring). Free. Available at corporate offices. To receive an issue,
send your request for the *Working
Parents Guide,* a self-addressed
manila envelope and $4.00 to
Family Publications, 37 West 72nd
Street, New York, NY 10023.

Y's

14th Street Y
Sol Goldman YM-YWHA of the
Educational Alliance
344 East 14th Street
New York, NY 10003
780-0800

Harlem Y - Jackie Robinson Youth
Center
181 West 135th Street
New York, NY 10030
283-8543

McBurney YMCA
215 West 23rd Street
New York, NY 10011
741-9210

92nd Street Y
1395 Lexington Avenue
New York, NY 10128
996-1100

Vanderbilt YMCA
224 East 47th Street
New York, NY 10017
756-9600

The West Side YMCA
5 West 63rd Street
New York, NY 10023
875-4112

The YWCA of the City of New York
610 Lexington Avenue
New York, NY 10022
755-4500

Volunteering

Jewish Community Center of the
Upper West Side
Volunteer Bank
15 West 65th Street
8th Floor
New York, NY 10023
580-0099

Mayor's Voluntary Action Center
788-7550

Volunteer Referral Center
745-8249

Volunteering in New York City by
Richard Mintzer (Walker &
Company, 1996)

Yorkville Civic Council
110 East 59th Street
New York, NY 10022
416-8250

For ideas on volunteering, some of
which are appropriate to do with
your children, and a source of
both national and New York City
organizations, see *How to Save the
Children* by Amy Hatkoff and Karen
Kelly Klopp (Simon &
Schuster/Fireside, 1992).

Chapter 8

NAVIGATING THE CITY

Navigating both the city's streets and its social nuances can, on occasion, be as challenging as driving the Amalfi Coast at night with a blindfold. In such a big city it is difficult not to feel lost at times. For anyone who has lived in Manhattan for any length of time, getting around town is second nature and not something about which to spend much time pondering. When living in Manhattan with kids, however, the number of trips we make around town seems to multiply, as does the amount of baggage we cart. In this chapter, you will find information about getting around town with your children both physically and socially, which we hope will make for smoother sailing as you navigate the island we call home.

Getting Around Town

Physically getting around New York requires an understanding of traffic flow, a great memory for which streets are under construction and a basic knowledge of the city's ever-changing landscape. Helpful extras, depending on your mode of transportation, might include: plenty of quarters or tokens, a MetroCard, small bills for taxi fares, a wallet-size street map and a good pair of walking shoes.

Getting from point A to point B does not have to be a test of your endurance due to the number of transportation options we have. There are subways, buses (school, activity and city), taxis, car services, or the family car. For the adventurous, bikes, rollerblades and scooters are available, although the number of individuals you can transport may be severely compromised. Last but not least there is the most reliable mode, your own two feet. Depending on the time of day you are traveling, and how important it is that you be on time, if you are going less than ten blocks and your children are good walkers or still in the stroller, it is generally faster to walk. No matter which mode of transportation you choose, if you are toting a tot or shuffling a school-aged kid around the city, it is advisable to take the path of least resistance.

▶ **Yellow medallion taxis.** New York City is known for many things: bagels, Central Park, hot dog vendors, the Empire State Building and of course those world-famous yellow cabs. Taxis now come in as many shapes and sizes as their drivers do, but a genuine New York City yellow cab will always have a medallion on the hood of the vehicle. The driver's name, license number and the medallion number must be displayed in the taxi and are usually located to the right of the meter on the dashboard or on the partition separating the front and back seats. The medallion number must also be displayed on the exterior of both rear doors, the roof light, the hood and the license plates.

Yellow medallion taxis are hailed on the street by pedestrians. Taxi fares are regulated and set by the Taxi and Limousine Commission (TLC). Rates are posted on the doors of the taxi and meters are required to be calibrated accordingly. There are special fares for trips to airports and rules governing the fares that may be charged for trips outside of the five boroughs, which are posted in the back seat of the taxi. Tipping is customary.

A yellow cab with its rooftop light illuminated (indicating that it is for hire) that stops to pick you up must take you to any destination within the five boroughs, although a driver is permitted to refuse to take you outside of New York City. A driver who asks you where you are going and declines to take you anywhere within city limits upon hearing your destination is in violation of the regulations governing the operation of yellow cabs.

The TLC has promulgated specific rules governing service, including the Taxi Riders Bill of Rights. The Taxi Riders Bill of Rights, which is required to be posted in the back seat of each medallion cab, states that as a taxi rider, you have the right to: direct the destination and route used; be taken to any destination in the five boroughs; a courteous, English-speaking driver who knows the streets in Manhattan and the way to major destinations in other boroughs; a driver who knows and obeys all traffic laws; air conditioning on demand; a radio-free (silent) trip; smoke and incense-free air; a clean passenger seat area and trunk. Refuse to tip if these basics are not complied with.

The TLC recommends that passengers abide by their suggested Basic Rules of Common Courtesy. Passengers are encouraged not to ask the taxicab driver to violate traffic laws (e.g., asking the driver to make a U-turn or exceed the speed limit) and to inform the driver of all stops and destinations at the start of the trip. The TLC asks that all fares be paid before the passenger exits the taxicab. It is illegal for a passenger to remove any stickers or take the passenger information maps from the interior of the cab.

The rules of the road. Taxi drivers get a bad rap in part because, from the viewpoint of the passenger, the whole taxi riding experience can be a rather arbitrary one. Some drivers ask you your route preferences, help you with your packages, know their way around town and are polite, while others seem to go out of their way to make your trip as unpleasant as possible. The problem is that no one really seems to know what the rules of the road are, and when the rules are known, they are inconsistently applied. As a result, passengers and drivers alike are not really clear as to what services are required to be, or appropriately, provided, which is further complicated by cultural diversity among drivers and passengers and the occasional less-than-perfect manners of some individuals.

According to the TLC, there are certain basic operating parameters that taxi drivers are supposed to follow. Knowledge of these guidelines affords you the opportunity to tip generously when service is above average, not to tip when you are dissatisfied, and to file a complaint against the driver if you are treated inappropriately. And, if you want your children to say please and thank you, remember to show them your good manners too.

How many kids can fit in a cab? You are with another parent and between the two of you there are four children. You hail a cab but when the driver pulls over and sees how many passengers you have in your group, he wants nothing to do with the whole lot of you. Was the driver being rude or does he have the right to refuse the fare?

A cab driver is only required to take three adults unless the driver determines it is safe to, and he chooses to, allow a passenger to sit in the front seat. There are supposed to be three seat belts available in the back for three passengers, whether they are children or adults. There is no formula to calculate how many children fit in a cab. For instance, two children do not necessarily equal one adult. So, if you are traveling by cab and your group includes two adults and two kids you are probably fine. If your gang is more than four, well, hope for an agreeable driver and tip accordingly.

Does the safety belt law apply to taxis? The law requires that seat belts be in working order and available for passengers to use. You and your child hop into a cab and a few blocks later the cab is pulled over by a police officer. Are you, by law, required to buckle up your child?

Among the joys of taxi riding, when you can find a taxi, is that you can slip in and out of the back seat without having to be responsible for the car. For many, it is a pleasure not to have to deal with the dreaded car seat. For most of us, for whom is it second nature in our own cars to buckle ourselves and children into our seats, in a taxi, the whole idea of buckling up is often as well received as a pothole.

In fact, parents are not required by law to use the safety belts for themselves or their children in a taxi, although the TLC recommends that all passengers be strapped in by a safety belt. Even though you are not in violation of the law if you are not wearing your seat belt, if you are injured in an accident, your not having worn a seat belt may affect your insurance claim or a claim against the driver. Ask your pediatrician for a recommendation on how to transport your small child.

How much is too much to ask of a cab driver? You went a little too far on your walk with your baby and it starts to rain. You attempt to hail a cab. After several minutes and the loss of the now-drenched paper shopping bag you were holding, you stand holding its contents and finally your luck changes. A cab comes to your rescue—or so you thought. You open the door, manage to put your belongings on the seat and start stripping down the stroller. You untangle the diaper bag, then the extra blanket, and you take off the rain cover only to find your child screaming. You lift your child from the stroller and then realize you cannot fold it correctly while holding the baby.

During this exercise the driver is looking more and more impatient. Holding the baby with one arm, you get the stroller to collapse and as you go to put the stroller in the front seat you hear the trunk pop open. You place the stroller in the trunk, get in the cab, shut the door and out of total frustration and exhaustion hardly get the address said before the driver says, "I can't hear ya." Most parents would agree that this situation should be grounds for having one's taxi license revoked, but is that the case?

As annoying as these kinds of situations can be, the driver is not required to assist a passenger or to allow the front seat to be used for cargo. Therefore a driver who gets out of the cab to assist you is certainly doing more than required. When you are in a situation where you are provided with only the most basic service and when clearly you could have benefited from some assistance, you may want to consider returning the favor and pay the driver only the basic fare.

To file a complaint. Do not hesitate to file a complaint against the driver with the TLC if: the driver was not driving safely, the driver did not know basic thoroughfares, the driver could not communicate in English, the physical condition of the taxi was poor or the driver was discourteous.

To file a complaint, the first step is to contact the TLC for a complaint form. You can either call the TLC Consumer Relations Unit at 302-TAXI, write to the TLC at 40 Rector Street, Fifth Floor, New York, NY 10006 or fax your correspondence to 676-1206. When writing, make sure to include the following necessary information: the medallion number, the driver's name and license number, the date, time and pickup and destination points of the ride and your mailing address and daytime phone. All complaints are confidential. Always remember to ask for a meter receipt when in a taxi because it contains the medallion number of the vehicle and the time of the ride.

▶ **Mass transit.** The bus and subway systems are so vast that if you are not already familiar with them, the thought of getting acquainted while you are trying to travel with your children may seem overwhelming. Fear not, mass transit does not take much savvy to master and there are advantages to using it. To begin with, taking the bus or subway can create an instant activity for your children because for most, especially young kids, it is an adventure. If you travel by subway, you do not have to deal with traffic or gridlock and can reach your destination quickly.

Using mass transit can save you a bundle because children under 44 inches tall travel free. There is no official limit to the number of children who can travel for free with a single adult. Note that when boarding a bus, you can use the bar that separates the bus driver's area from the passenger side as a rough height guide since it is approximately 44 inches from the floor of the bus.

There are a few things to keep in mind when using mass transit to better ensure that you make it to your destination safely. Strollers must be folded to board a bus or subway. On the bus, make sure the child is seated correctly in the seat. If you must stand, hold your child's hand in case of sudden stops and starts. The Department of Buses offers "The Insiders Guide," a free brochure that answers many of the questions you may have about the bus system. To obtain a copy of "The Insiders Guide" call the Bus Customer Relations Center, Monday through Friday between 7 a.m. and 5 p.m. at 718 927-7499.

When traveling by subway, ride the escalators to and from the subway platform with care. Strollers should be folded and children should hold a grownup's hand, not the handrail. Stand away from the sides because clothing can get caught as can shoes, shoelaces, sneakers, boots or sandals if you fail to step off. Never allow a child to run or sit on the steps or handrail of the escalator. The safest way to travel with your baby on the subway is to hold your child and fold the stroller before you enter the subway. If you do not fold the stroller while riding the subway, make sure to do the following: strap your child into the stroller, never place the stroller between closing subway doors, be aware of the gap between the platform edge and the train, engage the stroller brake while the train is in motion, keep the stroller away from the platform edge, and board the subway at the center of the train, in plain sight of the conductor.

Current fare for bus and subway is $1.50, payable in cash or tokens or by MetroCard. You can buy a MetroCard from any subway station, the St. George Ferry Terminal in Staten Island or at over 1,100 neighborhood newsstands, delis, groceries, banks, pharmacies, check cashiers and other stores. When you use the MetroCard, the fare will be automatically deducted and your remaining balance indicated. If you do not have enough money on your MetroCard to cover the fare, you cannot pay the additional amount needed with change or tokens. You can add money to your card at subway stations and at the St. George Ferry Terminal. As with tokens, the MetroCard cannot be replaced if lost or stolen. A MetroCard can be used until the expiration on the back of the card, after which you can transfer any remaining money to a new card at any subway station or the St. George Ferry Terminal.

For more information about MetroCard, free transfers and reduced student fares, you can call customer service at 638-7622 within New York City or 800 METROCARD outside New York City between 9 a.m. and 5 p.m. Monday through Friday or between 7 a.m. and 11 a.m. on weekends. Reduced fare benefits are available for senior citizens and customers with eligible disabilities, who can also obtain an application for a personalized photo-identification MetroCard by calling 878-7294 between 9 a.m. and 4 p.m.

For route and schedule information, you can get maps of the transit system from token booths, bus drivers and at approximately 4,000 other locations around the city, including libraries and museums, or by calling 718 330-1234.

▶ **Car services.** While it may seem frivolous to transport your children by hired car, having an account with a car service can be a great convenience. Although car services can be expensive—they are not subject to the yellow taxi rate schedule and each company sets its own rates—there are many reasons why parents have come to rely on them. For example, if requested, the car will wait for you while you pick up or drop off a child in bad weather. You can make reservations for a car to drop off and pick up you and/or your children at prearranged times, which can be enormously helpful when you need to get to and from hard-to-reach places during busy traffic times. Car services can be of great use when you have a very sick child, when the additional service makes an otherwise traumatic visit to the doctor easier to maneuver. In addition, car service drivers typically help you with your stroller and help load and unload your packages. In times of stress or just simply to make your busy life easier, a car service can be quite a mother's helper.

Car services and other for-hire vehicles differ from yellow medallion taxis, because they do not pick up passengers hailing from the street. The law requires that car service companies, vehicles and drivers be licensed by the TLC. In order to obtain a license: company owners must not have a criminal record in New York State, the company must have a legitimate place of business, the owners and location of the business must be on record with the TLC, the vehicle must be insured for the specialized job of carrying passengers for hire (other cars may not be covered or may have no insurance at all), vehicles must be inspected three times a year for safety defects, drivers must pass a physical that checks for conditions that could cause problems behind the wheel, and finally, all drivers must pass a New York State criminal record check.

All licensed car services should have cars displaying a diamond-shaped decal in the windshield. If you do not see the decal, do not get in. The cars bearing "Livery" plates are registered outside of the five boroughs and can drop passengers off in Manhattan, but cannot pick up fares within New York City. There are other cars for hire bearing "TLC" license plates (such as limousines), which are not supposed to pick up passengers in the street and are subject to regulations of their own. It is often hard to determine if a for-hire car looks legitimate or not. Certainly there are plenty of "gypsy" (i.e., unlicensed by the TLC) cabs driving the streets but for your own safety, it is recommended by TLC officials that you only take yellow taxis and prearranged licensed cars.

Names of car services can be found in the telephone book. When you call a car service company make sure to confirm that the service is licensed. Unfortunately, there is no governmental office to contact to get a list of licensed car services. Discuss rates, reservations procedures, how to open an account, whether they use vouchers, billing periods, identification procedures (are you given a car number in advance?), waiting time policies and last-minute requests. If someone other than a family member is authorized to request service, advise the car service in advance. You may have to try a few car services before you know which service is the most reliable, has the friendliest drivers, a fleet of vehicles in good condition and the most reasonable prices.

All complaints against drivers and services can be filed with the TLC in the same manner as complaints are filed against yellow cab drivers.

▶ **By car.** One of the many things suburban and urban parents have in common is the problem of transporting kids to school, activities and playdates. As your children's social circle expands and their activities and school friends begin to be further from home, family cars begin to hit the weekday streets. As long as you avoid midtown during business hours (where parking is hard to find), there can be many benefits to driving in Manhattan. Believe it or not, parking in a parking lot can often be cheaper than a round-trip taxi fare. If you are willing to park in the street, driving can be a downright bargain. In your own car, you can use age-appropriate safety seats, you can transport a lot of children with all of their gear, you can avoid getting stuck without transportation at inopportune times and yes, you can even car pool.

Some tips for city drivers: pay attention to parking signs or be prepared to pay a small fortune to the city in tickets; keep a roll of quarters hidden in your car or you will be forever begging people on the street for change; and when feasible, patronize the many stores and businesses that offer parking credits. By all means, if you do find yourself in the car often, make sure to stock it with creature comforts from home. This we have learned from our suburban friends: there is nothing like a few favorite snacks, books or toys (self-contained with no little pieces to fall between the seats) to keep kids busy when stuck in traffic or a change of clothing for your child so that an unexpected downpour or spill does not require you to retreat home.

The streets of New York are certainly not paved in gold, so there are many things to watch out for, including potholes, traffic, aggressive drivers, bicycles, emergency vehicles and pedestrians who sometimes dare you to hit them. It can get ugly, so take it easy and do not feel compelled to beat out the taxi drivers.

Getting Along in Manhattan

Increasingly, Manhattan is becoming a very child-friendly city. Almost everywhere you go there is something for children to do or, at the very least, to intrigue them. In most places children are accepted (or at least tolerated!) if not necessarily welcome. Unfortunately parents sometimes fail to realize their children's physical and emotional limitations or they simply do not bother to place limits on their children's behavior.

To improve the quality of your "out on the town" experiences with children you have to keep in mind that no one will ever think your child is as adorable and clever as you do. To some, your precocious three-year-old's antics might even be quite disturbing. However, if you respect that others may not have children of their own and therefore may not be very accommodating or patient with your children or that others may actually be escaping their own responsibilities of parenthood for a few hours, there really is not a place you cannot take children in New York. Here are some suggestions.

▶ **Restaurants.** If you are going to be dining at a restaurant that requires reservations and that would typically not be host to New York's youngest dining set, let the maitre d' know (in advance if possible) that your party includes a child or children. Generally, a table can be selected that will present the fewest distractions to others. With advance notice, the restaurant may be able to provide you with a child seat. Schedule your reservation for the early seating. Most children are not prepared to sit through a two-hour dinner starting at 8:30 p.m. Streamline your meal. A night out with young children is not the night to have a four-course dinner.

Make sure your children are aware of correct restaurant behavior before going out. It is not fair to the children to yell at them for sending the paper wrapper from the straw into orbit if you have not taken the time to discuss what is expected of them. Keep in mind that kids make a much bigger mess than adults (at least most of them), and though you may not be able to prevent the spilled grape juice you can take control over food fights.

The key to a successful evening is to pack distractions. Distractions come in many forms. Some are edible (do not rely on the restaurant to provide something your child is going to like) and some consist of activities for them to do with you or on their own. A strategy we have found useful with a very young child is for one adult to take the child outside or to an area where he or she can move around a bit for the time between placing your order and when food is put on the table. This tactic can help to postpone a child's limited table time attention span to the time when you need it the most—while you're eating. Dining with children may not be a relaxing experience, but it is a family one and that is reason enough for undertaking such an effort. You simply have to adjust your expectations and be aware that not everyone wants to pay $100 or more to eat with your child.

On the other end of the spectrum there are many informal restaurants that bend over backward to attract families. These restaurants tend to be decorated in a playful way providing an atmosphere that interests most kids. They usually have a children's menu, provide crayons and are very busy and noisy. These types of restaurants lend themselves to family dining. Keep in mind, however, that some kids have a hard time keeping themselves in control either due to the noise or the level of activity. Our suggestion for these restaurants? Again, distractions. They are the most important factor in achieving an enjoyable evening by helping to direct your child's energy and maintain focus.

Wherever you dine en famille, try to keep your child at the table. To allow children to wander among tables unattended is both dangerous for children and waiters carrying hot food and inconsiderate to other diners. If your child is melting down during the meal, be prepared to leave or take him or her outside for a little walk. If all else fails, order dessert early, buy everyone a round of drinks and tip well. For as cultured as most city kids are, there are few who have the manners to accompany their level of sophistication.

▶ **Performances.** There is a huge selection of shows performed by professionals geared for audiences of children that present wonderful opportunities to expose children to the arts. There is a vast array of alternatives including puppet shows, plays, dance performances, storytelling, films, all kinds of music, mime and even stand-up comedy by and for children. Taking your children to a performance provides a wonderful opportunity to introduce them to many new concepts such as being in a dark theater, focusing on a performance, listening and observing, doing without food and drink for a period of time, keeping quiet and, when they need to talk, remembering to whisper.

New York has an abundance of talented performers who mount children's productions. The beauty of these performances is that they are created to appeal to the younger set. They are typically short, the stories are not too complex, they are scheduled at child-appropriate times and they often include elements of audience participation or interaction. While children's shows are not always the most interesting to parents (especially when you are seeing productions that you have already seen with your older children), they are usually very interesting to your children and provide a great introduction to various forms of performing arts.

In addition to the performances created specifically for children, there are many other performances put on by the major adult-oriented cultural institutions of the city (such as opera and dance companies) exclusively arranged for children. Sometimes, productions that are otherwise primarily directed at adult audiences may offer tickets to dress rehearsals or other less formal previews that are suitable for children to attend. These options represent a perfect transition from the purely child-oriented performances to big time city culture, which can otherwise often create culture shock for your children. Generally the harsh reality of grownup show protocol and the length of grownup performances can be quite difficult for kids and parents alike without some advance preparation.

When you do venture beyond the kid-oriented selection of performances and bring your child to a grownup show, there are a few tricks to keep potential anxiety to a minimum. Children under eight usually do not last more than an hour and a half, so be prepared to leave at intermission. When possible, get tickets for a matinee rather than an evening performance. If you must go in the evening, avoid Friday and Saturday nights. Try to get aisle seats so that if you have to get up you can escape without requiring the entire row to get up with you. Bring lifesavers or other "quiet" candy.

It helps to be sensitive to the suggested age recommendations. Your preschool child may indeed enjoy pieces of "A Midsummer Night's Dream" but the attention span of a three-year-old rarely holds for the number of hours required to sit through the entire performance. It is also helpful to familiarize yourself with the content of a performance you plan on attending so that you do not end up at a show that is not appropriate for your child.

To find out about concerts, theater and other performances or cultural activities geared to children, the best sources are the newspapers, *New York* magazine, *Time Out New York*, and other local publications (see list at the end of Chapter 2). The museums frequently organize children's programs, as do other metropolitan cultural institutions (i.e., Carnegie Hall, Lincoln Center, City Center, etc.). *The Parents League Guide to New York and Calendar* also contains a great list of organizations and locations that have children's programming.

▶ **Out on the town**. If you are considering taking your child to a museum exhibition, a cruise around Manhattan, a day of shopping, or some other event or activity not particularly geared to children, your child will most likely be welcome as long as you are respectful and considerate of others. This requires a lot of effort because it is often difficult to contain an active, curious child or keep his or her interest during an activity not inherently interesting to children. On the other hand, it not fair to others to let your child run wild in an adult environment.

So what do you do when you want to do something more adult to which you want to take your child? The most important thing is to be realistic about what you think your child can handle and how hard you are prepared to work to make the outing pleasant for both you and your child. It is no fun to spend your leisure time chasing your kids through an exhibit you really wanted to see or stuffing them with cookies so you can have five minutes to whiz through an auction preview, and it is no fun for your child to be yelled at for doing what kids do. Even an activity that is family oriented, such as a cruise on the Circle Line, can feel like a voyage across the Atlantic if the children get bored.

What you can do is call in advance of attending events to make sure you can bring a stroller or baby backpack for an overtired child and find out whether it is appropriate to bring children at all, and listen to the advice. Parents can take turns; i.e., one parent takes the children outside while the other walks through the exhibit. You can also bring distractions, in the form of food, toys, books or anything else your child will enjoy and that will buy you some time. If your child is not doing well and is becoming disruptive and unhappy, be prepared to leave, regroup and try again another time.

Shopping is another activity that may be fun for adults, but unless you are shopping for toys or candy, most kids couldn't care less. One way to make a visit to a department store with a small child more tolerable is to make your first stop at a cosmetic counter to get a few samples in a small bag that the child can carry him or herself. And no, it's never to early to expose boys to a little grooming or styling advice. Make sure to have a morning or afternoon of shopping conclude with something your child wants to do. It is much easier for children to withstand the torture of shopping boredom with an activity they enjoy to follow.

▶ **The playdating game.** City kids do not typically run out of the house after school to play with the other kids on the block. While some kids are lucky enough to have playrooms in their building or a playground on their block, most city children see their friends during scheduled playdates. Even for the most socially adept adult, the world of playdating, and its attending etiquette, is elusive at best. There are no official rules nor is there a resource to which we can direct you for up-to-the-minute protocol. Instead, we conducted a highly unscientific poll of Manhattan parents about playdate "issues" and present to you these thoughts.

Making a date. Be sensitive to the fact that in some households the parent may not make playdate arrangements. When setting up a first playdate, ask with whom you or your babysitter should make plans to ensure that the plans you make end up on the family calendar and conflicting plans do not end up disrupting your schedule. Confirm playdates the evening before. Make sure that times and meeting locations, if outside the home, are clear.

Drop-off playdates. Usually sometime around kindergarten, drop-off playdates (i.e., where the child goes on a playdate without his or her parent or caregiver) become the norm. It is important to discuss with the other parent (or caregiver) what the plans are, who will be supervising the children and pickup arrangements. If the playdate is to be at your house, let the other parent know your plans for the playdate including what snacks or meals you will give the children, the activities you expect to do and whether you will be taking the children anywhere. Ask the other parent if their child has any special restrictions (no video games, TV, candy, etc.).

If the playdate is at the other child's house, confirm who will be picking up the children from school and how they will get to the next place, where they will be going and so forth. This way, for example, if you are not comfortable with the babysitter taking the children on the subway to a park in another part of town, you can do something about it. You should also let the other parent know about anything your child is not allowed to do (i.e., go to the corner store without an adult) or to have (i.e., soda or candy) or any allergies your child may have.

Do not assume that all parents share your views, so if there is anything specific you want to discuss, or think the other person may appreciate knowing if the playdate is at your house (i.e., that you will be going out and leaving the children with your sitter) do it before the playdate. Finally, if you are running late to pick up your child from someone else's house, call.

Remember to keep your child in mind when making plans. A plan or activity that sounds fantastic to you may be awful for your child. For example, if you are invited along with another family for a day at their club and then to dinner, make sure your child will make it the full eight hours or what sounds like a wonderful plan can turn into a horror show.

The blind playdate. It is not uncommon to meet a person through a friend or discover that a colleague has a child of around the same age as yours. Making a date to all do something together seems a natural thing, as everyone will have someone to "play" with during your date. This logic, however, does not always apply. As you remember back to days of blind dating, you might approach these kinds of situations with some careful planning. With babies this matchmaking usually works well, but for older kids it is the luck of the draw and when scheduling your first date you might keep it short and sweet to avoid a disaster.

The playdate disaster. There are playdates that seem to get off to a bad start or that dissolve into chaos and the kids begin to hit the wall, both figuratively and literally. Do not be afraid to call it quits before the time is up. If the child is not yet due to be picked up from your house, separate the children or introduce a neutral activity such as a video until things calm down. If the other parent was not there to witness the event, call and let them know what happened so they hear about the disaster from you first. It is much easier to reschedule a playdate that is not working out than to live through the event and potentially have two children who do not want to play together again.

Sharing. Despite the fact that most parents battle to get their children to share or to let a playdate go first or take a turn on the computer, there are generous kids out there who like to give away their toys, clothing, or whatever else is readily available. Though generosity is to be encouraged, you cannot allow your child to take home someone else's things or give away yours. Make sure to check with the parent or make arrangements to return the item(s) after they have been "borrowed."

At the opposite end of the spectrum, if your child has trouble sharing, consider letting him or her put away special toys before the playdate with the understanding that items not put away must be shared.

Cleanup. Nobody likes it but it is something we all need to help out with. Make sure that you let your children know you expect them to help, and if they are too young to take on the entire task themselves, show them how it is done.

Each family has different house rules. Your child should be aware of that fact and be prepared to follow them. When a child comes to your house for the first time, let him or her know in advance any particular rules you may have; for example, no playing in the living room or no food in the bedroom. For small infractions simply let the child know that in your house the particular behavior is not permitted and gently let him or her know you would appreciate it if next time he or she tries to remember. Remind your child that rules at someone else's house may be different from your rules and that he or she is expected to follow them. If, however, you find that a playdate in someone else's house leaves you or your child less than comfortable, try to schedule future dates at your house and avoid judgmental comments like, "I really don't think the kids should be playing Nintendo all afternoon."

Nobody likes to get sick. If your child has been under the weather, let the parent of the child he or she plans on visiting know. A choice in this situation is nothing less than a goodwill gesture, and in some cases can make you a friend for life.

Shorter is better. Children love to play, but a playdate that goes on too long leaves everyone unhappy. Whenever possible, err on the side of scheduling the playdate for too little rather than too much time. If the playdate is destined to be long (i.e., a sleepover), try to have some backup activities to keep the children happy or be prepared to hang out with them for a while until they settle back into a better rhythm.

The terrible triad. Threesomes are often difficult to handle, for adults as well as children. Too often, there is one child who feels left out and the playdate dissolves into a mess. If you have the choice, two or four children playing together works better than three. If there is no way around a triad, set some ground rules with the children at the beginning of the playdate so that everyone leaves with their feelings intact, and be prepared to be a referee.

There is no right or wrong way to organize playdates. The only rule of thumb is that the mission of the playdate is to set the scene for the children to enjoy the experience of playing together and have a good time. The best advice we can give, therefore, is to be sensitive to the children's needs and feelings. Be prepared to supervise and intervene as necessary, but most of all, enjoy the opportunity to watch them at play. It will not be long before you are banished from their kingdom, at least for part of the day.

Resources

Dining Out

City Baby by Kelly Ashton (City & Company, 1997)

Kids Eat New York by Sam Freund and Elizabeth Carpenter (The Little Bookroom, 1997)

Kids Take New York by Christine C. Moriarty (Book Happy Books, 1997)

Mass Transit

Bus and Subway Information and route information:

MTA New York City Transit
370 Jay Street
7th Floor, Room 702
Brooklyn, NY 11201
718 330-1234

To obtain a free copy of Department of Buses "Insiders Guide," call the Bus Customer Relations Center at 718 927-7499. M -F, 7 a.m. - 5 p.m.

For MetroCard information call customer service at 638-7622 within New York City or 800 METROCARD outside New York City. M - F , 9 a.m. - 5 p.m. Weekends 7 a.m. - 11 a.m.

For information about reduced-fare personalized photo-identification MetroCards for senior citizens and customers with eligible disabilities, call 878-7294. M - F, 9 a.m. - 4 p.m.

Outings with Your Children

The Cool Parents Guide to All of New York by Alfred Gingold and Helen Rogan (City & Company, 1996)

Kids Culture Catalog by the Alliance for the Arts, distributed by Harry N. Abrams, Inc.

Kids Take New York by Christine C. Moriarty (Book Happy Books, 1997)

New York's 50 Best Places to Take Children by Allan Ishac (City & Company, 1997)

Performances, Concerts, Theater, etc.

See the publications referenced in Chapter 2, *The Parents League Guide to New York and Calendar, Kids Culture Catalog* by the Alliance for the Arts, distributed by Harry N. Abrams, Inc. and *Kids Take New York* by Christine C. Moriarty (Book Happy Books, 1997)

Some specific ideas:

Aaron Davis Hall International, West 135th Street and Convent Avenue 650-6900

Abron Arts Center, Henry Street Settlement, 466 Grand Street 598-0400

Artsconnection, 120 West 46th
Street 302-7433

Atlantic Theater Company, 336
West 20th Street 645-8015

Brooklyn Academy of Music 718
951-4500

Carnegie Hall, 57th Street and
Seventh Avenue 247-7800

Chamber Music Society of Lincoln
Center 875-5788

Circle in the Square Theater, 1633
Broadway 307-2732

City Center Family Workshops,
130 West 55th Street 581-1212

Community Works Theater
Connections 459-1854

Czechoslovak-American Marionette
Theater 777-3891

Dance Theater Workshop, 219
West 19th Street 924-0077

Diller Quaile Rug Concerts, 24 East
95th Street 369-1484

Downtown Music Productions, 310
East 12th Street 477-1594

Film Society of Lincoln Center, 70
Lincoln Center Plaza, West 65th
Street 875-5610

Growing up with Opera 769-7008

Jazz at Lincoln Center, Alice Tully
Hall 875-5050

Joyce Theater,175 Eighth Avenue
242-0800

Kids at the Kaye, Danny Kaye
Playhouse, Hunter College
772-4448

Mazur Theater at Asphalt Green,
555 East 90th Street 369-8890

Little Orchestra Society 704-2100

Metropolitan Opera Guild
769-7022

Miss Majesty's Lollipop Playhouse,
39 Grove Street 741-6436

New Media Repertory Company,
512 East 80th Street 734-5195

New Victory Theater, 209 West
42nd Street 239-6200

New York City Ballet, New York
State Theater at Lincoln Center
870-5570

New York Philharmonic Young
Peoples Concerts, Lincoln Center
875-5656

New York Theater Ballet, 55 East
59th Street 679-0401

Paper Bag Players 362-0431

Pink Inc., Art in Motion 941-1949

Poppy Seed Players, 129 West 67th
Street 501-3360

Puppet Company, 31 Union Square
West 741-1646

Symphony Space Family Programs,
2537 Broadway 864-5400

Tada! Theater,120 West 28th Street
627-1732

Taipei Theater, 1221 Sixth Avenue
373-1850

Theatreworks/USA 647-1100

13th Street Theater, 50 West 13th
Street 675-6677

Tribeca Performing Arts Center,
199 Chambers Street 346-8510

West End Kids Productions
877-6115

Wings Theater Company, 154
Christopher Street 627-2960

Passport to the World of
Performing Arts, Lincoln Center,
70 Lincoln Plaza 875-5376.
Introduces children with disabilities to the arts.

Taxi and Car Service
Information

To get general information, file
complaints and make lost and
found inquires contact:

Taxi and Limousine Commission
40 Rector Street, 5th Floor
New York, NY 10006
302-TAXI Fax 676-1206

Chapter 4

DOCTOR, DOCTOR

Manhattan probably has the highest concentration of health care practitioners in the nation, if not the world. Whether you are seeking a pediatrician, family physician, specialist, therapist or homeopath, there are myriad professionals from whom to choose. Finding your way to the right person for the needs of your child and family takes some work on your part, but investing the effort and energy in times of relative calm can save you aggravation and anxiety, and perhaps even precious time, in times of illness or emergency.

New Yorkers tend to have very strong views about which doctors are "good." Because Manhattan is indeed the home of many world-renowned medical centers and famous physicians, it is easy to fall into the trap of seeking a celebrity doctor or a hot practice. Notwithstanding the lure of using a popular doctor or a medical star, the most fundamental issue in organizing health care for your family is finding competent practitioners who will pay attention to you, whose judgment you trust and with whom you can communicate about issues large and small.

In this chapter, we will guide you through the process of finding pediatric professionals, dentists and specialists. At the end of this chapter, you will find a list of resources to assist you in getting the best care for your children.

◤

About Pediatricians

For every neurotic New Yorker who has a Filofax filled with the names of specialists for all types of ailments and consults with a doctor for every sneeze, there is another New Yorker who has not seen a doctor since his or her last school-mandated physical. Whether you love to go to the doctor or go only under duress, once you become a parent, you will need a primary care physician for your child. Your infant will need regularly scheduled visits for immunizations, checking growth and physical condition and assessing development. In addition, there will be your fair share of visits for respiratory infections, rashes, stomach viruses and other things you could not have even imagined before you were a parent. As your child gets older, you will need a doctor to complete required forms for preschool, school, camp and other programs regulated by the health department.

▶ **Pediatrician vs. Family Physician.** Before beginning your search for a doctor, you need to decide whether you want a pediatrician or a family physician. A pediatrician is a doctor who has completed specialized training in pediatrics and only sees children. A pediatrician has particular expertise in dealing with children and childhood illnesses and is able to recognize and treat conditions ranging from the mildest to the most severe. By virtue of his or her practice, the pediatrician has a broad range of experience, will likely be well informed on the latest information in the specialty and have seen more unusual childhood diseases or behaviors, thereby broadening his or her diagnostic skills.

The family physician, a descendant of the general practitioner, on the other hand, does not limit his or her practice to children, but rather sees patients of all ages. Since family physicians tend to treat the entire family, they may be better able to spot emotional problems arising from family dynamics, be more aware of family conditions (such as allergies) and treat contagious illnesses that run through the family. Essentially, you must decide whether you prefer a specialist who treats only your children or more of a generalist who can be the primary physician for your whole family.

▶ **What type of practice?** Once you have decided what type of doctor you want, the next thing to think about is the type of practice you prefer. In Manhattan, the most common types of pediatric practices are individual or group. Solo practitioners maintain their own practices without partners. The advantage of the solo practice is that your child will always be seen by the same doctor, who will come to know you and your family very well. Individual practitioners must arrange coverage for times when they are unavailable. Most doctors tend to create coverage networks with colleagues affiliated with the same hospital so that in the event hospitalization is required, your child will be admitted to the hospital where your doctor has privileges.

While most solo practitioners make every attempt to be available to their patients at all times, it is not possible to always do so. Therefore the disadvantage of using a doctor with an individual practice is that there will be times when you must deal with a covering doctor who does not know you or your child and has no access to your child's records.

Some parents have found that covering doctors may be less inclined to see a child in the office during off hours and, if possible, prefer either to treat over the telephone, arrange to meet a very sick child in an emergency room or try to arrange for the patient's own doctor to see the child.

There tend to be two types of group practices. In the pure group practice, your child is a patient of the group rather than an individual doctor. While you may choose to see a particular group member for well visits, typically, your child will see whoever is available for a sick visit. In the other type of group practice, several doctors will share office space (and probably certain office personnel), but each doctor will maintain a separate practice. In this type of practice, the doctors will have a schedule of off-hour coverage among group members during which the patients of any group members will be seen.

The benefits of using either type of group practice are that a covering doctor will have access to your child's records, group practices tend to have extended office hours (evenings and weekends) so that you can take your child to a familiar office for an off-hour sick visit, and many groups have doctors with specialties, which can be helpful for additional on-site consultations. Over time, most parents and children become familiar with all of the doctors in a group practice.

There are also what are known as faculty practices, which operate in conjunction with, and are salaried by, a hospital. These tend to be more common at teaching hospitals and for specialty practices and are often located on or near hospital premises. Faculty practices tend to operate like group practices with a number of affiliated members.

▶ **Special credentials.** The American Board of Pediatrics, a national organization, certifies general pediatricians and pediatric specialists who complete an approved residency program and pass a written exam that the Board administers (this exam is in addition to the credentialing exam required by the New York State Board of Regents). Certification signifies that the doctor has achieved a certain level of competency and recognition in the profession. Certification used to be for life, but pediatricians certified after 1988 must be recertified every seven years. It is not necessary to be Board Certified to practice pediatrics in New York.

You may hear the term "Board Eligible" to refer to doctors who have complied with all certification requirements but have not sat for the certification exam. The Board no longer uses this term and if you inquire as to a doctor's Board status, you will only be told whether or not he or she is certified. You can find out if a pediatrician is Board Certified by calling the American Board of Pediatrics at 919 929-0461.

Board Certified pediatricians may also be members or fellows of the American Academy of Pediatrics. The Academy will provide lists of pediatricians in New York City who are Board Certified (a requirement of membership), as well as lists of members with particular pediatric subspecialties if you call the Academy at 800 433-9016. The Academy produces materials on many subjects pertaining to the health and care of children, which you can obtain for a nominal charge by sending your written request for information on a specific topic to the American Academy of Pediatrics, Department C, 141 NW Point Blvd, Elk Grove Village, IL 60007.

The American Board of Family Practice, also a national organization, certifies family practitioners who complete an approved residency program and pass a written exam that the Board administers (this exam is in addition to the credentialing exam required by the New York State Board of Regents). Board Certified family physicians must be recertified every seven years. It is not necessary to be Board Certified to be a family physician in New York. You can find out whether a family physician is Board Certified by calling the American Board of Family Practice at 606 269-5626.

The American Academy of Family Physicians, headquartered in Kansas City, Missouri, is an organization of family physicians/doctors who have completed a three-year residency in family practice at an approved institution. Academy members must complete 150 hours of continuing education every three years. You can contact the Academy at 816 333-9700 for a list of family physicians in New York City. The Academy can also provide you with information on anything from specific ailments to improving your relationship with your doctor.

▶ **Hospital affiliation.** Affiliation with a New York City hospital is not automatic and must be applied for by a doctor. Each hospital has its own criteria for granting hospital privileges—the right to admit and treat patients at the facility—to a physician. While all hospitals require that the doctor be licensed by the state, many require that he or she be Board Certified and/or be recommended by peers (or have professional references). In return for being granted privileges, most hospitals require the doctor to give something back to the hospital. In teaching hospitals, it may be a teaching requirement. In other hospitals, it may be some other type of service, such as seeing clinic patients. Because of the service obligation, as a practical matter, most doctors tend to only have one affiliation. While it is possible to practice without a hospital affiliation, the downside to using an unaffiliated doctor is that if your child needs to be hospitalized, your primary doctor can neither admit nor personally treat your child at the hospital.

▶ **Insurance.** Finally, before considering individual doctors, families must determine the specifics of their insurance coverage. Insurance coverage may permit an unlimited choice of doctors, provide lists of network doctors or limit choices to doctors at a specific facility. Each family must decide whether they will stay within insurance limits or use doctors for which all or a portion of fees will not be reimbursed. The good news is that there are so many terrific doctors in Manhattan that whatever your insurance coverage may be, you will in all likelihood be able to find a doctor who meets your needs.

▶ **Finding Dr. Right.** You may want to focus your search for a doctor on certain criteria such as the age or gender of the doctor, hospital affiliation, location of office, style of practice (formal or informal, group or individual), or you may prefer to meet a variety of doctors to see what suits you best. It is customary to interview one or more doctors before selecting one or bringing your child in for a visit. In fact, most expectant parents interview and select a pediatrician before their baby is born so that their own doctor can see the baby in the hospital following the birth.

To generate a list of prospective pediatricians, your first step is to seek referrals from people whose opinion you value. Excellent sources include your own physician, obstetrician or other medical specialists, friends, family and other parents. You can also get referrals from the American Board of Pediatrics or the American Board of Family Physicians. Most hospitals maintain physician referral services, but be aware that participants may pay the hospital to be included on such lists. Your health insurer may also provide a list of doctors covered in its network.

Once you have a list, schedule consultations with the doctors. Some doctors do not charge for interviews. However, it is becoming more common for doctors to charge for interviews due to the great number of families seeking consultations, which can take up a great deal of the doctor's time. You can expect the fee for a consultation to range from $50 to $100. Frequently, doctors who charge for the interview will apply the amount paid for the consultation against the first visit with the child. It is best to clarify the cost issue at the time you schedule the appointment.

▶ **The interview.** Your initial contact with a doctor's office provides your introduction to the practice. Were you treated courteously when making your appointment and upon arrival in the office? Was it easy or difficult to get an appointment (how full is the doctor's schedule)? Are the staff friendly and helpful? Look around the office. It should be neat, clean, have books and toys for children of all ages and be generally child-friendly. Is the office cheerful? Are the toys clean and in good repair? Is there a place to play while waiting? How long are patients kept waiting before seeing the doctor? Is equipment modern and up to date? What diagnostic equipment is kept in the office (e.g., for vision and hearing tests)? Are examining rooms pleasant for the children? Is the office formal (lab coats and nurses' uniforms) or more casual?

A question many parents ask is whether sick and well children are separated. While many suburban pediatricians have sick and well waiting areas, in Manhattan, where real estate is very dear, it is not often that you find a physician's office large enough to accommodate separate waiting areas. Also, segregated waiting areas may be difficult for parents to honor when bringing more than one child to the doctor's office. In most offices, very sick or contagious children are sent immediately to an examining room rather than remaining in the reception area. It is worth observing while you are waiting to see the doctor and asking the doctor how this is handled.

Before your meeting with a doctor, you may want to jot down your questions or the issues you want to discuss. Some ideas:

> ◪ You will probably be interested in the doctor's training and professional experience, specialties, credentials, certifications, professional memberships, continuing education and hospital affiliations.

◪ Ask how the practice runs. What are the scheduled office hours/ How is off-hour coverage handled (e.g., will the doctor meet you in the office over the weekend)? How can you reach your doctor in an emergency (i.e., beeper, service, voice mail)? Who will treat your child when your doctor is not available? If your child is admitted to the hospital, would your doctor be able to treat him or her? Discuss the doctor's rates for routine checkups, sick visits and consultations. If it is a group practice, can you choose which doctor you want to see for well or sick visits?

◪ Discuss office procedures. How are phone calls handled during office hours? Does the doctor have scheduled phone hours for nonemergency inquiries? Does the doctor use nurses or physician's assistants to answer certain questions and if so, under what circumstances are you put through to the doctor? Who performs various procedures such as taking blood, administering injections, conducting hearing and vision tests? What is the doctor called by the children? Are there give-aways for children, such as stickers?

◪ How interested is the doctor in behavioral, psychological and development issues? Does the doctor run and/or participate in parent support groups or educational seminars? For example, some offices sponsor groups for new parents. If groups are sponsored, who runs them and does the doctor participate? How involved does the doctor get in referrals for nonmedical issues such as speech therapy, psychiatric and psychological treatment, occupational therapy, and work with learning specialists? Some doctors take an active interest and role in helping parents of children with special issues while others prefer to refer to specialists and limit their role in non-medical treatments.

◪ Be sure to discuss any other issues that are of special concern to you or relevant to your situation. For example, you may want to know the doctor's views on breastfeeding, nutrition, use of bottles, toileting, when to begin classes for the child, sleep problems or reaching developmental milestones. If you are interested in nontraditional medicine, ask whether the doctor will support you in seeking alternative treatments. How does the doctor feel about prescribing medications?

▶ **The doctor–parent relationship.** According to Manhattan pediatrician Dr. Barry Stein, the most important feature of a sound doctor-parent relationship is trust. You will be relying on this person's judgment to tell you when your child is well and for diagnosis, treatment and guidance when your child is ill. You need to be able to communicate with your pediatrician and feel free to raise whatever questions and issues may be on your mind. If you feel intimidated and cannot fully express your concerns or if you feel that the doctor does not listen to you or is regularly unavailable, then you are not with the right doctor.

Providing good health care, however, is not the sole province of the doctor. Parents are an integral part of a team. It is unrealistic to expect your pediatrician to assess your child's total health and developmental profile from a 30-minute examination. You must alert the doctor to all matters—physical, psychological and environmental—which you think may impact your child's health. For example, stresses in the family (of which a child may be only subliminally aware) may contribute to such things as sleep disturbances, tantrums, withdrawal or eating problems.

It is also important to point out any changes in behavior or habits that you notice or differences between your child and his or her peers that you observe and about which you are concerned. To this end, the input of caregivers, teachers and other parents or family members can be quite relevant in assessing whether the behavior at issue is within normal ranges or requires further investigation.

Dr. Stein recommends that in advance of a visit to the doctor, parents should prepare a written list of questions, concerns and issues they would like to discuss. It may make sense to make a separate appointment with the doctor, without the child present, to talk about issues in greater depth or with respect to which it would not be appropriate to have the child in the room. The more information you provide to the doctor, the better prepared he or she is to assess your child's situation in the proper context and recommend a course of action.

Last, but certainly not least, your child must like the doctor too. Your child will inevitably have a relationship with his or her doctor, particularly as the child approaches adolescence. While all children will experience fear or anxiety about visits to the doctor at some time (or even every time!), how the pediatrician handles such situations is paramount. You will want a doctor who is kind, gentle and empathetic, relates well to children and attempts to assuage your child's fears rather than fuel them. You will also want a doctor who actually likes and listens to children, engages them and makes them feel comfortable. As Dr. Stein reminds us, a child can usually tell you whether the doctor is a good one.

▶ **Specialists.** There will likely be occasions when your child will need to pay a visit to a specialist of some type. The first source for referrals is your pediatrician, who can both direct you to the type of specialist you need and give you names. If you want more than one opinion, you should not hesitate to ask for more than one name. Your doctor should be able to recommend specialists from several hospitals.

You can do research on your own to find specialists. As with finding any medical professional, good sources include your own physicians, friends who have faced similar medical problems and other parents. Your insurance company may be able to provide you with names of specialists who are in their network. In some situations, school psychologists may be helpful in providing lists of specialists, particularly in the area of speech and learning problems. You can contact the professional organization of the specialty you need for a list of practitioners. If you are not sure how to find the relevant professional organization, the American Medical Association can help direct you to relevant Boards, Academies and other organizations as can the American Board of Medical Specialties (see resource list at the end of this chapter). You can network via organizations set up to deal with particular problems or diseases, parent support groups or the Internet. For resources relating to specific medical, mental health and learning issues, see the resources listed at the end of Chapter 9.

During times when you do need to work with a specialist, the relationship you have built with your pediatrician can be most valuable. The pediatrician can help you to understand and sort through various opinions, allay your, and your child's, fears, explain (and in some cases implement) treatment protocols and just generally be a supportive sounding board.

▶ **Alternative health care practitioners.** Parents interested in pursuing so-called alternative medicine methods to treat their children should be aware that there are no state licensing or certification procedures or requirements for most specialties. Parents are on their own in identifying suitable practitioners. One way to get information on a particular type of alternative treatment is to contact the relevant national or regional association in the practice area, which may set internal standards for its practitioners and will typically offer information to the public and refer people to members in the area.

Another potential source for locating alternative health care practitioners is the Office of Alternative Medicine, established by the Federal government and operating within the National Institutes of Health to study various alternative medical therapies. Finally, several medical institutions, including Columbia University College of Physicians and Surgeons and Harvard Medical School, are conducting research studies on various types of therapies and may be able to provide information to parents. A list of additional resources can be found at the end of this chapter.

■

About Pediatric Dentists

When your baby's toothless smile begins to fill with baby teeth, the furthest thought from your mind is going to the dentist. Prior to the tooth fairy's first visit though, your child's precious smile should be examined by a pediatric dentist. Manhattan parents are in luck because there are many pediatric dentists to choose from.

There is a big difference between a general dentist and a pediatric dentist. After graduating from an accredited dental school, pediatric dentists must complete two to three years of advanced training in children's dentistry from an accredited program. The pediatric dentist is specially trained to handle young children undergoing treatment and to spot developmental issues. Also, most pediatric dentists have created an office environment that not only makes the visits less threatening but actually makes visits entertaining.

▶ **Is it time to go to the dentist yet?** When asked when a child should first be seen by a dentist, Dr. Mark Hochberg, a Manhattan pediatric dentist who practices with Dr. Lou Cooper, said children, and particularly first children, are best seen by a pediatric dentist by age one. As Dr. Hochberg points out, "Would you take your child to the pediatrician for the first time at age three?"

At your child's first visit, the dentist will assess the growth and development of the teeth, counsel the parents about habits (sleeping with bottles, pacifiers, etc.) and discuss diet (formula, juice, fluoride and so forth). After the initial checkup, it is recommended that your child be seen by the dentist twice a year; i.e., every six months.

Assuming that subsequent children in the family benefit from what you have learned about dental hygiene the first time around and that you have an existing relationship with the pediatric dentist to address specific concerns, later siblings may not need to be seen before the age of two. It is a good idea to take younger siblings to the dental visits of older brothers and sisters so that they become familiar with the surroundings, the dentist and the checkup routine.

▶ **Finding a pediatric dentist.** Dental problems tend to arise without much notice. Even in the city that does not sleep, trying to find a dentist when your child has knocked out a tooth late at night is stressful at best. Therefore, it is worth collecting names of pediatric dentists and bringing your child in for an initial consultation early on.

Most parents find their way to a pediatric dentist's office after being referred by a pediatrician, friend or general dentist. In Manhattan, you can also contact the First District Dental Society at 212 889-8940, which can refer you to pediatric dentists in your neighborhood. Another professional association to call for referrals is the American Academy of Pediatric Dentistry at 312 337-2169, which will provide you with a list of members practicing in your area.

The American Dental Association (ADA) can provide consumers with information on particular dental problems and procedures. You can contact the ADA at 312 440-2500. The ADA produces written materials on many topics of interest to parents, which it will send to you upon request.

As is the case with finding a pediatrician, you will probably have many questions you want to ask the pediatric dentist about his or her credentials and training, office procedures for handling off-hours emergencies, who performs what procedures, how and what type of anesthesia is administered, how the dentist handles a frightened child, fees and office procedures and policies.

Although parents tend not to interview pediatric dentists before selecting one, it is possible to do so. In any event, when you visit the office, either with or without your child in tow, you would want to see an office that is child-friendly, cheerful and clean. It should have modern equipment and a variety of activities for children to get busy with in the waiting room. If your child has special needs, be aware that there are pediatric dentists with special training to treat mentally and physically challenged children, so be sure to ask whether the practice can meet your child's needs.

▶ **Your relationship with the pediatric dentist.** It is important for both you and your child to develop a good relationship with your pediatric dentist, particularly if your child will need to have various procedures, such as cavity filling, root canal or tooth extractions performed. Such procedures may be scary to your child (or to you!) and you will want to know that they are being done so as to minimize pain and maximize the possibility of your child having a positive experience.

For those of you with children well beyond the first visit, it is important to feel comfortable with how your child's care is being managed, especially because for many children, braces follow shortly after the tooth fairy has paid her final visit to your child. While braces are certainly not necessary for every child, for those who have to brace themselves for braces, there is nothing like a good pediatric dentist to lead the way. According to Dr. Hochberg, in general, orthodontics start when a child's dental age is approximately 10 to 10.5 years of age, although there is a trend toward earlier intervention. Dental age refers to the development of the mouth and may differ from the child's chronological age.

A pediatric dentist is usually the best source for finding an orthodontist. If you are not satisfied with the referral or want a second opinion, you can get additional names from your own dentist, your pediatrician or other parents. Additionally, you can call the American Association of Orthodontists at 800 STRAIGHT for a list of practitioners in your area or 312 993-1700 for general information. Keep in mind that you may get a different treatment plan from each orthodontist. A solid relationship with your pediatric dentist, based on your trust in his or her judgment, can help you sort through your options.

Whether or not your children are headed for the bright lights of Broadway, you will want their smiles to be bright and beautiful. So remember, start early and do not forget to floss.

▶ **Moving on.** A good rapport with a medical professional is built over time. If you are unhappy with some aspect of your child's care, by all means make an effort to resolve your issues with the doctor so that misunderstandings can be cleared up or feelings aired. If you determine that it is time to move on, there is no need to be uncomfortable. You must do what you think is best for your child. When you do change doctors, you will want to have your child's records transferred to the new doctor. Typically, you will need to request in writing that your files be sent to the new doctor. By law, the doctor is required to release your child's medical records within a reasonable time (interpreted by the State Health Department, Office of Professional Conduct, as 10–15 days). If your doctor withholds the records, you can contact the State Health Department, Office of Professional Conduct, Access to Patient Information, at 518 402-0814.

▶ **A final word on medical care in New York City.** We are extremely lucky to live in a city with some of the finest hospitals and medical talent to be found. There are scores of dedicated physicians in this city who help children and families every single day. Do not be disappointed if it takes more than one try to find the medical support you need for your children or the doctor to whom you and your child can relate. He or she, or they, are most definitely out there and with a bit of work on your part, you will find them.

Resources

Pediatric Care

American Academy of Family Physicians
8880 Ward Parkway
Kansas City, MO 64114
816 333-9700
www.aafp.org

American Academy of Pediatrics
Department C
North West Point Blvd.
Elk Grove Village, IL 60007
800 433-9016
www.aap.org

American Board of Family Practice
2228 Young Drive
Lexington, KY 40505
606 269-5626
www.abfp.org

American Board of Medical Specialties
47 Perimeter Center East
Suite 500
Atlanta, GA 30346
800 733 2267
800 776-2378 Certification Line
www.certifieddoctor.org

American Board of Pediatrics
111 Silver Cedar Court
Chapel Hill, NC 27514
919 929-0461
www.abp.org

American Medical Association
N. State Street
Chicago, IL 60610
312 464-5000
www.ama.assn.org

Manhattan Hospitals
Note: "full range of pediatric specialties" indicates that there are pediatric physicians handling a broad range of medical practice areas. Not all practice areas within each hospital are listed. If you want to know whether the hospital has specialists in a particular specialty that is not listed, contact the hospital's physician referral service or department of pediatrics.

Bellevue Hospital
462 First Avenue
New York, NY 10016
562-4141
Full range of pediatric specialties. Special pediatric programs include the Pediatric Asthma program (includes Eagle Circle exercise program), Pediatric Emergency Department and Child Life Program, Pediatric Resource Center, Reach Out and Read (ROAR, a literacy program), Perinatal Diagnostic Unit, children's psychiatric inpatient unit and Pediatric Infectious Disease Program.

Beth Israel Medical Center
First Avenue at 16th Street
New York, NY 10003
420-2000
and
North Division
170 East End Avenue
New York, NY 10128
870-9000
Physician Referral Service
800 420-4004
To obtain pediatric brochures
844-8300
Full range of pediatric specialties.
Special pediatric programs include
the Institute for Neurology and
Neurosurgery (North Division), the
Phillips Ambulatory Care Center,
Beth Israel DOCS (seven-day-a-
week immediate care facility,
1555 Third Avenue and 55 East
34th Street), Speechweb (hearing
and speech program), Pediatric
Music Therapy Program, Child Life
Program, neonatology, medical
genetics, critical and intensive care
unit, cardiology, child development, asthma, endocrinology and
hematology.

Cabrini Medical Center
227 East 19th Street
New York, NY 10003
995-6000
Physician Referral Service CABRINI
(222-7464)
Cabrini Medical Center does not
treat children on an in patient
basis but does maintain two primary care facilities (birth through
geriatric) at the Cabrini East Village
Family Practice at 97 East 4th Street
(979-3200) and Cabrini Haven
Plaza Family Medical Practice at
Avenue C and 12th Street (677-
2280).

**Gouverneur Hospital Diagnostic
and Treatment Center**
227 Madison Street
New York , NY 10002
238-7000
Special pediatric programs include
the walk-in clinic, adolescent
clinic, Reach Out and Read (ROAR).

Harlem Hospital Center
506 Lenox Avenue
New York, NY 10037
939-1000
Full range of pediatric specialties.
Special pediatric programs include
allergy and immunology, neonatology, hematology and oncology,
dentistry, surgery and ambulatory
care, Pediatric Resource Center,
Injury Prevention Program, Bike
Smart Program and Dance Clinic.
There are clinics for pediatric
genetics, dermatology, AIDS and
neurology. Harlem Hospital has
strong health education, preven-
tive services and community outreach programs (i.e., Horizon Art
Studio, Little League and Unity
Through Murals).

**Hospital for Joint Diseases
Orthopaedic Institute**
301 East 17th Street
New York, NY 10003
598-6000
Physician Referral Service 598-6727
Specialized hospital dealing with
orthopedics and rheumatology
including arthritis, bone disease,
Lyme disease and epilepsy. Special
pediatric programs include the
Center for Neuromuscular and
Developmental Disorders,
Children's Growth Disorder Center,
General Pediatric Orthopedics,
Ilizarov Limb Lengthening/Bone
Growth Center, Scoliosis Program,
Pediatric Rheumatology and
Allergy Program and the First
Chance Program (infant/toddler
special needs).

Hospital for Special Surgery
535 East 70th Street
New York, NY 10021
606-1000
Physician Referral Service 800 854-0071
Specialized hospital dealing with orthopedics and rheumatology. Special pediatric programs include specialties in Marfan's Syndrome, scoliosis, osteogenesis imperfecta, osteopertosis, familial dysautonomia, cerebral palsy, spina bifida, the Multipurpose Arthritis and Musculoskeletal Diseases Center and the Specialized Center for Research for Lupus.

Lenox Hill Hospital
100 East 77th Street
New York, NY 10021
434-2000
Physician Referral Service 888 RIGHT-MD (888 744-4863) (includes Appointment Schedule Assistance Program for appointments within 24 hours)
Full range of pediatric specialties. Special pediatric programs include The Babies Club and The Toddlers Club (parent information sessions lead by a pediatric specialist, 434-3152), the Neonatal Critical Care Unit and Neonatal Followup Program, Y.A.I/New York League LIFESTART Program (home-based early intervention program, 434-2991), Edward A. Davies, MD, Special Care Unit for acutely ill children, Pediatric Inpatient Unit, Health Education Center (free brochures, located at 76th Street and Lexington Avenue, 434-2980) and Tel-Med (a free telephone health information line, 434-3200), and pediatric orthopedics, trauma and ENT.

Manhattan Eye, Ear and Throat Hospital
210 East 64th Street
New York, NY 10021
838-9200
Physician Referral Service 605-3739 (speech and audiology), 605-3760 (Pediatric Eye Center), 605-3788 (ENT), 605-3784 (Learning Disabilities Center).
Specialized hospital. Special pediatric programs include the Pediatric Eye Center, the Learning Disabilities Center and pediatric practices in ENT, hearing, plastic and reconstructive surgery, communications disorders and audiology/speech.

Memorial Sloan-Kettering Cancer Center
1275 York Avenue
New York, NY 10021
639-2000
Physician Referral Service 800 525-2225
Specialized cancer hospital with specialties in all forms of pediatric cancers. Special pediatric programs include the Pediatric Day Hospital (to enable patients to live as normal a life as possible while in treatment), Kid's Express (support for children of parents with advanced or terminal cancer), SIBS (a support program for siblings of pediatric patients) and the Counseling Center (outpatient services located at 1246 Second Avenue).

Metropolitan Hospital
1901 First Avenue
New York, NY 10029
423-6262
Physician Referral Service 423-8131
Full range of pediatric specialties. Special pediatric programs include pediatric infectious disease and HIV programs, developmental pediatrics, Family Centered Asthma Program and adolescent psychiatric program.

Mt. Sinai Medical Center
One Gustave L. Levy Place
New York, N Y 10029
241-6500
Physician Referral Service 800 MD-SINAI (637-4624)
Through the Jack and Lucy Clark Department of Pediatrics, the Kravis Women's and Children's Center and the Maternal and Child Health Care Center, Mt. Sinai offers a full service children's "hospital within a hospital" unit within the Mt. Sinai Medical Center with a full range of pediatric specialties. Special programs include Meet Me at Mt. Sinai Pediatric Pre-operative Progam, Child Life Program, Through Our Eyes (a therapeutic video production program), a family-centered care approach for families living with an ill child, Neonatal and Pediatric Intensive Care Units, Young People's Diabetes Unit, Pediatric Pulmonary Center, Cystic Fibrosis Center, Apnea Center and pediatric cardiology, gastrointestinal, liver and nutritional diseases, surgery, ENT, genetics, neurology (including a neurofibromatosis center), etc.

New York and Presbyterian Hospital
(formerly Columbia Presbyterian Medical Center)
Babies & Children's Hospital of New York
3959 Broadway
New York, NY 10032
305-2500
Physician Referral Service 800 227-CPMC (800 227-2762)
Manhattan's only comprehensive children's hospital with specialties in all practice areas including the Pediatric Cardiac Care Center (cardiology and cardiac surgery), hematology/oncology, infectious diseases, genetics, dentistry, psychi-atry, surgery, autoimmune disorders, developmental pediatrics, Sickle Cell Center, orthopedics, Pediatric Urology Services, etc. Babies & Children's Hospital is at the hub of the Regional Perinatal Network, and offers a Child Life program for patients.

New York and Presbyterian Hospital
New York-Cornell Campus
(formerly New York Hospital Cornell Medical Center)
525 East 68th Street
New York, NY 10021
746-5454
Physician Referral Service 800 822-2NYH (800 822-2694)
Full range of pediatric specialties. Special pediatric programs include Perinatology Referral Center, Pediatric Critical Care Unit, Pediatric Endocrinology Division, Burn Center, Healthy Steps program for new babies, and pediatric allergy/immunology, child development, gastroenterology, infectious disease, mental health, neurology, hematology, cardiology, oncology, etc.

New York Eye and Ear Infirmary
310 East 14th Street
New York, NY 10013
979-4000
Physician Referral Service 979-4000
Specialized hospital. In addition to specialists in opthalmology and ENT, special pediatric programs include general care Eye Center and Pediatric Ear, Nose and Throat Center, Pediatric Glaucoma Clinic, bilingual speech therapy (English and Spanish), facial plastic and reconstructive surgery, ambulatory care, early evaluation and intervention services for children birth to three including developmental, feeding, vision, speech, language and audiology assessments.

New York University Medical Center
550 First Avenue
New York, NY 10016
263-7300
Physician Referral Service 263-5000
Full range of pediatric specialties. Special pediatric programs include Children's Cardiovascular Program, Children's Brain Tumor Program, Hassenfeld Center for Children's Cancer and Blood Disorders, Children's Rehabilitation Program, Children's Craniofacial Center, NYU-Bellevue Neonatal Program and Neonatal Comprehensive Continuing Care Service, Children's Cochlear Implant Program, Infectious Disease Services, Interventional Neuroradialogy, Children's Care Center, Pediatric Epilepsy Center, Neurogenetics Program, Pediatric Urology Program and pediatric allergy and rheumotology, endocrinology, dermatology, gastroenterology and nutrition, dysautonomia, surgery, etc.

NYU Downtown Hospital
170 William Street
New York, NY 10038
312-5000
Physician Referral Service 888 NYUD-DOC (888 698-3362)
NYU Downtown is primarily an acute care hospital. Pediatric care is mostly on an outpatient or clinical basis.

St. Clare's Hospital and Health Center
425 West 52nd Street
New York, NY 10019
586-1500
Physician Referral Service 265-8950 (Family Health Center)
St. Clare's does not treat children on an in patient basis but does maintain the full service (birth to geriatric) faculty practice. Clinton Medical Care Center located at 415 West 51st Street (scheduled to open spring, 1998) and the Family Health Center located at 350 West 51st Street (265-8950).

St. Luke's-Roosevelt Hospital Center
523-4000
Physician Referral Service 800 420-4004
Roosevelt Division
1000 Tenth Avenue
New York, NY 10019
St Lukes Hospital
111 Amsterdam Avenue
New York, N Y 10025
Full range of pediatric specialties. Special pediatric programs include the Child Life Program, the Pediatric Music Therapy Program, St. Luke's Pediatric Outpatient Clinic, endocrinology, gastronterology, hematology, oncology, pulmonary medicine, neurology, sickle cell disease, HIV/AIDS etc. The Joslin Center for Diabetes treats pediatric patients.

St. Vincent's Hospital and Medical Center of New York
13 West 11th Street
New York, NY 10011
604-7000
Physician Referral Service 888 4SVH-DOC (888 478-4362)
Full range of pediatric specialties. Special pediatric programs include the Cystic Fibrosis Center, Brian Wert C.H.I.L.D. Center (developmental issues), Child and Adolescent Psychiatric Program, Child Life Program, Parent Education Program, chronic disease management, allergy and immunology, cardiology, dermatology, developmental pediatrics, endocrinology, gastroenterology and nutrition, hematology and infectious diseases.

Alternative Medicine

American Association of
Naturopathic Physicians
601 Valley
Suite 105
Seattle, WA 98109
206 298-0125
Publishes a brochure available for a
nominal charge.

American Holistic Health
Association
P.O. Box 17400
Anaheim CA 92817-7400
714 779-6152
www.ahha.org

American Holistic Medical
Association
6728 Old McLean Village
McLean, VA 22101
703 556-9728/9245

National Center for Homeopathy
801 N. Fairfax Street
Suite 306
Alexandria, VA 22314
703 548-7790

Office of Alternative Medicine
National Institutes of Health
Bethesda, MD
888 644-6226

www.healthy.net Provides information and referrals in many practice
areas.

Dental Care

First District Dental Society
295 Madison Avenue
New York, NY 10017
889-8940

American Academy of Pediatric
Dentistry
211 East Chicago Avenue
Suite 700
Chicago, IL 60611
312 337-2169
http://aapd.org

American Dental Association
211 East Chicago Avenue
Chicago, IL 60611
312 440-2500
www.ada.org

American Association of
Orthodontists
401 North Lindberg Blvd.
St Louis, MO 63141
314 993-1700
800 STRAIGHT (800 787-24448)
www.aaortho.org

General Information

Association for the Care of
Children's Health
7910 Woodmont Avenue
Suite 300
Bethesda, MD 20814
301 654-6549

National Institutes of Health
www.nih.gov

National Library of Medicine
800 272-4787
MEDLINE http://igm.nlm.nih.gov

National Maternal and Child
Health Clearinghouse
2070 Chain Bridge Road
Suite 450
Vienna, VA 22182
703 821-8955
www.circsol.com/mch

Office of Professional Conduct
State Health Department
Access to Patient Information
518 402-0814

Office of Professional Discipline
One Park Avenue
6th Floor
New York, NY 10016
800 442-8106

Office of Professional Discipline
New York City Regional Office
State Education Department
163 West 125th Street
Room 819
New York, NY 10027
961-4369

Office of Professional Medical
Conduct
New York State Department of
Health
Entact Unit Suite 303
433 River Street
Troy, NY 12180
518 402-0836

Wellness Web
http://wellweb.com/index.htm

Appendix
Licensing Requirements for Professionals

The Board of Regents of the State of New York supervises the admission to and practice of the 38 professions, and the 31 special certification areas within those professions, recognized pursuant to Title VII of the Education Law of the State of New York. Licensed professions include such practice areas as health care, psychology, social work, engineering, accountancy, dentistry, architecture, pharmacy, optometry and so forth, but not the legal or teaching professions, which are regulated separately. Individual State Boards for the Professions, each consisting of members appointed by the Board of Regents, advise the Board of Regents with respect to matters of policy and practice for the particular professions.

The Board of Regents is responsible for: (1) professional credentialing, which includes evaluating the education and training of potential licensees, developing licensing standards, assessing of applicants' credentials, and developing and administering licensing examinations and issuing licenses; and (2) dealing with matters of professional responsibility, which include handling professional discipline, regulating issues of continuing competence and operating the Professional Assistance Program to help licensed professionals with substance abuse problems.

In New York, a professional license is effective for life unless revoked by the Board of Regents following a finding of professional misconduct or surrendered by a licensee voluntarily. Complaints of professional misconduct are handled by the Office of Professional Discipline for all licensed professions other than the medical profession. The main office of the Office of Professional Discipline is located at One Park Avenue, 6th Floor, New York, NY 10016. The toll-free hotline is 800 442-8106. The New York City Regional Office is located at the State Education Department, 163 West 125th Street, Room 819, New York, NY 10027, 961-4369. Allegations of misconduct by a physician, physician's assistant or specialist assistant (as defined by the Education Law) are handled by the Office of Professional Medical Conduct, New York State Department of Health, Corning Tower, Empire State Plaza, Albany, NY 12237, 518 474-8357.

The specific credentialing requirements for doctors, dentists, psychologists, social workers, audiologists, speech therapists, occupational therapists and other professions that might be of interest to parents are as follows:

Doctor: must be at least 21 years old, either a United States citizen or otherwise authorized to work in this country, complete appropriate preprofessional and medical education in a program in an institution acceptable to the State Education Department (and/or meet additional requirements if the person attended medical school outside the United States), hold a degree of doctor of medicine or osteopathy, have a minimum of one year of postgraduate hospital training, and pass the relevant written examinations. After January 1, 1991, an applicant for a license must complete a two-hour course in identify-

ing and reporting child abuse. As of July 1, 1994, all licensees must complete course work in infection control to prevent the transmission of HIV and HBV.

Dentist: must be at least 21 years old, either a United States citizen or otherwise authorized to work in this country, complete appropriate dental education including a doctoral degree in dentistry from a program in an institution acceptable to the State Education Department (and/or meet additional requirements if the person attended dental school outside the United States), and pass the written National Board Dental Examination and the Northeast Regional Board Examination practical examination. There are no work experience requirements. After January 1, 1990, dentists may not employ general anesthesia or certain types of sedation at other than a hospital without a special dental anesthesia certificate. After January 1, 1991, an applicant for a license must complete a two-hour course in identifying and reporting child abuse. As of July 1, 1994, all licensees must complete course work in infection control to prevent the transmission of HIV and HBV.

Psychologist: must be at least 21 years old, have a doctoral degree in psychology from a program in an institution acceptable to the State Education Department, have a minimum of two years of supervised experience, and pass the Examination for Professional Practice in Psychology of the Association of State and Provincial Psychology Boards. After January 1, 1991, an applicant for a license must complete a two-hour course in identifying and reporting child abuse.

Social Worker: must be at least 21 years old, have a master's degree in social work or its equivalent from a program in an institution acceptable to the State Education Department, and pass the written Social Work examination administered by the American Association of State Social Work Boards. There is no minimum work experience requirement except for applicants educated in foreign countries who must have two years of supervised experience in the United States.

Other professions:

Acupuncture: must be at least 21 years old, proficient in English, complete 60 semester hours at an accredited college or university, including nine hours in the biosciences and no less than 4050 hours of didactic, clinical and out-of-classroom study and 650 hours of clinical training, and pass the written and practical examination of the National Commission for the certification of Acupuncturists.

Audiology: must be at least 21 years old, have a master's degree in audiology or its equivalent from a program in an institution acceptable to the State Education Department, complete nine months of supervised experience, and pass the national examination administered by the Educational Testing Service.

Chiropractic: must be at least 21 years old, either a United States citizen or otherwise authorized to work in this country, complete a preprofessional and professional study program acceptable to the State Education Department, and pass the written and practical examination of the National Board

Examinations administered by the National Board of Chiropractic Examiners. After January 1, 1991, an applicant for a license must complete a two-hour course in identifying and reporting child abuse.

Massage therapy: must be at least 18 years old, complete high school and a massage therapy program acceptable to the State Education Department and pass a written examination.

Occupational therapy: must be at least 21 years old, have a bachelor's degree or graduate certificate or degree from a program in an institution acceptable to the State Education Department (and/or meet additional requirements if the person attended school outside the United States), complete six months of supervised experience and pass an examination administered by the Professional Examination Service.

Physical therapy: must be at least 18 years old, complete a physical therapy program in an institution acceptable to the State Department of Education and pass a written examination administered by LGR Examinations, Inc.

Speech-Language Pathology: must be at least 21 years old, have a master's degree from a program in an institution acceptable to the State Department of Education, complete nine months of supervised experience and pass a national examination administered by the Educational Testing Service.

Chapter 5

HOME SAFE HOME AND BEYOND

Non-New Yorkers tend to see our fair city as a very danger-ous place, with peril and temptation lurking around every corner. Those of us who have chosen to make this city our home have learned to accept the realities of living here and organized ourselves accordingly. Each of us develops our own ground rules for keeping safe in Manhattan: the neighbor-hoods in which we will walk at night, the hours we will ride the subway, the routes we take, the time of day we will visit the ATM and so on.

Once we become parents, however, we often see the city with new eyes. We begin to use parts of the city such as parks and playgrounds to which we may never have given much thought before. For those of us who are accustomed to spending business hours indoors in our places of work, we or our caregivers will be out and about with our children during those times in parts of the city where we may not have previously spent much time.

As we maneuver through town with our children and their paraphernalia, we realize that we are far more encumbered and hence less able to exit a precarious situation quickly. Whatever the case, we want to protect the vulnerable new lives for whom we are totally responsible and so suddenly need to think about how we want our children to travel and use the city and what will be safe not only for us adults, but for Junior too.

In this chapter, we will discuss safety within and outside of the home. We will look at dealing with emergencies. We will explore talking to your children about safety and how to help your older child safely navigate the city on his or her own. At the end of this chapter, you will find a list of resources relevant to making the city as safe as possible for your family.

◤

The City Life

From the moment your new baby crosses the threshold for the first time, your home transforms from one geared to adult living to a service center for your baby's needs. At first, the changes, though major, are relatively self contained. But whether you simply add a crib, changing table and basic baby supplies or go for all of the baby apparatus you can possibly squeeze in, you can be sure that your home will never be the same again. In a relatively short time, your baby will become mobile and your entire home will become one big playroom and field for exploration, playdates and activities.

▶ **Childproofing your home**. Childproofing your home is an important, ongoing activity for parents. You must continuously anticipate what skill your child will next master (climbing, opening doors, turning knobs, opening bottles, etc.) to prevent unnecessary accidents. Because childproofing is a process, you need to train yourself to survey your home on a regular basis and always be alert to what seemingly innocuous object could create a hazard both for your own child and other children who visit your house. Even if your child is the most cautious, obedient child, do not underestimate his or her natural curiosity. For example, your child may know not to put things in his or her mouth, but sometimes an object looks too good, or too much like candy, to resist.

To create a child-friendly environment, you do not need to remove everything from your home and pad the walls. But you do need to address conditions that could create danger for little people. The rule of thumb is to look at things from the point of view of your child. Get down on the floor and see what each room looks like to a crawling or toddling child. What is within arm's reach or can be moved or got around to get to something interesting? Look for sharp corners and objects, dangling cords and objects, free-standing objects that would be unstable if your child leaned on them, objects that your child could choke on, doors that lock or slam shut, things that could be pulled off of tables (including table-cloths) and counters, hinged tops that can slam on little fingers, slippery area rugs, and things that if turned on or off could be dangerous.

Some childproofing basics to keep in mind: move cleaning supplies out of reach (not just in a cabinet with a child safety lock); safeguard all poisonous, hazardous, flammable or toxic materials; keep plastic bags and electrical appliances out of reach; lock cupboards with appropriate child safety devices; carefully store scissors, knives, needles and sharp or heavy tools; safeguard windows and sliding doors; make sure you do not have poisonous plants in your home; remove matches and lighters; be alert to appliances that can burn or scald your child; and plug unused electric outlets with plastic safety plugs. All nursery and baby equipment should be checked for safety features. Toys should be evaluated both for age-appropriateness and safety.

The most important aspects in childproofing your home are to pay attention to detail and to practice, and teach your children, good safety habits. To help in your endeavors, most stores selling baby supplies as well as most hardware stores offer many products developed to safeguard your home. There are also a number of catalogues that feature home safety products, which are listed at the end of this chapter. For those parents seeking a professional opinion, there are childproofing services, also listed at the end of this chapter, which will pay a housecall, evaluate your home and supply and install childproofing devices.

Manhattan parents living in apartments should also be aware that pursuant to the Multiple Dwelling Law, building owners (landlords in the case of rentals and building owner entities in the case of co-ops and condominiums) are responsible for installing and maintaining window guards, at no charge to the tenant, in all apartments in which children under the age of ten reside. If you do not like the standard issue window guards provided in most apartment buildings, you can purchase customized window guards that may be more decorative.

▶ **Fire safety in your home.** There are two elements to fire safety: fire prevention and a plan of action to be executed in the event of a fire in your home. To prevent fires, it is necessary to inspect your home for potential fire hazards. Be sure to safeguard matches and lighters, carefully store flammable materials, be careful when lighting candles (particularly if there is a tablecloth underneath lit candles that can be pulled by a child), replace frayed electrical cords, do not overload electrical outlets or run wire under rugs or over nails, safeguard halogen light fixtures, do not cook while wearing sleeves that can dangle near burners or use towels as potholders near an open flame, and operate space heaters strictly in accordance with instructions. If you have a fireplace, be sure to have it professionally cleaned and checked annually and consider installing carbon monoxide detectors around your home.

By law, New Yorkers are required to have smoke detectors installed in our homes within 25 feet of each bedroom. If you live in a rental apartment it is the obligation of the landlord to install smoke detectors, though you will be responsible for their maintenance (i.e., changing the batteries). If you live in a co-op or condominium, it is your obligation to install and maintain smoke detectors inside your apartment. In addition to smoke detectors, you may also want to consider installing heat detectors in appropriate areas, which may set off an alarm before a smoke detector would.

In the event of a fire in your home, it is crucial to have a fire escape plan. Since many of us live in apartment buildings, it is important to locate and identify to children the fire stairs or fire escapes and to understand when it is or is not appropriate to use the building elevator. Plan your escape routes with your children and conduct periodic fire drills. It is also a good idea to post Tot Finder decals on your windows and doors to assist firefighters in rescuing your children in an emergency. If you have children old enough to follow directions, they should be taught to call 911 to report a fire and given instructions to meet at a designated meeting point in your immediate neighborhood in the event you are evacuated from your home by firefighters and become separated.

You can obtain written materials about fire prevention and safety by calling the New York City Fire Department at 718 999-0321/2056/2013 or contacting your local firehouse. You can also obtain materials (for a nominal charge) from the National Fire Protection Association at 11 Tracy Drive, Avon, MA 02322, 800 344-3555, www.NFPA.org. You can get information on safeguarding your home during storms from Con Edison.

▶ **A healthy home.** An important step in making your home safe for your children is to eliminate environmental hazards such as lead-based paint, asbestos, excessive dust mites and other allergens, water damage or moisture conditions that facilitate the growth of molds and harmful or toxic products. While it is not necessary to bring in a SWAT team to evaluate your indoor environment, it is worth considering whether there are issues that need to be addressed.

The presence of lead-based paint can create serious problems for infants and young children because it can cause lead poisoning. Since lead-based paint was in use up until 1978, many older apartments that have multiple coats of paint on the wall and trim (particularly around windows) can have lead issues. Lead poisoning can result in learning disabilities, neurological problems and physical illness. A child does not have to eat lead paint chips to be affected; inhaling the dust from lead paint can do the damage. Lead dust can be produced not only from renovations in your home, but from any disturbance (friction, scratching or impact, opening and closing windows, flaking or peeling, etc.) of surfaces covered with lead-based paint.

The dangers of asbestos have been well documented, so it is important to be sure that there is not exposed or friable asbestos in your home. The quality of the air in your home is not only meaningful to your family's comfort but can become crucial if you have a child with allergies, asthma or respiratory problems that can be caused or exacerbated by the presence of dust mites, airborne allergens or molds. It is a good idea to have ventilation systems and air-conditioning units periodically checked and cleaned by professionals.

Water quality is another area for potential inquiry. Older buildings in particular may have pipes made of lead or other metals that leak impurities into your drinking water. Recent reports of bacteria contaminating the water supply have led many families to consider installing water filtration systems in their homes.

If you are contemplating, or in the midst of, renovations, your contractor, architect or other professional can help you assess what kind of inspections or evaluations (in addition to those required in connection with your building permits) you may need to ensure the environmental quality of your home. If you are not involved in renovations, but are concerned and want to explore these issues, you can get information from a variety of sources including the City Departments of Environmental Protection, Health and Sanitation or retain a private consultant to evaluate your home. At the end of this chapter, you will find specific resources to help you in your inquiry.

◥

The Sidewalks of New York

New York City is home to more than eight million people. As such we live in close proximity to our neighbors. When we are not walking (or running!) we tend to travel by bus, subway and taxi. From very early on, our children are used to elevators, doormen, delivery people, public transportation and seeing many people from all walks of life throughout the day. As parents of New York children, it is incumbent upon us to teach our children age-appropriate city skills. The challenge is to do so in a way that reinforces safe and intelligent behavior without frightening them.

There are very few absolutes when it comes to safety rules. The trick is to teach your children not only specific words and actions, but also, and perhaps more importantly, strategies to deal with events for which they are not expressly prepared. While we want to protect our children against all harm, we cannot anticipate everything that can potentially happen. Rather, through open discussion, role playing and practice, we can help them develop good judgment and city street skills.

The development of safety rules is a process. The rules will change over time as your children become older and more capable and independent. Rules will adjust to address new concerns or in response to an incident that occurred in your home or someone else's or even as a result of a news story. When making your own safety rules, be sure to consider the age and temperament of your child and the level of responsibility he or she can handle. Balance your child's increasing need for independence against his or her level of maturity and what you believe is appropriate under the circumstances. Reinforce your rules with periodic reviews and updates and practice, practice, practice.

The best thing you can do for your children is to teach them how to observe situations, formulate a strategy, feel confident about their decisions and take decisive action appropriate to the situation. So take a deep breath and let's get started.

▶ **Home safety basics.** Even the youngest children need to be taught the basics of home safety, such as rules for answering the telephone and doorbell and how to use the telephone. As soon as children are able, they should learn their full names, their parents' names, and their addresses and phone numbers. You can point out landmarks in the neighborhood to help them identify where they live.

Children should be instructed early on in how and when to use 911 and given other important telephone numbers to be used whenever needed. It is valuable to teach your children your work numbers, your cellular phone or beeper numbers, how to call the doorman or superintendent for your building, and numbers for neighbors and others (relatives and friends) who can help in an emergency.

Telephone numbers should be prominently displayed for children and caregivers in more than one location. For children who are not yet reading, you can identify phone numbers with symbols or pictures (e.g., a police car or fire truck) or a photograph of the person whose number it is. If your telephone has a speed dial function, you may find it easy to use, although your child will still need to memorize certain important numbers for use outside of your home.

You will probably want to develop some specific home safety rules of your own. Such rules should be clearly communicated to all caregivers, housekeepers and babysitters who work in your home. Even very young children should be taught safety rules because occasions may arise, even if you are at home (i.e., when you are in the shower, or in the event of an emergency), where they should know what to do. On the other hand, young children need to understand their limits. One curious three-year-old we know let himself out of the house while his mother went to the bathroom and took the elevator to the lobby alone. Happily the doorman stopped him at the door and safely returned him home before his mother had even realized that he had gone.

Whatever type of rules you devise, think about the kind of situations that are relevant to your children and how you want them to be prepared. Some ideas:

◪ Telephone. How should the telephone be answered? What information may your child give to friends or strangers (e.g., who is home, when you will be home, whether you have a home security system or alarm)? Would you prefer that calls go on the answering machine rather than be answered by a child or employee?

◪Answering the door. To whom may your child open the door? What should they say before they open the door (who is it?) or if they are not going to open the door (i.e., we are not expecting a visitor now)? Must visitors be announced by the doorman? What if someone rings the bell who was not announced by the doorman? What about the service door? What about delivery people? If your building has a buzzer system, under what circumstances may your child let someone into the building?

◪Apartment building personnel. What employees are allowed in the apartment and when (only when you have called for a repair, if the superintendent has called in advance, during work hours)? Where in the building may your child go with an employee (bicycle room, basement, elevator, lobby, no place)?

◪ Leaving the house without an adult. When may the child leave and where may he or she go (to the garbage disposal, the laundry, the elevator, the lobby, no place)? If the child is allowed to leave the house alone, who must be told that he or she is leaving and for how long may he or she go out?

◪ Things children may do without direct supervision. Cooking? Using kitchen appliances? Using electrical appliances (e.g., hair dryer) or tools? Taking a bath or shower? Opening windows? Climbing on a chair to reach something?

▶ **Home alone.** Sooner or later, the day will come when you agree to let your child or children stay home for some period of time without an adult in the house. The issue tends to arise when children are somewhere between eight and ten years old. Even if you do not consider it appropriate for your child to be alone in the house at that age, odds are some parents in your child's class will have deemed it so for theirs. By early adolescence, you can be sure that your child will be asking, if not demanding, the opportunity to stay home without you for some period of time.

Leaving your child home alone is a very controversial issue. We are not expressing a view as to whether or not you should do this. While you certainly do not have to, and we are not necessarily recommending that you do, acquiesce, if you do want to permit your child to be alone in the house, do so in an informed (as to both you and your child!) and deliberate manner. Remember, there is no rule that you must leave your child home alone or any prescribed age at which being left home unattended is mandated. Your decision as to when to leave your *older* child alone in the house is strictly a family matter. *It is never appropriate to leave an infant, toddler, or very young child alone or in the care of another child.*

If you are ready to try leaving your child home alone, some considerations:

■ Is your child ready? Consider whether your child: wants to be alone; is not afraid to be alone; has good problem-solving skills; is responsible and self-motivated; can recognize a problem and take action; follows instructions and the rules; would feel comfortable seeking help (from a neighbor, by phone, calling 911).

■ Make sure your child is prepared. Teach him or her: basic first aid; emergency procedures; what to do if there is a fire; how to reach you, another adult, building personnel or police or firefighters; how to handle phone calls, visitors or deliveries; what to do if you are late coming home. Make sure your child has one or more adults to call upon if there is a problem (neighbor, friend, doorman, etc.) and that he or she has a way to reach you (beeper, cellular phone, all your phone numbers). As you develop contingency plans, make sure to review them with your child and rehearse different scenarios. Do not leave your child alone if you do not have adequate household security or your neighborhood or apartment is not safe for an unattended child, and do not leave a very young child alone or in the care of another child.

■ Start slowly. Get your child acclimated to staying home alone in stages. Start with very brief trial runs (e.g., five minutes) when you are very nearby (perhaps just outside the door or in the lobby) and build up gradually. Take small steps as appropriate, talk to your child about his or her feelings and experience and modify the plan as necessary.

■ If your child will be coming home from school (or other activity) to an empty house, establish procedures for your child to check in with you or another designated adult upon arrival home and how to contact you if his or her schedule will change. Make certain your child always has, and can safeguard, a key and if he or she loses or forgets the key, knows how to access a spare key. Instruct your child not to enter the house if the door is open or not properly locked or, if applicable (i.e., a ground floor apartment or brownstone), if windows are open or broken.

▶ **Out alone.** The need for independence takes root early among sophisticated city children. Your children will likely be asking for some modicum of independence somewhere around eight years old. At that age, the request may be simply to go to a public restroom without you or to take the elevator in your apartment building or wait for a friend or the school bus in the lobby alone. By the age of 11, however, your child will likely be asking to take a public bus or walk to school or even to go to a local store, coffee shop or movie with friends. Whether or not you want to let your young adolescent out without an adult, you can be sure that by sixth or seventh grade, the peer pressure will begin to build.

For most of us, letting go is one of the hardest things we will ever do. The news stories make us very aware of potential dangers to children, which unfortunately have escalated in recent times. As a result, we are naturally reluctant to send them out without our protection. On the other hand, at some time or another, we must prepare our children to fend for themselves because eventually, it will become inappropriate for us to escort them everywhere. A child with no street experience becomes an easy victim.

Regardless of our feelings on the subject, they will turn into teenagers and young adults before too long and will need to have street-smart skills. Therefore, even if we only let our children out under very limited circumstances and with very strict conditions, and we do not do it until they are older, we still need to think about how to prepare them, and ourselves, for that momentous occasion.

If the subject of venturing out alone has not yet arisen, or you have a very young child, it is still important for your child to be prepared for situations where an adult is not present, even if only for a moment. For example, your children should know what to do if they become separated from you, the caregiver, their teacher or other adult with whom they are supposed to be. They need to know how to conduct themselves if approached by a stranger in a store, on the street, in a crowd, at the park or anywhere else. They need to be empowered to protect themselves against potential molestation or sexual abuse. As much as we may not want to have to discuss these issues with our children, as responsible parents, it is our duty to give them the tools to protect themselves.

There is a great deal of literature (for both adults and children) and a number of videos available on the topic of safety. There are even self-defense courses, videos and books for children. In talking to your children about safety, some topics you will probably want to include are:

> ◪ Street safety. Children should pay attention, look alert and self-confident and walk with a purpose. Whenever possible, they should walk in a group or with a buddy, stick to well-lit, well-traveled areas, avoid construction sites, empty or closed stores and deserted buildings, and not take shortcuts through the park (stick to streets). Children should know how to use a

public telephone and make collect calls. Money should be kept out of view. If in trouble, a child should shout "help," "call the police," or "fire" to attract attention. Work out strategies for dealing with strangers and what to do if being followed on foot or by a car.

■ Getting around. Teach your children the basics about crossing the street, following traffic signs and rules and being alert to vehicles whose drivers cannot see them or are backing up. If your child uses a bicycle, skateboard or in-line skates, make sure he or she uses appropriate safety gear, rides safely and understands how to conduct him or herself in traffic (pedestrian and vehicular).

■ Transportation. Bus, subway and taxi safety are extremely important. Children riding the bus or subway alone should be instructed on specific procedures such as avoiding isolated bus stops, having extra tokens or a MetroCard on hand, staying clear of the platform edge and riding in the car with the motorman (usually the center car). Children using taxis should only take yellow cabs or cars from a telephone car service (making sure not to get into an unmarked car or car service car that cannot identify by name the person they are supposed to pick up). The Parents League recommends that children riding in taxis always carry about $3.00 of "escape money" that can be quickly handed to a driver as the child exits the taxi at a traffic light if he or she is uncomfortable in the taxi.

■ Communication. As beepers, cellular phones and even high-tech walkie-talkies become more available and accessible, you may want to consider using technology to remain in contact with your older child as he or she begins to be out and about without you.

▶ **Safety programs in Manhattan.** The Parents League has been a leader in dealing with safety issues. The Parents League produces "Safety Guidelines for Kids, Parents and Teens," a tip sheet that provides extremely useful, New York-specific advice for families, important phone numbers and resources and information on how to report a crime. *In an emergency, a crime or missing child should be reported immediately by calling 911.* In a nonemergency situation, crimes should be reported to your local police precinct (a list of Manhattan precincts can be found at the end of this chapter).

The Safe Haven Program, begun in the 1970s by the Parents League in conjunction with the East Side Chamber of Commerce, registers merchants who agree to provide a sanctuary to a child or adult who is in danger or otherwise feels threatened. Safe Haven participants display a distinctive yellow and black sticker in their window or on the door and receive training (from either the Parents League if located in the 19th Precinct or the local precinct in other areas) to assist the person in need by providing shelter, allowing or making a telephone call (either to the police or someone else) and giving help. The Safe Haven Program has recently expanded to include apartment buildings on routes commonly traveled by school children. It is well worth educating your children to locate Safe Havens and choose a route along which Safe Havens can be found.

There are several Safe Haven networks throughout the city. On the Upper East Side, the program is coordinated by the Parents League and has more than 500 participants. On the Upper West Side, the program is coordinated by the Westside Crime Prevention Program and has more than 300 participants. If there is not a Safe Haven Program in your area, you can start one through your local schools, neighborhood associations or local precinct. The Parents League has prepared written guidelines to help start a Safe Haven Program, which you can get by calling 737-7385. The Parents League also maintains an active Speakers Bureau, which sends speakers to talk to students, community groups and parent associations about safety.

The Safety Net program is an organization made up of the Parents League and 28 member schools, representatives of which meet to share safety and safety patrol information. The Safety Net works with police and community officials and organizations to improve street safety. The Parents League will provide information about forming safety patrols to schools upon request.

School safety patrols play an important role in making the streets safe for our children. The public school system, through the Board of Education, has its own security force, which includes school crossing guards and internal security guards. Some public schools supplement with parent volunteers to assist at drop-off and pickup times.

The private schools tend to have very active safety patrol networks staffed by parent volunteers. Each school handles the situation differently, but most schools maintain a daily safety patrol force that works in conjunction with school administration and security personnel. Local police precincts work closely with parent safety patrol organizations, via their community affairs office or other outreach personnel to address student safety issues.

A number of precincts have developed so-called safe corridors, which are designated routes commonly traveled by students from neighborhood schools that will be specially patrolled by police during specific hours (typically before and after school and perhaps during lunch periods). Your child's school safety patrol or your local precinct can advise you whether there are any safe corridors in your neighborhood.

Your local police precinct can be another resource when it comes to safety. Precincts all have community affairs officers and youth officers who can provide valuable information to concerned parents. These officers will send personnel to address parent and student groups, and may have written materials, about safety issues. The precinct youth officer can also provide referrals to various social services and community resources, information on individual programs and help parents with troubled children. The precinct can even be a resource for activities as diverse as roller hockey sports leagues and the Boy Scouts' "Explorer Program."

Most local precincts will help parents assemble a child identification package that includes fingerprints and front and side view photos of your child. While New York City police will not keep an identification kit in police files, you can bring your child to the station house where they will take the photos and fingerprints of your child for you to safeguard at home. Call your local precinct to see if they will assist you in putting together your kit. If you assemble an identification kit, you may also want to include a description of any identifying marks (e.g., birthmarks, scars, chipped tooth, etc.) or characteristics (e.g., handedness, pitch of voice or a tendency to giggle or lisp), a lock of hair, and frequently updated measurements, clothing and shoe sizes and a photo.

Every fire department in New York City is also a safe haven for children through the Firecap program. Under this program, every firehouse and fire truck is considered a safe haven for a child or adult. The Firecap decal consists of a white square, bordered in black, with a red helmet in the middle and two children holding hands, and says "If you're in trouble, or if someone's bothering you, say NO and get away. You can always go to a firefighter or firehouse for help." When someone comes to them for help, they will notify appropriate authorities and take the necessary steps to help the person in need.

▶ **A final thought.** Preparing ourselves and our children for unpleasant or dangerous situations is a very tough thing to do. We do not even want to imagine our children in peril without us there to protect them. The reality is that we live in a very busy city where accidents can easily happen, crime is certainly not unknown and our children can be vulnerable targets. For that reason, we must help our children develop the judgment and have the tools to feel secure and help themselves. We urge every parent to spend time thinking about these issues, accessing the many available resources the city offers to aid in that endeavor and educating and working with their children to keep them as safe as possible.

◪

Emergencies

The last thing a parent wants to think about is coping with an emergency. However, the best thing you can do in the event of an emergency is to be prepared. This does not mean that you have to live your life waiting for the moment when your lifesaving, self-defense or other survival skills are put to the test, but it does mean that you and the members of your household, which includes your children, caregivers and housekeepers, have a current working knowledge of how to handle themselves and what to do if an emergency occurs.

▶ **Medical emergencies.** It is extremely important for you and those who take care of your children to be prepared to handle a medical emergency. At the very least, you should have a well-stocked first aid kit in the house, a book or two about how to handle various medical emergency situations (falls, burns, wounds, nosebleeds, bites, seizures, fevers, etc.) and a list, posted at or near each telephone, containing important emergency phone numbers such as your work and cellular numbers, the pediatrician (or any other doctor your family uses), the dentist, poison control, and a family member, neighbor or friend who should be called if you are not available. It is also wise for you and any caregiver you employ to be trained in CPR and other emergency techniques such as how to treat a choking victim, and that such training be regularly updated.

In the event of a medical emergency, many parents would prefer to have their regular pediatrician treat the child than to be taken by ambulance to an emergency room. Manhattan pediatrician Dr. Barry Stein advises that you quickly assess the situation and decide whether you have time to call your own doctor. In the case of a dire emergency, you should call 911 before anything else. If you have the choice, try to have the ambulance take your child to the hospital with which your doctor is affiliated (see below). If the situation is not dire, you can call the doctor and ask to be met or called at the emergency room or for the doctor to call ahead to the emergency room on your behalf so that you can be met by an appropriate specialist (e.g., an orthopedist if a broken bone is suspected). **If you are not sure how bad the situation is, do not waste time trying to decide, call 911.**

Another important element of preparation is to keep an envelope in your home that contains directions to the closest emergency room and/or to your doctor's hospital, cab fare to get to the doctor's office or hospital and a signed consent form authorizing treatment of your child. Keep in mind that in some circumstances, the doctor or emergency room cannot administer treatment without parental consent. Your consent form should state that your child may receive treatment if deemed necessary by his or her physician or the hospital physician in the event that you cannot be reached. It should also include any pertinent information about allergies, chronic conditions, medications taken regularly by the child and medical insurance.

▶ **EMS.** The New York City Emergency Medical Service (EMS), which operates under the auspices of the City Health and Hospitals Corporation, is the primary emergency medical care provider in the city. EMS operates a fleet of more than 350 ambulances that are deployed throughout, and constantly patrol, the five boroughs. There are both basic and advanced life support ambulances that provide on-site medical care and transportation to hospitals. Whenever an ambulance crew requires the advice of a physician, the crew can contact a Telemetry Control Unit staffed by a physician, which can monitor, review and direct the treatment protocol of the crew.

Basic ambulances are staffed with two emergency medical technicians who can perform CPR, bleeding control, administer oxygen, deliver a baby, immobilize the spine, apply antishock trousers and use a semiautomatic defibrillator. Advanced life support ambulances are staffed with two paramedics. In addition to the basic services, paramedics can perform more invasive procedures involving defibrillation, EKGs and the insertion of intravenous lines and endotracheal tubes.

When you call 911 for an ambulance, your call is routed to the high-tech EMS communications center in Maspeth, Queens, for triage and dispatching of an ambulance. EMS will transmit information directly to a mobile data terminal located in the dispatched ambulance. The ambulance you get will either be an EMS unit, a Voluntary Hospital Unit or a Volunteer Ambulance. Voluntary Hospital Units are owned and operated by private hospitals and receive no funding from the city. The participating private hospitals have contractually agreed to be dispatched via the 911 system and be subject to EMS rules (although they can determine their own billing rates). Volunteer Ambulances are operated by unpaid volunteer ambulance corps. Volunteer Ambulances are typically only called upon by EMS during peak hours or in the event of major multi-casualty situations.

If you need an ambulance, you can call 911. Once your call is routed by the police operator to EMS, be sure to give the EMS operator all relevant information and the telephone number of the phone from which you are calling. Be certain not to hang up until the EMS operator tells you to so that the automatic location indicator and automatic number indicator can be activated and all relevant information can be obtained. If possible, have someone meet the ambulance to lead the crew to where the patient is located. Remember to only use 911 for a true emergency.

Once you are in an ambulance, you have a limited ability to direct EMS to the hospital of your choice. EMS is required to take you to the closest 911 Receiving Emergency Facility (an emergency room certified by EMS and relevant state authorities). You can request that EMS take you to a specific hospital, which EMS will endeavor to do only under the following circumstances: the patient is not in extremis and the hospital you request is *not more than* either (1) ten minutes from the closest hospital to which you would have otherwise been taken or (2) 20 minutes from where the ambulance picks you up (i.e., not more than 20 minutes of total travel time).

The decision as to the medical condition of the patient and the estimated travel time is in the discretion of EMS, not you. As an example, if the ambulance picks you up at 14th Street and Fifth Avenue, the closest hospital (i.e., within 10 minutes of travel time) would be St. Vincent's. If you requested New York University Medical Center (at 33rd and First) and it was not rush hour, your request could probably be honored if EMS determined they could get there in under 20 minutes. If you requested Mt. Sinai Medical Center (at Madison Avenue and 100th Street), your request would be denied.

At the end of this chapter, you will find a list of Manhattan emergency rooms, New York City trauma centers, burn centers, replantation units, snake bite facilities and hyperbaric chambers.

▶ **Reporting a crime.** There are two types of situations involving crimes, emergencies and nonemergencies. In an emergency situation, the crime is in progress, or if not actually still in progress, the person or persons who committed the crime may still be in the vicinity. In a nonemergency situation, the crime has been committed and some amount of time has elapsed.

It is important to report crimes because police resources are allocated on the basis of reported criminal activity in the precinct. If crimes do not make it into official statistics, additional police presence or investigative resources will not be assigned or anticrime measures undertaken. From the point of view of city officials, a crime that is not reported did not happen.

You should report a crime in an emergency situation by calling 911. Patrol cars are dispatched by 911, so calling the local police precinct will delay police response. Your report should include as much information as you have about what happened, where it happened and descriptions of the perpetrator(s). The information you provide will be broadcast over the police radio. *A missing child should be reported immediately.* The responding officer will interview the victim and witnesses, if any, and file a complaint. A detective will be assigned if appropriate under applicable police procedures.

You can report a crime in a nonemergency situation by contacting the relevant local precinct. Assaults can generally be reported by telephone although robbery complaints must be filed in person. The complainant will be interviewed and a detective will be assigned if appropriate under applicable police procedures.

▶ **In case of a fire.** The New York City Fire Department recommends the following in the event of a fire in an apartment building:

◪ Get Help. Call 911 to report smoke, a fire or a suspected fire. If you are able, leave the area immediately and call from a safe location.

■ Smoke. If you smell smoke, call the fire department and, if applicable, activate the building fire alarm system. Since smoke rises, stay low. If you cannot escape, use wet towels or tape to seal the door and room vents. Open a window, but do not break it as you may need to close the window to prevent smoke from a lower floor entering through your window.

■ Escape. Identify fire exits in your building and locate fire exits in any unfamiliar building. Plan two ways out of the building and what you will do if you cannot escape. Do not use the elevator to escape a fire. Develop and practice a family escape plan. The safest escape may be to stay where you are and await help. Stay calm.

■ Alarm. Do not depend on someone else to call the fire department. Always call the fire department even if you think the fire is out. Do not depend on the building alarm system as it may not be directly connected to the fire department or may not be functioning.

■ Prevention. Complain to your building management if you notice blocked fire exits, locked fire doors, fire doors wedged open or trash stored in fire exits.

■ If your clothes catch fire, Stop, Drop and Roll.

For additional information on fire safety and prevention, you can contact the New York City Department Office of Public Safety and Education at 718 999-0321.

▶ **Don't panic.** While there is surely a great deal of potential for accidents to occur or for our children to land in dangerous or unsafe situations, in many ways, our lives in New York City are no more or less vulnerable than anywhere else in the country. We cannot and should not scare ourselves or our children away from partaking in the fun and pleasure of living in this city. What we can and should do is take reasonable precautions at home and, when we are out, be prepared and give our children the tools and security to handle the situations we and they may encounter.

Resources

Childproofing Services

Baby Proofers Plus Inc.
Summit, NJ
628-8052 (New York City office)

Baby Safe Inc.
444 East 86th Street
New York, NY 10028
396-1995

Childproofers Inc.
800 642-4654

Child Safe Homes Inc.
718 433-1446

CPR Training

American Heart Association
661-5335
AHA will provide a list of hospitals and other organizations offering CPR training. Be sure to ask for the organizations that offer training to individuals as opposed to those offering certification to medical personnel.

American Red Cross
150 Amsterdam Avenue
New York, NY 10023
787-1000
Health and Safety 875-2222
Regional course registration
800 514-5103

Babysaver CPR and Child Safety
Parent/Family Education Program
Beth Israel Medical Center
First Avenue at 16th Street
New York, NY 10003
420-4479

14th Street Y
Sol Goldman YM-YWHA of the Educational Alliance
344 East 14th Street
New York, NY 10003
780-0800

Jewish Community Center of the Upper West Side
15 West 65th Street
8th Floor
New York, NY 10023
580-0099

Lenox Hill Hospital
100 East 77th Street
New York, NY 10021
434-2273

92nd Street Y
1395 Lexington Avenue
New York, NY 10128
996-1100

St. Luke's Roosevelt Hospital Center
1000 Tenth Avenue (Roosevelt Hospital)
Amsterdam Avenue at 114th Street
(St. Luke's Hospital)
523-6222

St. Vincent's Hospital
Infant CPR
Maternity Education Program
153 West 11th Street
New York, NY 10011
604-7946

Tot Saver
School of Continuing Education in
Nursing
Mt. Sinai Medical Center
5 East 98th Street
Box 1144
New York, NY 10029
241-7050

Vanderbilt YMCA
224 East 47th Street
New York, NY 10017
756-9600

West Side YMCA
5 West 63rd Street
New York, N Y 10023
875-4112

Emergency Rooms (ER)

Bellevue Hospital
(911 receiving facility)
462 First Avenue
562-4141
ER entrance on the corner of First
Avenue and 27th Street. Bellevue
maintains specific pediatric emergency facilities staffed with a member of the Child Life Program.
Pediatric Trauma Unit, Trauma
Unit, Replantation Unit, Spinal
Cord Injury Center

Beth Israel Medical Center
(911 receiving facility)
First Avenue and 16th Street
420-2000
ER entrance on 16th Street
between First and Second Avenues.
Beth Israel maintains specific pediatric emergency facilities.
170 East End Avenue (911 receiving facility)
870-9000
ER entrance on East 87th Street off
of East End Avenue.

Cabrini Medical Center
227 East 19th Street
995-6000
ER entrance on 20th Street
between Second and Third
Avenues.

Gouverneur Hospital Diagnostic and Treatment Center
227 Madison Street
238-7000
No ER but a walk-in clinic for treatment and diagnosis on Madison
Street between Clinton and
Jefferson Streets.

Harlem Hospital Center
(911 receiving facility)
506 Lenox Avenue
939-1000
ER entrance on Lenox Avenue
between 135th and 136th Streets.
Harlem Hospital maintains specific
pediatric emergency facilities.
Trauma Unit

Hospital for Joint Diseases Orthopaedic Institute
301 East 17th Street at corner of
Second Avenue
598-6000
Specialized hospital. ER for private
ambulance only, not serviced by
EMS. Entrance through main
lobby. Immediate care center for
broken bones, sprains, etc.

Jacobi Medical Center
1400 Pelham Parkway South
Eastchester Road
Bronx, NY 10461
718 918-5000
Hyperbaric center and snake bite
center

Lenox Hill Hospital
(911 receiving facility)
100 East 77th Street
434-2000
ER entrance at 120 East 77th Street
between Park and Lexington
Avenues. Lenox Hill maintains specific pediatric emergency facilities.

Manhattan Eye, Ear and Throat Hospital
210 East 64th Street
838-9200
Specialized services for eye, ear, nose or throat emergencies. ER entrance through main hospital entrance on 64th Street between Second and Third Avenues.

Metropolitan Hospital
(911 receiving facility)
1901 First Avenue
423-6262
ER entrance on 97th Street between First and Second Avenues. Metropolitan maintains specific pediatric emergency facilities.

Mt. Sinai Medical Center
(911 receiving facility)
One Gustave L. Levy Place
241-6500
ER entrance on Madison Avenue between 100th and 101st Streets. Mt. Sinai maintains specific pediatric emergency facilities staffed with a member of the Child Life Program.

New York and Presbyterian Hospital (911 receiving facility)
Columbia-Presbyterian Campus
(formerly Columbia Presbyterian Medical Center)
622 West 168th Street
305-2500
ER entrance on 168th Street between Broadway and Ft. Washington Avenue. Columbia-Presbyterian Campus maintains specific pediatric emergency facilities.
Pediatric Trauma Unit

New York and Presbyterian Hospital (911 receiving facility)
New York-Cornell Campus
(formerly New York Hospital Cornell Medical Center)
525 East 68th Street

746-5454
ER entrance on 68th Street between York Avenue and the FDR Drive. New York-Cornell Campus maintains specific pediatric emergency facilities.
Burn Center, Trauma Unit

New York Eye and Ear Infirmary
310 East 14th Street
979-4000
Specialized services for eye, ear, nose or throat emergencies. ER entrance on Second Avenue between 13th and 14th Streets.

New York University Medical Center (911 receiving facility)
550 First Avenue
263-7300
ER entrance on First Avenue at 33rd Street.

NYU Downtown Hospital
170 William Street
312-5000
ER entrance at 170 William Street between Beekman and Spruce.

St. Clare's Hospital and Health Center (911 receiving facility)
425 West 52nd Street
586-1500
ER entrance on 52nd Street between Ninth and Tenth Avenues. Because St. Clare's does not treat children on an inpatient basis, EMS does not bring pediatric patients here. The ER will treat a walk-in pediatric patient but seriously ill pediatric patients will be transferred to St. Vincent's as soon as possible.

St. Luke's-Roosevelt Hospital Center (911 receiving facility)
523-4000
St. Luke's
111 Amsterdam Avenue
ER entrance on the corner of 113th and Amsterdam Avenue. St. Luke's maintains a pediatric emergency room.
Trauma Unit

Roosevelt Division (911 receiving facility)
1000 Tenth Avenue
ER entrance on West 59th Street between Columbus and Amsterdam Avenues. Roosevelt maintains a specific pediatric emergency department.

St. Vincent's Hospital and Medical Center of New York (911 receiving facility)
153 West 11th Street
604-7000
ER entrance on Seventh Avenue between 11th and 12th Streets. St.Vincent's maintains special pediatric emergency facilities.
Trauma Unit

Fire Safety

New York City Fire Department
9 Metrotech Center
Brooklyn, NY 11201
718 999-2000 (headquarters)
718 999-0321 (public safety and education department)
718 999-2056/2013 (public information—Fire Department and EMS)
718 694-2713/2730 (Firecap program)

National Fire Protection Association
11 Tracy Drive
Avon, MA 02322
800 344-3555
www.NFPA.org (includes a list of publications)

Home Safety and Health

ConEdison
General Information 338-3000 or 460-4600
Corporate communications 460-2115 (for copies of ConEdison pamphlets)
Gas emergency 683-8830
Fallen power lines, damaged electrical equipment or hazardous conditions 338-3000

Healthy Home Environmental (private consultant)
79 Pomona Road
Suffern, NY 10901
888 466-3620

New York City Department of Environmental Protection
59-17 Junction Blvd.
Corona, N Y 11368
718 595-6579
718 DEP-HELP (24-hour complaint number for water, sewer, air, noise)

New York City Department of Health
125 Worth Street
New York, NY 10013
442-9666 (general number)
788-5290 (external affairs)
Special services:
City health information 788-5381
Heat complaints 960-4800
Lead hotline BAN-LEAD (226-5323)
Lyme Disease Hotline
518 474-4568
Ozone alert 800 535-1345
Pest control 718 956-7107/8
Pollen count 800 223-6837
Radiological health 676-1580
Smoking enforcement and regulations 442-1840
Water complaints 718 595-3510
Window falls prevention program 676-2140/1

New York City Department of Sanitation
Bureau of Waste Prevention, Reuse and Recycling
PO Box 156
Bowling Green Station
New York, NY 10274
219-8090
Publication on hazardous home cleaning materials

New York State Department of Health
Nelson Rockefeller Empire State Plaza
Albany, NY 12237
518 474-7354
Metropolitan Regional Office
5 Penn Plaza
New York, NY 10001
613-4900
800 458-1158 (environmental health information)

U.S. Environmental Protection Agency
Washington, DC
202 260-2090 (general number)
800 490-9198 (general number)
202 260-5922 (publications)
www.epa.gov

www.knowlead.com (Lead poisoning information)

Poison Control

Poison Control Center
POISONS or VENENOS or 866-8603

Police Information

General information 374-5000
Child Abuse Hotline 800 342-3720
Crime victim services 577-7777
Crimestoppers 577-TIPS
Domestic violence 800 621-4673
Sex crime report unit 267-RAPE

Precincts have a list of neighborhood pharmacies that are open 24 hours.

1st Precinct
16 Ericsson Place
334-0611

5th Precinct
19 Elizabeth Street
334-0711

6th Precinct
233 West Tenth Street
741-4811

7th Precinct
191/z Pitt Street
477-7311

9th Precinct
321 East Fifth Street
477-7811

10th Precinct
230 West 20th Street
741-8211

13th Precinct
230 East 21st Street
477-7411

Midtown South Precinct
357 West 35th Street
239-9811

17th Precinct
167 East 51st Street
826-3211

Midtown North Precinct
306 West 54th Street
767-8400

19th Precinct
153 East 67th Street
452-0600

20th Precinct
120 West 82nd Street
580-6411

Central Park Precinct
86th Street Transverse
570-4820

23rd Precinct
164 East 102nd Street
860-6411

24th Precinct
151 West 100th Street
678-1811

25th Precinct
120 East 119th Street
860-6511

26th Precinct
520 West 126th Street
678-1311

28th Precinct
2271 Eighth Avenue
678-1611

30th Precinct
451 West 151st Street
690-8811

32nd Precinct
250 West 135th Street
690-6311

33rd Precinct
2120 Amsterdam Avenue
927-3200

34th Precinct
4295 Broadway
927-9711

West Side Crime Prevention
Program 866-8603

Product Catalogues

One Step Ahead
800 274-8440

Perfectly Safe
800 837-KIDS

The Right Start
800 548-8531

Safer Baby
800 356-0654

Safety 1st
800 964-7744

www.kidsafe.com

www.safensoundkids.com

www.safetysuperstore.com
800 683-7233

Product Safety

Auto Safety Hotline
800 424-9393

Center for Auto Safety
2001 S Street NW
Suite 410
Washington, DC 20009
202 328-7700

National Highway Traffic Safety
Administration
US Department of Transportation
Washington, DC
800 424-9393 Safety Hotline

Juvenile Products Manufacturers
Association
609 231-8500
www.jpma.org

U.S. Consumer Product Safety
Commission
Washington, DC 20207
800 638-CPSC
www.cpsc.gov

Safety—General Information

Kid Protection Network
PO Box 516
Middlefield, CT 06455
860 347-0408

MPI
PO Box 6960
Villa Park, IL 60181
888 840-SAFE
Publishes *Kids Safe and Sound* and
Home Safe and Sound available for
$1.50 each

National Center for Missing and
Exploited Children
2101 Wilson Blvd.
Suite 550
Arlington, VA 22201
800 843-5678

Parents League of New York
115 East 82nd Street
New York, NY 10028
737-7389
Safe Haven Program, Safety Net,
Safety Tips, Speakers Bureau

www.safebaby.net

www.safekids.org

Self-Defense Classes for Children

Children's Safety Project
Greenwich House
27 Barrow Street
6th Floor
New York, NY 10014
242-4140

Prepare, Inc.
147 West 25th Street
New York, NY 10001
800 442-7273

www.seriouskidstuff.com

Chapter 6

IN SEARCH OF MARY POPPINS

Arranging child care for our families is one of the most difficult and complicated aspects of modern parenting. When we cannot be with our children ourselves, we want them to be in the care of loving, responsible and competent individuals who will take care of their needs, look out for their welfare and provide a safe, stimulating environment. Yet, when it comes to our ideas about caregivers, many of us have an image of a caretaker based on fictitious television and movie characters, such as Alice from *The Brady Bunch*, Mr. French from *Family Affair*, Maria from *The Sound of Music* and, of course, Mary Poppins. At the other end of the spectrum, today's media has left us with images of the dire consequences of selecting the wrong caregivers.

In short, we are looking for that mythical caretaker who has the patience of a saint, brilliant parenting skills, excellent judgment and a doctorate in education, is a licensed paramedic able to cope with any medical emergency and is a great friend and playmate for the kids. While most of us do of course manage to find satisfactory child care arrangements, it is usually the result of having become more realistic along the way.

In general, there are three types of child care alternatives available to parents. First, there is the in-home caregiver. The in-home caregiver can work on a live-in or live-out basis and is typically either a nanny, combination housekeeper/caregiver, au pair or hourly babysitter. Second, there is in-home group care, also known as family child care. In this type of situation, the caregiver provides child care services in her own home. Under New York law, any person caring for three or more unrelated children in her home for more than three hours per day, other than her own children, must be registered or licensed. Third, there are day care centers, which provide care for a number of children in a group environment in a special facility. Day care centers in New York must be licensed.

In deciding what kind of child care is most appropriate for your family, it is essential to consider several factors: what stage of development your child is at; the number of children you need care for; your budget; your own scheduling needs and flexibility; your preferences and priorities; and the benefits and limitations of the various types of child care. This chapter will help you to identify your needs, establish your priorities and direct you through the process of selecting the right child care for your family. At the end of this chapter you will find a directory of resources for your easy reference.

▶ **At each stage of development, your child has different needs.** An infant is dependent on a caregiver for food, comfort, company and diaper changes. It is important to the development and sense of security of the infant that its needs be addressed promptly. As the baby gets older and develops motor skills and the beginnings of language, it becomes necessary to provide stimulation and enrichment beyond tending to his or her physical needs and providing nurturing care. For the mobile baby and toddler beginning to explore, the safety of the environment becomes more challenging. There needs to be opportunity for the child to walk, climb and run as well as to manipulate many types of toys, indoors and out. The preschooler must have ample opportunity for socialization with other children. School-age children have their own needs. They still need a certain degree of physical care (meals, baths, etc.), but will require a different type of supervision of playdates and homework and transportation to and from after-school activities.

If you have two or more children, it is important to acknowledge their different developmental needs and organize child care accordingly. For example, it may not work to send an infant on the playdate of an older child or to have an older child forgo activities because of the baby's nap schedule. It is advisable to evaluate your child care alternatives and prioritize your and your child's needs on an annual basis. For example, your quiet and sweet baby nurse may not be the person who will do well chasing an active toddler at the playground. Or the skills of the wonderful nanny who cared for your preschoolers may be underutilized when your children are in school all day.

▶ **What's out there?** In comparing the various types of child care available, a parent must have realistic expectations about what each alternative offers and does not offer. In-home care offers flexible hours and can be extremely convenient for parents. The child is in his or her own home with his or her own toys. If the child is sick at home, no special arrangements need to be made. The parents and caregiver can organize a routine (i.e., naps, mealtimes, outings) that is specifically tailored to the child. Parents can enroll the younger child in classes attended with the caregiver to create opportunities for socialization. Parents and caregivers can also make playdates and take the child to the park or other play areas (public or private) to make the child's day active and fun. The caregiver can pick up older children from school and transport them to their after-school activities and playdates.

On the other hand, in-home caregivers are unsupervised, unregulated and unlicensed. The quality of the care is a direct function of the experience, personality and competence of the caregiver. In-home care can be more expensive than other alternatives. Because of the intimacy of having a caregiver in the home, the parent/caregiver relationship can be quite complicated. The convenience factor can become severely compromised when the caregiver is late for work, calls in sick, goes on holiday or quits without warning.

Group care, in the form of family care or day care centers, offers a regulated and licensed environment. Children are in a social environment that is consistent and likely to be structured. In group situations with more than one caregiver, the caregivers are supervised or at least not alone. Group care providers often have special training, or the facility may be accredited by national associations. There can be a curriculum for the children and specific activities geared to the age levels of the children. The cost can be quite reasonable.

Although the caregiver/child ratio is regulated by law, the group care option offers less one-on-one time between child and caregiver and, if care is provided by several people, the child may not have the opportunity to form a bonded relationship with a particular individual. If a child is ill and cannot be brought to day care, the parent must make other arrangements, which can be quite difficult to do on short notice. Group care usually has regular operating hours and drop-off and pickup times that are not generally flexible and rarely cover nighttime hours. There is typically a routine for meals, snacktimes and rest periods, which are set for the group and may not specifically accommodate a particular child's needs or schedule.

▶ **What does it cost?** The cost of child care can be quite unexpected for the uninitiated. For full-time in-home caregivers, salaries typically range from $300 to $900 per week (plus room and board for live-ins) depending on the job description and caregiver qualifications. Average salaries range from $300 to $450. Au pairs typically cost approximately $200 per week. Family child care and day care can cost between $100 and $350 per week. Some lucky parents have day care services either provided on-site by employers at no cost or at a subsidized cost. Hourly babysitters usually get between $7 and $15 per hour plus transportation home at night, although it may be possible to hire high school students or mother's helpers at somewhat less per hour. Most of the private schools and some of the colleges and universities located in Manhattan, as well as the Parents League (a nonprofit organization of parents and independent schools), maintain a registry of students interested in babysitting.

Whatever type of child care you ultimately choose, the goal is to obtain the best quality care available to meet your needs and your budget. The person with whom you leave your children is your surrogate in your absence and so should be a valued and respected member of a parenting partnership. Child care is not a place to find bargains. Unfortunately, in the child care business, you really do get what you pay for. This is *not* to say that a highly paid nanny is necessarily a better quality caregiver than a lesser paid caregiver who does housework. It is to say, however, that when a caregiver or child care facility is willing to be paid substantially below market rate, there are serious questions to be asked and reference checking to be done.

In-home Caregivers

If you have elected to hire an in-home caregiver, it is important to determine exactly what job you are attempting to fill. Although this may sound like a foolish exercise, in fact, in the realm of in-home child care, there are a range of functions that a family may want to delegate to one or more employees. The potential employee also is likely to have a view on what tasks she is willing or unwilling to perform. We say "she" because, according to the International Nanny Association (INA), more than 95% of in-home caregivers are women.

In addition to caring for the children, the typical household jobs are cleaning and laundry, cooking, shopping, and doing errands. The issue becomes whether the employee will do all, any or some of these tasks for just the children, for the whole family or some combination thereof.

▶ **In-home alternatives.** With the intention of providing a framework for discussion, it is helpful to identify four basic categories of in-home child care: nanny, combination caregiver and housekeeper, au pair (American or foreign) and babysitter. These terms have no formal or legal definitions and are often used interchangeably. For our purposes however, we have based our definitions of the different types of in-home child care on the terms most commonly used in Manhattan and the terms used by the INA.

◾ Nanny. The INA defines a nanny as a full-time employee who is hired to handle all tasks related to the care of children and whose duties are restricted to the domestic chores related to child care, such as preparing meals for the children, children's laundry and cleaning children's rooms. The nanny may or may not have had formal training, but usually has actual experience. Her work week ranges from 40-60 hours and she generally works unsupervised. She can live in or live out.

◪ Combination caregiver and housekeeper. This person provides full-time or part-time child care and domestic help for a family. In addition to caring for the children, she is typically responsible for some level of house cleaning, laundry and cooking and may also do family errands. She usually has actual experience. She works the same range of hours as a nanny, is usually unsupervised and can live in or out.

◪ Au pair/American. According to the INA, an American au pair lives with a family, handles light housekeeping chores and has full-time child care duties. She typically works under the supervision of a parent and works a 40-60 hour week.

◪ Au pair/Foreign. A foreign au pair works in this country under the provisions of a special one-year cultural exchange visa. Au pair programs are federally regulated by the United States Information Agency. The intention of the au pair program is to provide a young European woman or man with the opportunity to live with a host family and provide up to 45 hours per week of help with child care and household chores in exchange for a modest stipend/salary (approximately $150 per week). The host family is required to provide the au pair with $500 toward and time off to attend an educational program. The particular conditions of an au pair's employment are specified by the terms of the program with which he or she is affiliated. By law, au pairs are required to have eight hours of child safety and 24 hours of child development instruction, and pass a reference and criminal records check before placement with a host family. The average cost for an au pair, including program fees, stipend, transportation and educational expense, is $200 per week.

◪ Babysitter. The INA defines a babysitter as a person who provides supervisory, custodial care of children on an irregular full-time or part-time basis. In New York, babysitters are usually paid on an hourly basis for actual time worked.

▶ **How to find an in-home caregiver.** The key to finding a caregiver is to network, network, network. The most typical methods for finding applicants are word-of-mouth recommendations, advertising and employment agencies. As will be discussed in greater detail, no matter where you find a potential employee, you must fully check her references and background before hiring her to care for your children.

Word of mouth. Many families find their employees via word of mouth. Most caregivers have friends or relatives to recommend. Other parents can be a great source of candidates too, as can bulletin boards in pediatricians' offices, schools, the Parents League office and other facilities catering to children (i.e., children's gym classes) or families. Almost any time that parents gather and talk it is possible to generate a list of names of potential candidates as well as both welcome and less-than-welcome advice on getting through the search process. When relying on word-of-mouth sources, it is best to get names from people whose judgment you trust and who personally know the individual they are proposing.

Advertising. Another popular method is to advertise in local newspapers. Most parents who go this route have a view on which papers yield the best applicants and which papers are favorite places to list their job. The most used are the *New York Times* and the *Irish Echo,* a local newspaper that comes out every Wednesday. The newspapers not only have listings for job opportunities, but also contain sections on situations wanted. Newspapers are widely used by caregivers of all nationalities as a job source. Other possibilities include foreign language publications (i.e., Polish, Russian and Spanish), which reach specific ethnic populations.

There are three tricks to advertising for caregivers: drafting your job description, handling the volume of responses and screening applicants. Your job description must be clear and specific. Indicate the qualifications required, the number of children to be cared for, other duties included in the job description, hours and salary. If, for instance, you only want someone who is legally allowed to work in this country or with a certain amount of experience, say so. The more detailed your advertisement, the less calls you will get from unsuitable candidates and the better the pool of applicants from which you can choose. It is helpful to peruse other advertisements for ideas before you place your own.

No matter what your ad says, be prepared for an onslaught of phone calls. You may well receive in excess of 100 responses if your ad presents an attractive job description or salary. One veteran of this process actually sets up a temporary voice mail service when she hires a new caregiver. If you plan to screen calls with an answering machine, say so in your ad, because many applicants will not leave messages on a machine. When screening calls, work up a basic telephone interview (more about this later), which an applicant must pass before being invited in for an interview. This will save you from wasting time meeting unacceptable candidates.

A concern about hiring through the newspaper is that the person comes to you totally unscreened—she has not been interviewed or her background checked, however superficially, by anyone in the employment business. Consequently, since you have no intermediary to rely on to screen the applicant, you must carefully do your own investigation and use caution before letting someone into your home. Many parents who regularly use this method arrange to meet applicants in a public place such as the lobby of the apartment building or a coffee shop for an initial screening. Others arrange to have the children out and another adult (both parents, a friend, relative or neighbor) present in the house for a first interview. Once you are satisfied that an applicant is an appropriate candidate, you can invite her back for a subsequent interview and to meet the children.

Agencies. This leads us to the domestic help employment agencies. The main reason a family will turn to an employment agency is that the agency will screen applicants, supply candidates that will meet your needs, check references, provide advice and guidance through the search process, serve as an intermediary in negotiating terms of employment and provide additional candidates if the placement does not work out. For this service, the typical fee is either 10% of the employee's annual salary or from one month's to six weeks' salary. Fees are not generally negotiable.

Most agencies offer a limited guarantee with respect to placements. If a placement does not work out during the guarantee period, the agency will either provide a replacement or refund all or a portion of the fee. If possible, it is advisable to have a written agreement with an agency regarding fees and guarantees.

The key to using an agency is to find a reputable one run by professionals. Wendy Sachs, former president of the INA, recommends these tips for identifying a good agency:

◪ Investigate the reputation of the agency by asking friends, colleagues and other parents who have used that agency. Personal recommendations and referrals are very helpful. Make sure that the agency is licensed to do business in the jurisdiction. How long has the agency been in business? Has the agency had violations or citations against it? Is the agency an INA member?

◪ Understand the fee schedule and refund and replacement policy in the event the placement does not work out.

◪ Understand the screening process used by the agency and be clear about what information the agency will provide to you and in what form it will be provided. How does the agency recruit applicants, how are references checked (phone, mail), how far back does the agency go (age, years of employment, school records), is there a written application or report, does the agency require any health checks, is an applicant sent out for interviews before references are confirmed, does the agency do a criminal check?

☑ What services does the agency provide? Each agency has its own practices with respect to placement and follow-up and even training, so understand what the particular agency does.

☑ Availability of the placement staff can be important when you are in the throes of a search. Does the agency run a full-time business or will your calls be answered by a machine? Will you work with a single counselor?

While it may be difficult to get clear answers from an employment agency or independently confirm the answers you are given, it is certainly worth initiating the dialogue and getting whatever information you can about the agency, its practices and its track record.

The INA asks that its member agencies adhere to a certain level of professional practices to provide the best and most reliable service to their clients. These include disclosing how candidates are interviewed and their references checked, and offering a written fee agreement to parents and prompt refunds when the placement does not work out. Equally as important, the INA recommends that agencies respect the applicants, accurately describe jobs and families so that applicants and parents are better matched, help families and caregivers develop an employment agreement and make the applicant aware of the fee policy to which the family is subject. According to Ms. Sachs, who also is the CEO of the Philadelphia Nanny Network and owner of NannyCheck (a New York City consulting service for screening and interviewing nanny applicants for families), in her experience, the more information made available to both applicants and families, the more likely the placement will work out for both parties.

In New York, domestic employment agencies are regulated under the State General Business Law (fees, refunds), and the New York City License Enforcement Law (licensing by the Department of Consumer Affairs), Consumer Protection Law (prohibits misleading and deceptive practices) and the Human Rights Law (discrimination). The fees that an agency may charge an employer are not set by law except in the case where (1) the agency specifically recruited a domestic or household employee from outside the continental United States, in which case the fee may not exceed 11% of the employee's first full year's wages (of which not more than 25% may be charged the employee) or (2) the agency receives a fee from the employee, in which case the fee for a placement may not exceed 10% of the first full month's salary if no meals or lodging are provided, 12% of the first full month's salary if two meals per day are provided and 18% of the first full month's salary if three meals per day and lodging are provided.

If an agency does not receive a fee from the job applicant, the fee is determined by agreement between the employer and employment agency. Essentially, the agency is free to charge families looking for domestic help whatever the market will bear. You are not entitled by law to a refund if the placement goes awry unless the applicant also paid a fee to the agency, in which event the General Business Law has specific provisions. Since most employment agencies placing caregivers do not charge applicants and therefore have placement fees paid by the employers, your right to a refund will be a matter of contract. If the agency represented a refund policy to you and fails to live up to its promise, you may file a complaint with the City Department of Consumer Affairs at 42 Broadway, New York, NY 10004, 487-4444.

Agencies are not required by law to check more than one reference or to perform any other background screening of an applicant. Agencies will vary in their screening and background checking procedures and their vigilance in contacting references and verifying immigration status. It is therefore important to make the effort to determine what exactly the agency does and does not do and supplement their efforts with your own. No matter what any agency tells you, it is always wise to contact references and confirm other information yourself. Again, however, if an agency does represent to you that it investigated the qualifications of an applicant in any way and/or has done a background check, you can complain to the City Department of Consumer Affairs if you were deceived or misled by such representations.

Pursuant to the City Human Rights Law, an employment agency cannot discriminate on the basis of age, race, creed, color, national origin, gender, disability, religion, marital status, sexual orientation or alienage or citizenship status. The agency is therefore not supposed to get this type of information from applicants or honor discriminatory requests by a potential employer. This law, however, does not apply to an employer with less than four employees. Thus, while you are not supposed to ask an agency to send you applicants who are of a certain age, race, religion and from a certain country, you may reject individuals who do not meet these criteria.

To find out whether an agency is licensed or to get a current list (for a nominal charge) of agencies licensed to do business in New York City, you can contact the City of New York Department of Consumer Affairs, 42 Broadway, New York, NY 10004, 487-4444. The department will not release a list of agencies with outstanding violations against them. However, you can call the department and ask whether a particular agency has outstanding violations against it.

Included at the end of this chapter for your reference is a list of a number of local agencies (licensed as of the date of this publication) and agencies that handle national or regional placements. Please note that we do not recommend any particular agency and should you decide to work with an agency, we urge you to clarify its policies, procedures, fee structure as well as the depth of their background checks of applicants.

Au pairs. If you want to hire a foreign au pair, you must go through one of the eight agencies authorized by the United States Information Agency to place au pairs in this country. Because of the unique visa status granted to au pairs, you cannot hire an au pair on your own. The au pair agencies have their own recruitment personnel and a staff of local counselors to work with au pairs and their host families. The hiring and interviewing procedures followed and services offered by the agencies will differ somewhat. If hiring an au pair, it may be wise to contact more than one agency to determine which suits your preferences and standards.

You can get more information about the au pair program by contacting the United States Information Agency at 202 619-4355 or by directly contacting the au pair agencies which are listed at the end of this chapter.

Nanny schools. Another method for finding a caregiver is through nanny schools. There are currently 13 schools and colleges offering nanny training programs certified by the American Council of Nanny Schools. To be certified, a program must provide 200 classroom hours and 100 "laboratory" hours in subjects such as child development, communication, family studies, nutrition, behavior and guidance, planning activities, CPR and a supervised "practicum." Nanny schools offer placement services and will provide a certificate of completion and transcript of grades to graduates. To obtain a list of certified nanny training programs, contact Joy Shelton, President of the American Council of Nanny Schools, Office A-74, Delta College, University Center, MI 48710, 517 686-9417. At the end of this chapter you will find a list of nanny training programs (not all of which are certified by the American Council of Nanny Schools) that will help arrange placements in New York City.

▶ **Interviewing basics.** Before inviting an applicant to your home, it is useful to conduct a screening over the telephone. During this call, you can describe the job (number of children, basic duties, hours/days) and salary, clarify the individual's qualifications (i.e., experience, immigration status), and confirm her availability to begin work. This is a good time to state any prerequisites you have for the job such as swimming, driving, cooking, traveling or nighttime babysitting. You may want to ask some open-ended questions such as "Why are you seeking a child care job?" to get a feel for the type of person she is. If the person meets your threshold requirements, you can schedule the interview.

When interviewing, first impressions do count. Your prospective caregiver should be punctual (or have handled being late with an acknowledgment, phone call or very good excuse), be dressed appropriately, have good manners and be able to communicate in your language. The particular qualities you are seeking will depend in large part on your own priorities. Some parents prefer a high-energy, enthusiastic and jolly person while others favor a calm, steady and sensible personality. A person's age, experience, education level, household skills, sense of humor, culture and common sense are all relevant to the role this person will have in your family.

An interviewing technique we have found very effective is to prepare a written application for prospective employees to complete. The application can include basic information (name, address, driver's license, passport number, education, etc.), a health questionnaire, information about prior employment, and references. Be sure to examine originals of all legal documentation. An application provides a less personal way to ask hard questions such as whether the person has been arrested or convicted, uses alcohol or drugs, and get information about family background and outside commitments (such as caring for their own young children or other dependents). This is also an easy way to obtain a signed release to conduct a criminal check if you elect to do so. You can include questions about the person's philosophy about discipline, handling anger, hypothetical situations, why the person wants the job, leisure activities and long-term plans. In addition to the answers provided, you can assess the person's communication and comprehension skills. The application serves as an excellent starting place for your discussion with the applicant.

One of the most important elements of the interview is to establish an employment history of the applicant. Wendy Sachs suggests developing a timeline of the person's work experience since the age of 18. All gaps in employment should be explained and job references should be verifiable. A red flag should go up in your mind when a person has had an abundance of short-term jobs, cannot remember who she worked for (or the names and ages of the children), has long unexplained gaps in employment and/or cannot provide a way to contact references.

There are many qualities to seek in a caregiver. The INA has developed a list of basic competencies for a caregiver that provides an excellent checklist for families seeking an in-home employee. While it is not possible to find the perfect nanny, it is worth seeking a person who has as many of the following characteristics possible: is observant and consistent; can articulate a philosophy of work, maintain confidentiality, follow instructions, perform basic tasks, plan and prepare meals for the children, care for a moderately ill child, act in an emergency, create and maintain a safe and healthy environment, communicate with children, observe safety rules, provide appropriate play and learning experiences for the children, support parents' preferences and their right to privacy, maintain basic hygienic standards (bathing, hand washing, brushing teeth) and recognize her role as part of a team and the parents as the ultimate authority. She should also have a professional attitude and appearance, decent judgment, initiative, good manners, use proper language, and be able to execute appropriate management techniques (discipline, organization and supervising activities).

On a more personal level, it is also important to find a person who expresses a similar philosophy to your own and who you think will be compatible with your family in terms of habits, neatness, flexibility, organization, food choices and style of interacting with children. There is no formula to ensure that the person you hire will meet all of your criteria, but your intuition can be a powerful tool in making a choice. If you feel comfortable and positive, by all means pursue the process. If you feel uncomfortable and negative, listen to your instincts—they probably are right.

In all cases, it is wise to meet with an applicant you are considering hiring more than once, and if at all possible, to have both parents (or any other adult whose judgment you trust or who is part of the household) present or available during one of the meetings. A call-back interview offers a useful opportunity to collect information, gain a sense of the person's disposition and confirm your original feelings.

It is also critical that you see how the individual interacts with your children, whether for a brief introduction or an extended play session. Some parents conduct the full interview with the child present, while others find this distracting and bring in the child for only a portion of the interview. Still other parents prefer to have a trial period (a weekend or several workdays) with a caregiver before making an offer to the person, the advisability of which is a function of how your children deal with strangers and handle transitions.

Checking references. Once you have narrowed down your search, it is crucial to check completely all references given to you and confirm the specifics of the information you were given with respect to job responsibilities, length of employment and reasons for leaving. Ask the reference questions regarding the caregiver's attitude, performance and competence. Go back to your own priorities and confirm that the caregiver has the qualities you seek. It is worth asking former employers what problems they might have had with the employee and whether they would hire her again. You may also want to verify that the reference is valid and not just a friend or relative of the applicant. For example, you can confirm that the reference has the job title you were given by calling his or her office.

Current wisdom in the caregiver industry is that it is appropriate to do a background and criminal record check on a prospective caregiver before she begins work in your home. Some employment agencies will perform this valuable service as part of their own screening process, in which case you should ask for a copy of the written report. Many families hire a private investigation firm to conduct a search of the applicant's criminal, driving, and credit records, as well as a search of credit bureau databases to determine whether a social security number is valid. The cost of a search can range from $100-500 or even more depending on the number of jurisdictions involved and the depth of the search. For an additional cost, some agencies will also verify other information, such as attendance at educational institutions or foreign visa and passport information (to the extent information is public). A list of agencies that can conduct records searches can be found at the end of this chapter.

While there is no such thing as a national criminal check, in certain states it is possible to perform statewide checks, while in others, including New York, searches must be conducted at the county level. A criminal records search will reveal felony and misdemeanor convictions and must be conducted for each jurisdiction where the prospective employee has lived or worked. The driving records search, available if the applicant has a driver's license, will verify address, physical description and birthdate as well as reveal license suspensions or penalties for driving under the influence or other driving-related offenses. The credit report verifies addresses (current and prior) and employment and will give you information about the applicant's behavior (excessive indebtedness, financial responsibility, collections).

When hiring an agency to do searches, be clear on how far back in time the various searches will go and the number of jurisdictions being reviewed. Remember, New York City alone has several counties, which must be searched separately. Note that neither you nor a nanny employment agency can screen a potential babysitter through the New York State Central Child Abuse and Maltreatment Registry.

The prospective employee must sign a release to enable you to arrange for a records search. The agency that you retain to do searches can provide you with a release form to be signed by the applicant. You may want to contact agencies at the start of your search so that you have the release form available during your interviews with prospective employees.

While asking for a release may feel awkward, if conducting a search will make you feel more confident in your decision, it is well worth it. If an applicant will not sign such a release, it may be an indication of a problem in her history and should be considered a warning signal. It is important to remember that searches are not fail-safe. They will not pick up crimes committed under an alias or in a jurisdiction that was not searched.

▶ **Health Screening.** You may want to consider requiring your new caregiver to have a physical before beginning employment in your home. If this is a precondition to employment, many parents handle the situation by sending the caregiver to the parent's doctor at their expense. For parents who elect to require a physical exam, Manhattan pediatrician Dr. Barry Stein suggests a screening for TB (and other communicable diseases) and a routine exam, which would indicate if the caregiver has any physical conditions or limitation or takes any medication that would affect her ability to do her job.

▶ **Becoming an employer.** Choosing to hire an in-home caregiver comes with certain legal obligations applicable to your role as an employer. Your first duty is to hire someone who is legally allowed to work in this country. This means that the person is either an American citizen, has a valid Alien Registration Card (a "green card") or has an Employment Authorization Document. You are required to verify that the employee is eligible to work here by having the employee complete the employee section of the Immigration and Naturalization Service (INS) Form I-9, Employment Eligibility Verification, which is held by the employer. You can obtain this form by calling the INS at 800 357-2099 (employer hotline) or 800 870-3676 (forms) to obtain the INS Handbook for Employers. Civil penalties for employing an illegal alien start at $2500 and can go much higher, even resulting in criminal penalties. There are additional penalties under federal and state tax laws if the person was paid "off the books."

Because many of the applicants for in-home child care are in fact undocumented aliens, a question frequently asked by parents is whether it is viable to sponsor a potential candidate for permanent residency in this country. While this is certainly an option, the process is time consuming, labor-intensive and expensive (approximately $5000-10,000). For more information on the sponsoring process, see the Appendix to this chapter.

▶ **Taxes.** Your next obligation is to determine whether you have to pay employment taxes. Even though many caregivers want to be paid "off the books," as an employer, you may not be able to offer them that option legally. You can learn more about your responsibility as an employer by calling the Internal Revenue Service at 800 829-1040 (24-hour information line) or requesting a copy of the IRS "Household Employer's Tax Guide" by calling 800 829-3676 (forms and publications).

In addition to federal tax liability, a household employer may have state tax liability for a household employee. For state tax information, you can call 800 225-5829 or 800 972-1233 or write to the NYS Department of Taxation and Finance, Taxpayer Assistance Bureau, W. A. Harriman Campus, Albany, NY 12227. Information regarding state unemployment insurance is available from NYS Department of Labor, Unemployment Insurance Division, State Office Bldg Campus, Albany, NY 12240, 518 457-6339. Information regarding workers' compensation and disability insurance is available from State Insurance Fund, 199 Church Street, New York, NY 10007, 312-9000.

As with any matters relating to tax liability or benefits, it is wise to contact the IRS or state taxing authorities directly or consult a tax lawyer or accountant for advice and assistance with filings. You can also contact a private payroll/tax service specializing or with expertise in domestic employment matters, a list of which you can find at the end of this chapter. For more information about taxes and domestic help, see the Appendix to this chapter.

▶ **Living with your caregiver.** Congratulations. You have made it through the search and interview process and have finally hired an in-home caregiver. Whether she lives in or lives out, you must now incorporate this person into your family life and learn to be a team. You are also a manager of your household and must employ managerial skills in your role as an employer.

The employment relationship with your caregiver is unlike any you may have experienced in your working life. First and foremost, the object of her employment is what is most precious to you—your children. You are trusting her with their welfare when you cannot be at home. Second, there are aspects of childrearing about which you may be passionate, and it is crucial that your wishes be followed. You should keep in mind that there may be some areas in which you are ambivalent or even unsure of your views, potentially affecting your ability to give clear direction. Third, the locus of employment is your home, the most personal and vulnerable place imaginable. Your caregiver will know things about your life that you may not even share with close friends. She will see you at your best and your worst, your most capable and your most confused. She must be your partner, support and trusted surrogate when you are not present. This is a huge responsibility to delegate and for the caregiver to accept.

With this in mind, we have compiled some thoughts on living with your caregiver based on our own personal experience and that of our friends:

◪ Your relationship is first and foremost an employment relationship. Terms of employment should be clearly expressed, preferably in writing, and reviewed and updated on a regular periodic basis. Periodic reviews are useful tools for airing out tensions and dealing with situations before they get out of hand. Open and honest communication will serve you well.

◪ Your caregiver is not your personal property. She is an employee and a person with her own personality, priorities and personal life. Even if she lives in your home, she is entitled to her privacy. She may become like a member of your family, but she still has her own commitments and relationships outside your home. As hard as it may be, a balance must be found between the personal and professional relationship you have with your caregiver.

◪ Respect and honor this line of work. Treat it professionally. It is useful to have agreed-upon benefits such as paid vacation time, paid holidays, paid sick leave, bonuses or overtime and transportation home at night. It is customary to provide two weeks paid vacation. You may want to consider having one week accrue every six months during the first year of employment. Be clear about your vacation policy and when she can or cannot take vacation time so that your caregiver can organize her own life. Agreeing to a certain number of paid sick days and holidays per year can avoid sticky situations about when to dock pay for days off.

■ Your caregiver is not superwoman either. It is hard and sometimes tedious work taking care of children and doing household chores. Be realistic about how much can really be done in a day, the rhythm of spending the day with kids and how long it takes to do things. For live-in employees in particular, because the hours tend to be long, schedule reasonable break times. Working without breaks over long periods of time leads to burnout. An overworked, stressed-out caregiver is not likely to be patient, calm or alert.

■ Be clear about your expectations of conduct on the job. You may want to consider having written house rules. You cannot assume that your caregiver has exactly the same sensibilities as you do. Even the best caregiver will have different judgments from yours on various issues. Some good rules we have seen: no smoking or drinking during work hours (or in the house at any time); no meeting friends or boyfriends while on the job; dressing appropriately for work (no high heels and miniskirts in the park); no wearing headphones while with the children; rules about with whom the children may be left (no one other than the caregiver or certain named adults); rules about where the children may or may not be taken (subways, other peoples' cars or homes); in homes with older children, rules about whether (or under what conditions) children may be left alone in the house or are allowed to go out alone; a list of parks the children may go to and until what time; rules about food choices and television; use of your telephone during work hours and for long distance calls; and curfews and guest privileges for live-ins. Arrangements for daily household expenses (car fare, money for snacks, etc.) should be determined in advance. Be clear about how you will provide the caregiver with money for daily expenses related to the job and what receipts you expect to have for expenses.

■ Work as a team. Discuss how to handle discipline, tantrums, sibling fighting and other behavioral issues as well as household basics such as snacks, television, naps, play time, playdates and such so that your child will be given a consistent message. If you are going to have a caregiver, you must let her do her job, but you should be in agreement about the parameters of her authority. While she must support you, you must also support her, particularly in front of the children, so that your household will be harmonious.

■ You are the boss, they are your children and it is your home. You should never feel like an outsider in your own home or be made to feel by your caregiver that your parenting skills are less than adequate. While your caregiver may have excellent recommendations or input on issues relating to the children (which should surely be encouraged), and it is essential to give her the authority and opportunity to do her job, you make the final policy in your home. We have seen many high-powered, capable parents be reduced to tears and worse by caregivers who have taken over the household. When this happens, it is time to reassert yourself and take control. Even if it means saying goodbye to the caregiver, in the long run it may be a healthier choice for your family.

■ Consider sending your caregiver to courses or programs to enhance her skills. Many nursery schools conduct seminars for caregivers and classes can be found at local parenting centers (see Chapter 7). Such programs are informative and eye-opening and can be very useful to the caregiver, improving her job performance. Many caregivers appreciate the opportunity to learn and enjoy being acknowledged as a relevant member of the household.

■ Be a thoughtful and generous employer. Say thank you for a job well done and, when called for, show your appreciation with appropriate raises, bonuses or intangibles (i.e., time off). Remember that your children are watching how you treat people. The person at issue here is someone to whom they are probably very connected. It can be a great opportunity to teach your children about kindness and respect.

▶ **Surveillance cameras.** In recent years, there has been a growing trend to use surveillance cameras in the home to monitor job performance of caregivers. This is a subject about which many people have strong opinions and about which the law is not terribly clear. For some, cameras offer the only way to really "know" what happens when they are not home, in terms of the caregiver's interaction with her charges and her time management skills. For others, camera surveillance without the knowledge or consent of the caregiver is considered an unacceptable invasion of privacy.

Parents wishing to use a surveillance device may want to consider notifying the caregiver that they may use a hidden camera from time to time without advance notice. Certain caregivers will be willing to accept this, but others may become irate at the thought of being "spied on" and resign.

While a tape showing negligent or abusive treatment of a child provides obvious cause for termination, a tape that shows nothing outrageous or upsetting does not necessarily mean all is well either. Even though a hidden camera can indeed reveal a great deal of information, parents should use it as a tool for monitoring a situation and not as a substitute for their own intuition and vigilance. Surveillance tapes, when used, should be one element of a full evaluation of your caregiver. Moreover, if your instincts tell you that there is a problem, do not wait for evidence, but take action as soon as possible.

For information on renting or buying a surveillance camera for your home, see the resource list at the end of this chapter.

▶ **Breaking up is hard to do.** The impetus to change your child care arrangement can come from many different directions. The decision is often clear, such as needing to let go of a caregiver who is unqualified or not performing up to par. Sometimes, however, the situation is more complicated. Perhaps the children are older and the job description has changed. Perhaps the relationship is tense or uncomfortable or has become too familiar. Perhaps the caregiver's personal life is interfering with her work. Or perhaps the relationship has simply soured and no one is happy anymore.

In any such situation, it is time to review the situation, sit down with your caregiver and act on your decision. In some cases, it may be possible to rework the job description to accommodate changes in the family (new baby, children attending school full-time, parent going back to work or leaving a job, moving, etc.), resolve disputes or otherwise set the relationship back on course. When the situation cannot be rectified, or if the caregiver is endangering the children in any way, it is time to move on and end the relationship as amicably as possible.

Many parents are reluctant to make a change, preferring the known, however unsatisfactory, to the unknown. Other families are anxious about disrupting their children's lives or their own schedules or forcing their children to lose a caregiver to whom they are attached. Unfortunately, there is never a convenient or optimal time for a transition. However, prolonging a situation that is not working out is probably more detrimental to the family than letting a caregiver go. Whatever your situation, if you treat the relationship and the caregiver respectfully, you will likely find that irreconcilable differences do not always have to end in an ugly divorce.

The experts agree that in general, a child can well tolerate saying goodbye to a caregiver as long as the parents are sensitive to the feelings of the child and handle the situation appropriately. Remember that no matter how unsatisfactory the caregiver was in your eyes, your child may, at least in the beginning, miss the caregiver with whom he or she spent a great deal of time.

Much of how to orchestrate a departure has to do with the circumstances of the caregiver's leaving, the relationship between the caregiver and child and your own personal style. While some families give a caregiver departing on good terms a party and a gift and encourage an ongoing relationship, others prefer a farewell with less fanfare and limit subsequent contact. However you choose to arrange things, keep in mind that your child and caregiver may have a strong bond and that the child's feelings need to be considered. If a new caregiver will be on the scene, the family needs to give her a chance to integrate into the family without undue interference from the former caregiver.

◢

Group Child Care

If you have decided that group child care is the right choice for your family, there are two alternatives: in-home care, known as family child care, where the caregiver provides child care services for several children in her own home; and group day care, known as day care centers, where child care services are provided in a special facility. The New York City Department of Health, Bureau of Day Care is responsible for the regulation and licensing of all group care facilities that care for children up to the age of six. There are also private organizations that provide additional accreditation, and sometimes support and training services, to licensed facilities. While unlicensed facilities do exist, particularly with respect to family care services, it is recommended that parents avoid these situations.

▶ **Prioritizing your needs.** Before you get on the phone or start visiting day care facilities, it is worth spending some time thinking about what you want out of a group care facility. Some considerations:

■ During what days and hours do you need care? What about holidays?

■ Does the facility have flexible or fixed drop-off or pickup times? Can you commit to an exact time or do you need a contingency capability if you must work late or go to work early?

■ Do you need the facility to be within walking distance, on a public transportation route, near home or near your workplace?

■ What are your feelings about the number of children being cared for and the number of caregivers present?

■ Do you prefer a more school-like setting or a homey feeling? More professional or more nurturing? Educational or custodial?

■ Do you want your child to be with children of mixed ages or in a group with less age range?

■ Can the group accommodate siblings of different ages?

■ Do you want the caregivers to have the type of educational training that is required in day care centers but not family care facilities?

■ Do you want a setting that is structured or more laid-back? Do you want there to be a curriculum or more free play?

■ Do you have a preference for a facility that is part of a network or a community agency?

■ Do you want the caregivers and/or children to be multilingual?

■ What preferences do you have about the methods of working with children? Scheduled or demand feeding for infants?

Food choices? Access to television or videos during the day? Discipline? Naps? Outdoor play? Toilet training? Reading? Field trips? Independent play or one-on-one activities with an adult?

◪ Is your child more comfortable in small groups or large groups? With one adult or several adults? In large open spaces or more intimate spaces?

◪ Is your child very active, needing a lot of opportunity for outdoor activities, or does your child prefer more quiet play? Is your child sensitive to noise? Does your child need a lot of adult stimulation or does he or she prefer to play independently or with other children with minimal adult intervention?

Having developed a checklist of your basic priorities, you can decide whether you are more interested in family care or a day care center.

▶ **Family Day Care.** Individuals caring for more than two unrelated children in their homes for more than three hours per day must register with the City Department of Health as family day care providers. Family day care providers care for children in their own homes. By law, family day care providers can take care of up to six children, including their own, of at least six weeks of age and under the age of 12. If there are no children under the age of two, the provider can care for six children. If there are any children under the age of two, the provider may only care for five children. If the provider receives special approval and passes an inspection by the Department of Health, she may care for an additional two children of school age. The provider may not care for more than two children under the age of two at any one time.

Another category of family day care is group family day care. In this case, the provider may provide care in her home for seven to 12 children, including her own, of at least six weeks of age and under the age of 12, provided that she has at least one assistant. If there are no children under the age of two, the facility can accommodate 12 children. If there are any children under the age of two, it can have a maximum of ten children. No more than four children under two years old and no more than six children under three years old can be cared for at the facility at any one time.

Under New York law, to become a registered family care provider, an individual must be at least 18 years old, attend a city-run orientation program, have at least one year of child care experience, be screened through the New York State Central Child Abuse and Maltreatment Register (as must all assistants, emergency coverage personnel and other adults in the home), complete a comprehensive written application and medical form and certify that she has never been convicted of a felony. Although the facility must meet certain safety requirements, note that registered family care homes are inspected on a random basis, not as a prerequisite to registration. Providers are also required to receive 15 hours of training during the first year in operation and every two years thereafter.

In addition to meeting the registration requirements for a family care provider, a group family care provider must operate her facility on either the first or second floor of an apartment building or her own single-family dwelling, and such facility must have two exits. The facility must pass an inspection by the New York City Department of Health, an educational consultant and a fire safety inspector.

Family day care offers a more intimate environment and may be less expensive than a day care center. Because the provider is working out of her home, there is a greater possibility for flexibility in organizing pickup and drop-off times. With the right provider (a loving person with great time management skills) and a small number of children, there may be opportunity for developing a bonded relationship between caregiver and child. The children can have ample opportunity for socialization and interaction in a home-like environment.

There are potential drawbacks to consider. If the provider is ill or has her own emergency, how is coverage handled? If the caregiver works alone, she is unsupervised. It may be difficult to arrange for outdoor play or activities (and transportation to and from activities) outside the home. The caregiver may have limited resources for providing play materials or separate areas for rest and play. Because the facility is in her home, her own household obligations may need to be attended to during her workday. Depending on the age range of children in the facility, it may be difficult to organize and monitor age-appropriate activities, meals and schedules for each child. If the caregiver does not have any assistants, it is important to consider the effects of the isolation and stress associated with caring for many children on the caregiver's patience, alertness and ability to be creative.

▶ **Group Day Care.** All out-of-home day care programs caring for more than six children under six years old must be issued a permit by the City Department of Health. An initial permit is issued for a six-month period, at the end of which the facility is evaluated and a subsequent permit is issued. One-year permits are issued for programs that include children under the age of two. Two-year permits are issued for programs for children between the ages of two and six years old. Licenses must be displayed at the facility. The relevant regulations cover facilities known as child care centers, day nurseries, day care agencies, nursery schools, kindergartens, play schools or any other facility that meets the definition, whatever its name.

To obtain a permit, the program must meet minimum requirements for physical space, equipment and teacher/child ratios. The premises must pass an inspection by the New York City Fire Department, Buildings Department and Public Health Sanitarian. The director and teaching personnel must be either New York State certified teachers or have other specified training, education and experience. The staff and children must supply evidence of certain health screenings and immunizations. There are also permit requirements pertaining to food service, snacks, rest periods, admissions policies and transportation. All personnel must be fingerprinted and screened for criminal convictions and pending criminal actions and screened with respect to the New York State Central Child Abuse and Maltreatment Register. Each prospective employee's three most recent employment references must be checked.

Because the permit criteria are more stringent for group care facilities than for family day care facilities, the group care facilities may offer families a higher level of service, feeling of security and professionalism. Caregivers must have professional training or education in the field of child development. With more personnel on the premises, caregivers are supervised and do not handle all situations alone. Physical premises are likely to be larger, contain more play materials and perhaps even an outdoor play space. Depending on the facility, there may be a curriculum for the older children and more structured activities for the younger set. If a particular caregiver cannot come to work, there is staff available to cover her duties and the overall operation of the facility is not disrupted. Since group care centers care for a larger number of children than family day care providers, there is ample opportunity for your child to socialize with children of his or her own and other ages, and siblings can generally be accommodated.

On the other hand, the group care facility may have specific operating hours and be less flexible for parents. Facilities may be closed for holidays or vacation periods, leaving parents without day care coverage during those times. Because of the number of children being tended, there may be less opportunity to accommodate the specific needs of an individual child and the environment may be less personalized. There may be several adults responsible for caring for young babies so that your own baby may not have a close relationship with a particular person. If there are a large number of children being cared for at the center, it may be overwhelming or too stimulating for your child.

▶ **How to find a day care facility.** Whether you have decided on family day care or a day care center, or you would like to look at both before making a final decision, you must set about finding a facility that meets your needs and where you feel comfortable leaving your child. A first course of action is to ask friends, colleagues, neighbors or your pediatrician for recommendations. To obtain a list of registered and licensed facilities or family day care providers and/or group care centers, you can contact the Bureau of Day Care at 676-2444. They will generate a list by zip code. If you want to know whether a particular facility has any outstanding violations, you can make a specific request by writing to the Secretary, Department of Health, 125 Worth Street, Room 604A, Box 31, New York, NY 10013. Unfortunately, you cannot receive a list of all facilities with pending violations. Your written request must include your return address and telephone number.

If you are interested in getting personalized assistance in finding a facility, you can contact a Child Care Resource and Referral Agency (CCRR). CCRRs are private community organizations that provide a variety of services to parents in connection with child care services. They are funded in part by the New York State Department of Social Services. In general, a CCRR will provide detailed information, usually from a computerized database, about the child care and early education providers and programs in the community. CCRRs have trained counselors who provide advisory services (for free or at a nominal cost) for parents seeking child care services.

While a CCRR does not actually place the child, the counselors can provide lists of registered and/or licensed providers, direct families to the type of care that will best meet their needs, provide information on choosing a facility and assist in sourcing social services, financial aid and services for families with children with special needs. CCRRs will make referrals, but not recommendations.

CCRRs are involved in providing training and other services or technical support to child care providers and creating networks of providers with the intent of generally upgrading the child care services in the community. They may be involved in conducting research, developing child care public policy and exploring public and private funding sources to expand the availability of child care services. The CCRRs provide excellent written materials in the form of brochures, checklists and tip sheets to help parents evaluate and select a facility.

Most CCRRS are members of the National Association of Child Care Resource & Referral Agencies (NACCRRA). Its mission is to promote and develop a high quality national CCRR system and offer guidance to policy makers on improving child care services. NACCRRA provides members with technical support, professional education and conferences, develops a policy agenda and is engaged in advocacy activities. NACCRRA also publishes *The Complete Guide to Choosing Child Care*, which can be purchased by contacting NACCRRA Publications, 1319 F. Street NW, Suite 810, Washington, DC 20004, 202 393-5501.

The CCRRs that service Manhattan are: Child Care Inc., 929-7604; Child Development Support Corp., 718 398-2050; Chinese American Planning Council, 941-0030; Committee for Hispanic Children and Families, 206-1090; Day Care Council of New York, 213-2423; or Day Care Vacancy, Agency for Child Development, 718 367-5437. The Agency for Child Development, which also administers all publicly funded day care in New York City, can provide you with information regarding eligibility for publicly funded day care services and Head Start programs.

Another excellent resource in the search for quality child care is Child Care Aware, a joint venture of NACCRRA, the Child Care Action Campaign (CCAC), and the National Association for Family Child Care (NAFCC). The mission of Child Care Aware is to "improve the quality of child care in America by supporting professional development and training of providers, and by educating parents to recognize and choose good child care." By calling Child Care Aware's parent hotline, 800 424-2246, you can receive, at no cost, a referral to the CCRRs in your region, brochures and other materials to help you find and choose a facility, as well as checklists for evaluating child care services.

Other potential sources for locating day care services are the UJA Federation of New York Resource Line at 753-2288, which provides free and confidential information about day care, camps and other programs, and the Catholic Charities of the Archdiocese of New York, Family and Children Services at 371-1000, which will direct you to services offered by Catholic charities.

▶ **Selecting a quality child care facility.** Once you have developed a list of potential child care providers, a telephone screening is in order. You can establish that the facility has openings and get basic information about the number of children enrolled, their ages and the age distribution, the ratio of caregivers to children, how long the facility has been in operation, the hours during which care is available and the cost. This initial screening will assist you in deciding which facilities warrant a visit.

It is essential that you observe several facilities in order to develop a basis for comparison. It is best to visit when children are present. The bottom line is to find a facility that is safe, has a sufficient number of appropriate caregivers, will provide an environment with adequate stimulation for your child and where you feel comfortable leaving your child. During your visit you should observe the caregivers and children, see the entire facility and any outdoor play areas and be shown a copy of the license or registration certificate. If possible, meet with the particular personnel who will be caring for your child.

In evaluating a child care provider, you may want to consider the following:

■ Is the facility part of any networks or does it have any other accreditation or affiliations? Accredited facilities voluntarily meet quality standards developed by national organizations. The caregivers in these facilities usually are required to attend continuing education programs, which can raise the level of services provided to your child. Day care centers may be accredited by the National Association for the Education of Young Children (NAEYC). You can obtain a list of accredited facilities by contacting the NAEYC at 1509 16th Street NW, Washington, DC 20036, 202 232-8777. Family care providers may be accredited by the NAFCC. You can contact the NAFCC for information at Suite 900, 206 6th Avenue, Des Moines, IA 50309, 515 282-8192.

■ Ask for parent references and check them. Talking with other parents who have children at the facility is a great way to check out the quality of the care.

■ Ask how drop-off and pickup are handled and how caregivers deal with separation issues. Ask about procedures for visiting your child during the day. Under New York law, parents must be able to see their children or take them out of the center at any time. Determine how security issues are handled. To whom will the provider release your child? Who has access to the facility during the day?

■ Determine whether the provider has scheduled conferences or is available to meet with you at your request. Are parents involved in the facility? Do the caregivers report to parents about the child's activities daily or weekly? The willingness of the provider to meet with parents can be a good indicator of the philosophy of the caregivers and the level of communication to which they aspire.

☑ Does the facility provide meals or do parents send in meals? What foods are served and what happens if your child does not want what is offered?

☑ Is the physical facility clean, bright, cheerful, organized and well-ventilated? Are there a variety of toys and materials as well as areas for different types of play? Where do children play outdoors? Where do children rest or relax? What is the typical day for the children? What is the noise level?

☑ Are any personnel trained in CPR and first aid? Where are fire exits? What are fire procedures (escape routes, fire drills)? Are there window guards, gates or doors at stairwells, safety plugs on electrical outlets? Could a child leave the facility unobserved? What are the procedures for handling a sick child?

☑ Do the children seem busy and happy? Do the caregivers seem engaged and happy? Do they seem to enjoy the children? Are children held or comforted? Are caregivers talking and playing with the children? Is the atmosphere nurturing and relaxed? How is discipline handled? What about toilet training? Assess the program through your child's eyes. Does this seem like a fun and interesting place to spend your days? The CCAC suggests avoiding a facility where children seem to be wandering around or run to any adult who comes into the room.

☑ What is the training and background of caregivers? How long have employees been at the facility? Is there much employee turnover? What is the ratio of caregivers to children? In general, the fewer children a single adult has to care for, the better for your child. The CCAC suggests that for each adult, there should be no more than three to four infants or toddlers or four to six two-year-olds or seven to eight three-year-olds, or eight to nine four-year-olds or eight to ten five-year-olds or ten to 12 school-age children. State law limits the number of children one adult can care for to the following: ages two months to 12 months, four children; ages 12 months to two years, five children; ages two years to three years, five children; ages three years to four years, ten children; ages four years to five years, 12 children; ages five years to six years, 15 children.

▶ **Once your child is in day care.** No matter what your level of due diligence in selecting a facility, there is no absolute guarantee that the situation will work out as you hoped. Accordingly, keep up your vigilance by visiting the facility as much as possible, perhaps by arriving early for pickup or making surprise visits when you have the chance. Talk with the caregivers as much as possible and ask for feedback about your child. Keep up a dialogue with parents of the other children being cared for and find out about their feeling about the level of care and the experience of their children.

Be sensitive to your child's behavior. Is he or she happy to be dropped off? What is he or she like when you pick him or her up? If your child can talk, ask about his or her day and listen to what he or she says. Does he or she like going to day care, has he or she made friends, does he or she bring home projects or sing songs learned during the day? Be alert to changes in your child's behavior and look into the reasons for the change.

If you feel it is warranted, you can file a complaint against the child care provider by calling the New York City Department of Health, Bureau of Day Care at 676-2444.

As with any other types of child care, assess your needs on

an annual basis to make sure that the choices you have made continue to be appropriate.

▶ **Summer Care and Before- and After-School Care.** When seeking resources for summer or before- and after-school care, the CCRRs can often direct you to programs in your neighborhood. Child Care Aware has tip sheets and the CCAC has booklets to help you get started in your search and provide information in helping you select an appropriate program. You can contact Child Care Aware by calling the parents' hot line at 800 424-2246 and CCAC at 239-0138. The Parents League is a good source for summer programs, and your child's school may be able to direct you to early morning and after-school programs.

When evaluating programs for school-age children, the same criteria used for assessing other day care programs apply. You may also want to consider whether the program arranges field trips, the type of time allocated and supervision available for doing homework, how snacks are handled, and transportation to and from school if the program is not at your child's school.

Resources

In-Home Childcare

International Nanny Association
(INA)
900 Haddon Avenue
Suite 438
Collingswood, NJ 08108
609 858-0808
www.nanny.org
Publishes the International Nanny
Association Directory (contains
information on nanny training
programs, placement agencies and
special services) and other
brochures and material on in-home
caregivers.

Parents League of New York, Inc.
115 East 82nd Street
New York, NY 10028
737-7385

Au Pair Agencies

Au Pair Care
San Francisco, CA
415 434-8788

Au Pair/Homestay
Washington, DC
202 408-5380

Au Pair in America
Greenwich, CT
203 869-9090

Au Pair Intercultural
Portland, OR
503 295-7730

Au Pair Program USA
Salt Lake City, UT
801 255-7722

EF Au Pair
Cambridge, MA
800 333-6056

EurAuPair Intercultural Child Care
Programs
Laguna Beach, CA
714 494-4100

Interexchange Au Pair
New York, NY
924-0446

*Nanny Background Searches (B) and
Surveillance Services (S)*

Baby Safe Inc. (B, S)
444 East 86th Street
New York, NY 10028
396-1995

Babywatch Murray Hill (B, S)
New York, NY
889-1494
Will also screen and interview job
candidates.

Babywatch Corporation (S)
Spring Valley, NY
800 558-5669

Care Check, Inc. (B)
1056 Fifth Avenue
New York, NY 10028
360-6640
Will also screen, interview and
check references of job candidates
as well as help structure nanny
position.

ERS Employer's Reference Source
(B)
Marietta, GA
800 800-ERSI (800 800-3774)

Innovative Personnel Strategies
(psychological screening)
Napa, CA
888 477-8378

Kid View Inc (S)
Manhasset, NY
800 339-7146

Mind Your Business, Inc. (B)
Maplewood, NJ
888 869-2462
Will also check references and
arrange for psychological and drug
screening of candidates.

NannyCheck
New York, NY
717-0446
Will screen, interview and check
references of job candidates as well
as help structure nanny position.

Nanny Check Inc (B, S)
50 Broad Street
Suite 1600
New York, NY 10004
742-0340

Nannyvision (B, S)
551 Grand Street
New York, NY 10002
677-2776

PFC Information Services, Inc. (B)
Oakland, CA
510 653-5061

Rothman Consulting LLC (B, S)
235 West 75th Street
New York, NY 10023
580-7077/7041

RSI (B)
1495 Third Avenue
New York, NY 10028
517-4609

*Nanny Employment/Placement
Agencies*

New York City:
A Choice Nanny (INA member)
130 West 57th Street
New York, NY 10019
246-KIDS (246-5437)

Adele Poston/Park Avenue/Bonfield
Domestic Agencies (INA member)
16 East 79th Street
New York, NY 10021
879-7474, 737-7733, 288-1010

A. E. Johnson Agency
681 Lexington Avenue
New York, NY 10022
644-0990

All Home Services
2121 Broadway
New York, NY 10023
799-9360

Austin Agency Inc.
71-09 Austin Street
Forest Hills, NY 11375
718 268-2700

Avalon Registry
PO Box 1362 Radio City Station
New York, NY 10101
245-0250

Babysitter's Guild
60 East 42nd Street
Suite 912
New York, NY 10017
682-0227

Best Domestic Services Agency, Inc.
(INA member)
10 East 39th Street
Suite 1126
New York, NY 10016
685-0351

Best Placement Inc.
234 Fifth Avenue
4th Floor
New York, NY 10001
689-5671

Domestic Care Specialist, Inc. (INA
member)
180 Broadway
Suite 10-02
New York, NY 10038
346-0873

Elite Nannies Inc.
70-09 Austin Street #203
Forest Hills, NY 11375
718 544-9800

Fox Agency
30 East 60th Street
New York, NY 10022
753-2686

Frances Stewart Agency
1220 Lexington Avenue
New York, NY 10028
439-9222

London Agency
767 Lexington Avenue
New York, NY 10021
755-5064

Loving Care Agency
310 Madison Avenue
Room 1111
New York, NY 10019
599-5702

Moms Services, Inc.
177 East 87th Street
Suite 201B
New York, NY 10128
410-6700

Pavilion Agency Inc. (INA member)
15 East 40th Street
Suite 900
New York, NY 10016
889-6609

Perfect Fit Home Services Ltd.
155 West 72nd Street
New York, NY 10023
579-3665

Pinch Sitters (places temporary or
occasional sitters)
799 Broadway
Suite 204
New York, NY 10003
260-6005

Plaza Domestic Agency
136-21 Roosevelt Avenue
Flushing, NY 11354
466-1662

Professional Nannies Institute (INA
member)
501 Fifth Avenue
Suite 908
New York, NY 10017
692-9510

Sterling Domestics Inc.
310 Madison Avenue
New York, NY 10017
661-5813

Town & Country
157 West 57th Street
New York, NY 10019
245-8400

Working Solutions, Inc.
51 East 42nd Street
Suite 151
New York, N Y 10017
922-9562

Regional or National Services:

A Mother's Resource
Larchmont, NY 10538
914 834-7353

An Extra Pair of Hands
800 756-0567

All American Nanny, Ltd. (INA
member)
Virginia Beach, VA
800 3-NANNYS (362-6697)

At Your Service Agency (INA member)
Tenafly, NJ
201 894-5339

Beacon Hill Nannies, Inc. (INA
member)
Newton Centre, MA
800 736-3880

Child Care Services of Wisconsin
(INA member)
Wauwatosa, WI
414 782-7882

Choice Care Agency (INA member)
Tucson, AZ
520 322-6966

Heartland Caregivers (INA member)
Missoula, MT
800 866-NANNY

I Love My Nanny, Inc. (INA member)
West Hartford, CT
860 243-2222
www.ILoveMyNanny.com

Midland Nanny Placement (INA
member)
Waterloo, IA
319 232-0026

Nannies of Nebraska (INA member)
Norfolk, NE
402 379-1898

Nannies Plus, Inc. (INA member)
Morris Plains, NJ
800 752-0078

Neighborhood Nannies, Inc. (INA member)
Haddonfield, NJ
800 590-KIDS (800 590-5437)

New York Nanny Center (INA member)
Port Washington, NY
516 767-5136

Oregon Nannies, Inc. (INA member)
Eugene, OR
541 343-3755
www.parentsplace.com/shopping/nanny/jobs

Nanny Health Insurance Services

Richard A. Eisenberg Associates
Newton Centre, MA
800 777-5765

Nanny Professional Development

American Red Cross
Child Care Course
Various Locations
800 514-5103 (regional course registration)

Nanny Enhancement Course
Best Domestic Services
30 East 42nd Street
Suite 1517
New York, NY 10017
685-0351

Nanny Training Program
An interactive training program to be used at home. The kit includes a video, workbooks and reading materials for the caregiver and parents.
888 626-6921

NannyWise/Amy Hatkoff
19 East 88th Street
New York, NY 10128
534-5623

Nanny Training Programs that Place Graduates in New York City

American Council of Nanny Schools (ACNS)(will provide list of certified programs)
Joy Shelton, President
Office A74 Delta College
University Center, MI 48710
517 686-9417

American Nanny College, Inc. (ACNS Certified)
4650 Arrow Highway
Montclair, CA 91763
909 924-7717

Delta College (ACNS Certified)
Nanny Training Program
University Center, MI 48710
517 686-8736

DeMarge College, Inc. (ACNS Certified)
3608 N.W. 58th Street
Oklahoma City, OK 73112
405 947-1534

English Nanny & Governess School, Inc. (ACNS Certified)
30 South Franklin Street
Chagrin Falls, OH 44022
216 247-0600

Hocking College Nanny Academy (ACNS Certified)
3301 Hocking Parkway
Nelsonville, OH 45764
614 753-3591 x2186 or x22

Lake Land Community College
5001 Lakeland Blvd.
Mattoon, IL 61938
217 234-5295

NMSU, Dona Ana Branch Community College (ACNS Certified)
Box 30001, Dept. 3 DA
Las Cruces, NM 88003
505 527-7630

Northeastern Oklahoma A & M
College
Child Development
200 I Street, NE
Miami, OK 74354
918 540 6265

Northwest Nannies, Inc. (ACNS
Certified)
11830 SW Kerr Pky. #100
Lake Oswego, OR 97035
503 245-5288

Southeast Community College
8800 O Street
Lincoln, NE 68250
402 437-2455

Starkey Nanny Advancement
Program (SNAP)
1996 Starkey International
Institute
1350 Logan Street
Denver, CO 80203
800 888-4904

Sullivan College (ACNS Certified)
2659 Regency Road
Lexington, KY 40503
800 844-1354

Tri-State Nannies Training &
Placement Agency
5 Cannon Brook Lane
Norwalk, CT 06851
203 847-3929

*Tax and payroll information and
services*

Internal Revenue Service
800 829-1040 (24-hour information line)
800 829-3676 (forms and publications)

NYS Department of Labor
Unemployment Insurance Division
State Office Building Campus
Albany, NY 12240
518 457-6339

NYS Department of Taxation and
Finance
Taxpayer Assistance Bureau
W. A. Harriman Campus
Albany, NY 12227
800 225-5829 or 800 972-1233

State Insurance Fund
199 Church Street
New York, NY 10007
312-9000

Breedlove & Associates, Inc.
Golden, CO
800 723-9961

GTM Payroll Services
Albany, NY
800 929-9213

Home/work Solutions, Inc.
Sterling, VA
703 404-8151

Nanny Tax, Inc.
50 East 42nd Street #2108
New York, NY 10017
867-1776

Group Care

New York City Department of
Health
Bureau of Day Care
2 Lafayette Street
22nd Floor, Box 68
New York, N Y 10007
676-2444

Secretary
New York City Department of
Health
125 Worth Street
Room 604A, Box 31
New York, NY 10013

*Child Care Resource and Referral
Agencies (CCRAs)*

Child Care Inc.
275 Seventh Avenue
15th Floor
New York, NY 10001
929-7604

Child Development Support Corp.
352-358 Classon Avenue
Brooklyn, NY 11238
718 398-2050

Chinese American Planning
Council
365 Broadway
First Floor
New York, NY 10013
941-0030

Committee for Hispanic Children
and Families
140 West 22nd Street
Suite 301
New York, NY 10011
206-1090

Day Care Council of New York
10 East 34th Street
New York, NY 10016
213-2423

Day Care Vacancy
Agency for Child Development
30 Main Street
Brooklyn, NY 11201
718 367-5473

Other Resources

Catholic Charities of the
Archdiocese of New York
Family and Children Services
1011 First Avenue
New York, NY 10022
371-1000

Child Care Action Campaign
330 Seventh Avenue
17th Floor
New York, NY 10001
239-0138

Child Care Aware
Parent Hotline 800 424-2246

Citizens' Committee for Children
of New York, Inc.
105 East 22nd Street
New York, NY 10010
673-1800
Advocacy organization

National Association of Child Care
Resource & Referral Agencies (NAC-
CRA)
1319 F Street NW
Suite 810
Washington, DC 20004
202 393-5501

National Association of Family
Child Care (NAFCC)
206 Sixth Avenue
Suite 900
Des Moines, IA 50309
515 282-8192

National Association for the
Education of Young Children
(NAEYC)
1509 16th Street NW
Washington, DC 20036
202 232-8777

UJA Federation of New York
Resource Line
130 East 59th Street
New York, NY 10022
753-2288

**To report known or suspected
child abuse or neglect by a
caregiver call the NYS Child
Abuse and Maltreatment
Register 800 342-3720**

Appendix

In-home Employees

Sponsoring an undocumented immigrant. The process for sponsoring a domestic employee begins with filing an application for labor certification of the potential employee with the New York State Department of Labor (NYSDL). The application includes a written employment agreement between the sponsor and applicant pursuant to which the sponsor agrees to pay the applicant a prevailing market wage (currently deemed to be $365 per week for a live-out and $370 per week for a live-in) and written references showing that the applicant has at least one year of paid prior employment for the same type of work for which she is being sponsored.

During the next three to eight months, while the NYSDL reviews the application, the matter is assigned a case number and the sponsor is required to advertise to fill the position. The sponsor must forward resumes of, and report back on, all interviews with potential applicants to the NYSDL. If the NYSDL agrees that no suitable candidate was available, the application will be forwarded to the United States Department of Labor.

It takes between six and 18 months for the United States Department of Labor to process the application. If the application is not rejected, a Labor Certification will be issued. Once the Labor Certification is issued, a petition must be filed with the INS. Approval of the petition generally takes up to two months.

That, however, is not the end of the story. Even if the applicant has been approved for green card status by the INS, she still has to get into the quota system pipeline. Under the United States immigration laws, domestic workers (which include nannies, governesses, and housekeepers) are considered unskilled or semiskilled workers. The current immigration quota system permits the granting of green cards to 10,000 workers in this category per year. Since the annual number of applications in this category is well in excess of 10,000, with the existing and ever-growing backlog, an application submitted under this quota this year will take approximately 12 years to process.

It is important to point out that during the sponsorship period, the applicant for a green card is not supposed to work for the family that is sponsoring her. This rule is routinely broken by families who decide to take the risk of paying civil penalties in the event they are caught by the INS. However, with the recent attention to potential political appointees who hired illegal aliens and pending legislation to make it harder than ever for unskilled workers to get green cards, this course of action cannot be recommended and should be discussed thoroughly with an immigration lawyer.

Interestingly, cooks and butlers are not considered to be unskilled or semiskilled workers and so are not subject to the quota system and can be processed on a more reasonable timetable. Accordingly, many parents attempt to sponsor caregivers under these and other skilled job titles. Some employers attempt to hire the person to be an employee of a family-owned business rather than as an employee of the individual family. Needless to say, the laws are strict, and sponsoring an individual under misleading or fraudulent conditions can subject the employer to serious civil and even criminal penalties. The first step for anyone interested in pursuing sponsorship is to retain an experienced immigration lawyer specializing in this type of situation.

Taxes. It is important to ascertain whether you are responsible for paying taxes with respect to your in-home employees. If you pay the employee cash wages of $1000 or more in the calendar year, you are required to pay Social Security and Medicare taxes. The taxes for the employer and employee are 7.65% (6.2 % for Social Security and 1.45% for Medicare). The employer is responsible for payment of both the employer's and employee's share of these taxes. The employee's share can either be withheld from her wages or paid from the employer's own funds.

If you pay the employee cash wages of $1000 or more in any calendar quarter, you must also pay federal unemployment tax. This tax is not withheld from the employee's wages. It is paid from the employer's own funds. An employer is not required to withhold federal income tax from a household employee's wages but may agree to do so. If your employee is eligible for an earned income credit (available to certain workers who have a child or children living with them), you may have to make special advance payments of her earned income credit along with her wages.

You will need to obtain a federal employer identification number (which is different from your social security number) in order to process tax filings and report federal household employment taxes with your individual federal tax return. You can learn more about your responsibility as an employer by calling the Internal Revenue Service at 800 829-1040 (24-hour information line) or requesting a copy of the IRS "Household Employer's Tax Guide" by calling 800 829-3676 (forms and publications).

In addition to federal tax liability, a household employer may have state tax liability for a household employee. As under federal law, you are not required to withhold New York State or New York City taxes, but you may agree to do so. Unlike federal law however, New York still has quarterly filing requirements. If you pay the employee cash wages of $500 or more in any calendar quarter, you must also pay state unemployment tax. Finally, if you employ a domestic employee who works 40 or more hours per week for you, you are subject to the Workers Compensation Law and Disability Benefits Law and must provide each eligible employee with these benefits.

For state tax information, you can call 800 225-5829 or 800 972-1233 or write to the NYS Department of Taxation and Finance, Taxpayer Assistance Bureau, W. A. Harriman Campus, Albany, NY 12227. Information regarding state unemployment insurance is available from NYS Department of Labor, Unemployment Insurance Division, State Office Bldg. Campus, Albany, NY 12240, 518 457-6339. Information regarding workers' compensation and disability insurance is available from State Insurance Fund, 199 Church Street, New York, NY 10007, 312-9000.

Surprisingly, if your caregiver is not legal, even though it is illegal for you to employ her, you are still supposed to make the necessary filings and pay employment taxes with respect to her employment, and she is supposed to file a tax return. The IRS will assign your caregiver a taxpayer identification number (different from a social security number) to process her return. The IRS claims not to share this information with the INS. Needless to say, if this is your situation, you should consult a tax professional.

Notwithstanding the foregoing, there are certain situations where you may not have to pay taxes with respect to your domestic help. If an individual is not an employee but is a bona fide independent contractor (as defined in the tax law and regulations) you will not have filing or payment obligations. You should consult with a tax advisor to determine whether your situation meets the technical requirements for this tax treatment.

Not all the news about taxes is bad. You may be eligible for a child and dependent care tax credit if you incur expenses to care for a child under the age of 13 so that you can work or look for work. Also, your employer may have a flexible spending arrangement (or reimbursement account) pursuant to which you can receive certain tax-free reimbursements for dependent care or a cafeteria plan that allows employees to receive dependent care assistance benefits from the company.

As with any matters relating to tax liability or benefits, it is wise to contact the IRS or state taxing authorities directly or consult a tax lawyer or accountant for advice and assistance with filings. You can also consult a tax service specializing or with expertise in domestic employment matters.

Chapter 7

THE ENLIGHTENED PARENT

E ach generation is subject to historical factors that make its parenting experience unique. For this generation of parents, technological advancements, the increase in the number of dual-career households, the explosion of information and the change in our culture's general attitude toward children all affect the way in which children are raised today. Things simply are not as they were when the parents of today were kids being raised by their parents.

Certainly more is known about child development and the processes of how little people become adults. Never has information about parenting been so plentiful, accessible and potentially conflicting. Parent organizations, professional groups and individuals in private practice disseminate information through lectures, workshops and discussion groups. There are radio and television shows, videos, magazines, books, computer software and websites dedicated to the topic of parenting. The abundance of theories, strategies and general advice has translated into a new business category, and today the business of parenting is big business.

Big business, however, is not necessarily a bad thing. Information can be a great comfort to new parents adjusting to their changing lifestyles as well as to seasoned parents moving through the different stages of parenthood. Attending programs and joining support groups can be both interesting and informative. The opportunities for parents to gain perspective and understanding, as well as to connect with others, can truly enhance the ability to parent lovingly and productively while making it more fun in the process.

Most parents today look beyond traditional avenues of support to the new world of knowledge, packaged and marketed to an audience accustomed to having the answers. Whether you are an information junkie or just an occasional user, the mere existence of the information around us has made parenting a more intellectual endeavor, and potentially an enlightening experience.

One thing to keep in mind as you seek out all that there is to know, the ultimate parenting manual or authority does not exist, no matter where you look for it. There simply is no right way to parent. Our society defines, through the many laws we have created to protect children, what we cannot do to our children. But no one can spell out exactly what we must do to help them grow to be balanced, healthy and happy people.

Our only advice: be an educated consumer. Almost any point of view can be validated by an "expert," so make sure to use your good judgment when evaluating the information you receive, as well as the credibility of the source. If you are uncomfortable with the advice you get or if a recommendation proves ineffective, even if it came from a highly respected source, have faith in yourself and continue your search.

Following is a list of some of the parenting resources available in Manhattan. The list includes individuals and organizations that offer group-oriented programs rather than individual counseling (although some on the list may offer individual sessions). Note that we do not recommend specific individuals, businesses or services, nor have we attempted to check or validate their credentials for the services they offer. Good luck!

◪

Resources

The following resources offer lectures, seminars, workshops and/or group programs. Some organizations listed offer groups for caregivers as well. Call for information on the specific kinds of programs each organization provides.

14th Street Y
Sol Goldman YM - YWHA
of the Educational Alliance
Parenting and Family Center
344 East 14th Street
New York, NY 10003
780-0800 extension 239

Central Synagogue Parenting
Center
123 East 55th Street
New York, NY 10022
838-5122

Child's Play
East Side - Central Presbyterian
Church
593 Park Avenue
New York, NY 10021
West Side - Rutgers Presbyterian
Church
236 West 73rd Street
New York, NY 10023
838-1504
(Parents only)

The Early Childhood Development
Center/Nina R. Lief, M.D.
163 East 97th Street
New York, NY 10029
360-7803

East Manhattan Toddlers/Irina
Pigott, M.A.
208-210 East 18th Street
New York, NY 10003
475-8671

Elizabeth Bing Center for Parents
164 West 79th Street
New York, NY 10024
362-5304

Groups for Mothers/Dr. Beverly
Amsel
165 West End Avenue, #1E
New York, NY 10023
362-5903

Jewish Board of Family and
Children's Services/Child
Development
120 West 57th Street
New York, NY 10019
582-9100

The Jewish Community Center of
the Upper West Side
15 West 65th Street, 8th Floor
New York, NY 10023
580-0099

The New Center for Modern
Parenthood
Dr. Eleanor Morin Davis,
Psychologist/Psychoanalysts
3 Rutherford Place
New York, NY 10003
982-7733

The Parent Child Center/New York
Psychoanalytic Society
247 East 82nd Street
New York, NY 10028
879-6900

Parent Guidance
Workshops/Nancy Samalin
180 Riverside Drive
New York, NY 10024
787-8883

Parenting Center - 92nd Street
YM-YWHA
1395 Lexington Avenue
New York, NY 10028
415-5611

Parenting Horizons/Julie A. Ross,
M.A.
405 West 57th Street #1F
New York, NY 10019
765-2377

Parenting Resource Center,
Inc./Virginia Stowe, M.S.N.
1088 Park Avenue
New York, NY 10128
423-0532

ParentWise/Amy Hatkoff
19 East 88th Street, Suite 5H
New York, NY 10128
534-5623
(Various locations)

The Rhinelander Center
350 East 88th Street
New York, NY 10128
876-0500

Sackler Lefcourt Center for Child
Development
17 East 62nd Street
New York, NY 10021
759-4022

Sckool for Parents
20 West 64th Street, Suite 34P
New York, NY 10023
877-8700

The SoHo Parenting Center
568 Broadway, Suite 205
New York, NY 10012
334-3744

These hospitals offer a variety of
prenatal, sibling, parenting, toddler and family programs. Call for
details.

Beth Israel Hospital
Parent and Family Education
Center
First Avenue at 16th Street
New York, NY 10003
420-2999

New York and Presbyterian
Hospital
New York-Cornell Campus
(formerly New York Hospital-
Cornell Medical Center)
525 East 68th Street
New York, NY 10021
746-5454
Healthy Steps 746-0498
Preparation for Parenthood
746-3215
Health and Wellness Seminars
(sometimes relevant topics)
746-5454, ask for Department of
Pediatrics

New York and Presbyterian
Hospital
Columbia-Presbyterian Campus
(formerly Columbia Presbyterian
Medical Center)
141 Ft. Washington Avenue

New York, NY 10032
Babies & Children's Hospital of
New York
3959 Broadway
New York, NY 10032
305-2500

Lenox Hill Hospital
Parent Education Program
100 East 77th Street
New York, NY 10021
434-2273

Mount Sinai Medical Center
Maternal Child Health Care
Center/Parent Education Program
1 Gustav Levy Place, Box 1153
New York, NY 10029
241-8909

New York Medical College
Center for Comprehensive Health
Care
163 East 97th Street
New York, NY 10029
360-7872

New York University Medical
Center
Parenting Institute at NYU Child
Study Center
550 First Avenue
New York, NY 10016
263-6622

St. Luke's Roosevelt Hospital
Center
Parent/Family Education
Roosevelt Hospital
1000 Tenth Avenue
New York, NY 10019
St. Luke's Hospital
Amsterdam at 114th Street
New York, NY 10025
523-6222

Saint Vincent's Hospital & Medical
Center of New York
Parenting Education Program
153 West 11th Street
New York, NY 10011
604-7646
(Programs for children under three
only)

**The following are specialized
resources:**

Childrens' Rights Council/Fathers
Help Hot line
431-7724
(Non-custodial parent groups)

Fatherhood Project
465-2044

The Fourth Trimester
182 East 79th Street, Suite A
New York, NY 10021
348-6308
(New mothers support group)

Gilda's Club
195 W. Houston Street
New York, NY 10014
647-9700
(Cancer support groups/organized
by age)

NannyWise/Amy Hatkoff
19 East 88th Street, Suite 5H
New York, NY 10128
534-5623
(Various locations)

National Organization of Mothers
of Twins Club and Higher Order
Multiples
NOMOTC, P.O. Box 23188
Albuquerque, NM 87192-1188
800 243-2276

The New Mommies' Network/Lori
Robinson
769-3846
(New mothers support group)

New Mothers Luncheon/Ronni
Soled
744-3194
(New mothers support group)

New Parents Circle/Ann Profitt,
M.A.
41 East 11th Street
New York, NY 10003
938-0139
(Various locations)

New York City Parents In Action
426-0240
(Conducts programs through
various schools and independently)

Parent Helpline/NY Foundling
Crisis Nursery
472-8555

Parents Anonymous, Inc.
Claremont, CA
909 621-6184

Single Mothers By Choice
988-0993

Single Parent Resource Center
31 East 28th Street
New York, NY 10016
951-7030
(Offers programs for the single
parent, conducts seminars and has
support services)

Single Parents Group
14th Street Y/Sol Goldman
YM - YWHA
of the Educational Alliance
Parenting and Family Center
344 East 14th Street
New York, NY 10003
780-0800 extension 239

Toll Free Parent Resources:

Child Abuse Hot Line
800 4-A-Child
(24-hour advice and referral
service)

Family Resources
800 641-4546
(Support and information)

PIRC-Parent Information Research
Center
800 342-7472
(General information, crisis intervention and referrals)

National Parent Information
Network
800 583-4135
(Handles parenting questions)

Parents without Partners
800 637-7974
(Support network)

**Web Sites for parents to
browse:**

http://npin.org/ (Parent information clearinghouse)

http://parenthoodweb.com

www.hbwm.com (Home Based
Working Moms)

www.family.com (Disney)

www.parentsoup.com

www.parenttime.com

www.parenting-qa.com

www.tnpc.com/parenttalk/index.
html

www.zerotothree.org

Chapter 8

FROM ABC TO ERB

Contrary to popular belief, it is neither necessary nor possible to sign your child up for school at birth, and there is no direct track from preschool to the Ivy League. Facing the process of enrolling your child in the school of your choice does, however, create some interesting challenges for even the most sensible parent. Finding the right school for your child can be daunting, but the difficulty has more to do with the learning curve involved in the application process than it does with how competitive Manhattan schools truly are.

School today is quite different from the institutions we attended in the 1950s, 1960s and 1970s. School administrators have applied current educational theory to their curricula and day-to-day operations in surprisingly different ways. Private schools have worked hard to differentiate themselves from one another and thus offer a wide range of educational

options. The New York City public school system also contains many alternative school models and programs to consider. The diversity of educational opportunities available for
city kids is such that long before it is time for school, parents
need to become familiar with the ABCs of education today.

In addition to understanding how schools differ,
Manhattan parents must work through an admissions
process that is unique to this city and become familiar with a
system that appears to be arbitrary, complicated and at times
incomprehensible. We are here to help you do your homework.

This chapter is organized into sections on preschool, ongoing private school and ongoing public school. The sections
cover the general procedures and timetables for admissions,
information on the application process and recommendations for getting through this exhausting process and maintaining your perspective. Sample checklists are included,
which are designed to assist you in organizing your efforts. A
list of resources and references is included at the end of the
chapter.

◢

The Bottom Line

Deciding where to send your child to school can feel overwhelming. Very few of us come to the process fully informed
or even totally clear about what we want. We all want to
send our children to the best school possible. At the very
least, we want to find a safe place with qualified individuals
in charge who will provide a rich, stimulating social and academic environment. But we may want more, a lot more. We
may want a school that espouses values similar to our own or
with a family community with which we feel we can connect. We may have particular interests that we want reflected
in the curriculum: foreign languages, technology, athletics,
the arts, ethnic diversity, community service, gender equity

or religious affiliation. We may have our own views about traditional versus progressive education and public versus private schools.

There is probably no school that can fulfill every item on your wish list, so you will need to prioritize. When you visit schools, as you inevitably will, observe carefully and ask questions. Here are some factors you may want to consider when visiting and reading about schools and talking with parents about the schools their children attend. This list was culled from parents, educators, nursery school directors, principals and ongoing school admissions officers and can be helpful when looking at programs from toddler groups to middle schools.

◪ Location. To what extent do you want the school to be located near your home or workplace? How will your child get to and from school? Is busing available and if so, commencing at what age? Who monitors the busing process? If you have more than one child, can you manage the logistics of getting children to and from different schools? Will you be able to attend school programs and teacher conferences conveniently, or pick up your child in an emergency or if your regular arrangements fall through?

◪ The physical plant. Is the school orderly, neat, clean and cheerful? Do classrooms have age-appropriate activities and equipment in a stimulating environment? Is the children's work displayed? Are classrooms child-friendly? Do children have easy access to restrooms (and for little ones, can they go to the bathroom alone or do they need to be accompanied)? Are there opportunities for outdoor play and indoor physical activity? Do the children need to leave the building to get to other parts of the school? Is the building in good repair?

◪ Faculty. What is the child/teacher ratio? How many children are in a typical class? What kind of professional qualifications do teachers and administrators have? Do teachers have professional development opportunities? What is teacher turnover like? How do teachers interact with children?

■ Security. What kind of security measures are employed around the school building and grounds? How are drop-off and dismissal of children handled? Is play equipment safe and well-maintained? Do the children use public playgrounds and parks and if so, how are they supervised and transported to and from? Does the school accommodate early drop-off or late pickup?

■ The classroom. Do children seem happy and engaged? Do children seem well supervised? How is a child's progress measured? How many times during the year do parents have formal teacher conferences and written reports? What forms of enrichment and remediation are offered on-site? Are classes grouped by age or is there some mixing of age groups? For the younger set, how does the school handle the separation process and what kind of transition schedule is used to allow children to become familiar with the classroom, teachers and other students (home visits, phasing into a full schedule)? If meals and/or snacks are served, are they nutritious? What kind of extras are offered: music, art, swimming, dance, cooking, woodworking, etc.? For ongoing schools, when do the children begin getting homework, grades and tests? How is the school day structured?

■ Philosophy. Is the school's stated philosophy evident in its environment? Does the school's style or ambiance feel comfortable to you? Is the school formal or informal? Does the school welcome parents' involvement and in what ways? Is there an active parents association? Are parents expected to do fund-raising for the school? Is the school responsive to the needs of individual children? Is the school culturally diverse? How does the school accommodate children with special needs? How are disciplinary issues handled? Is there a specific policy? What is the student population and what is the projected growth of the school? For older children, is there a school code of ethics, a dress code or school uniform, and is community service part of the curriculum? How does the director relate to parents? What kind of extracurricular and after-school activities are offered by or at the school? For schools with a religious affiliation, how is religious training integrated into daily activities?

▰ Curriculum in ongoing schools. Does the school prepare a written curriculum guide or other materials to explain the curriculum? How much time is dedicated to social studies, language arts and reading, math, science, "specials" (i.e., music, art, movement, etc.), foreign language, library periods and gym? To what extent do children move among different classrooms and teachers during the day? How does the school teach reading and what is expected of students? What percentage of students are tutored? What type of extracurricular activities are offered (e.g., athletic teams, orchestra or singing groups, clubs) and for what age children? When and how is technology used in the classroom?

▰ Cost. With respect to nonpublic school, what is the tuition and what payment plans or schedules are available? Are parents expected to contribute to an annual fund to support operating budgets or a capital campaign? Does the school offer financial aid or accept students whose tuition is paid via non-profit organizations? What percentage of children receive financial aid? Is the school committed to maintaining a financial assistance program?

When looking at schools, keep notes on your impressions from your tours and meetings with school officials and compare them with written materials prepared by the schools to see whether they are consistent. It is also interesting to observe drop-off and dismissal of children to see how the system works. Follow your instincts. Schools have different personalities and will likely evoke a response from you on more than just an intellectual level. You want a place where you believe your child will fit in as well as grow and a program you believe can meet its stated goals. Since school becomes a family affair when you have young children, it is also important that you feel the school creates a community of which you would like to be a part. You will find that some places just feel right or can be eliminated because they feel so wrong.

You will probably have other concerns that you will want to explore as you gather information about and visit schools. Remember, the schools want to attract new students as much as you want to find a place for your child. Feel free to ask your questions and do your research as thoroughly as you need to feel you can make an informed and reasoned choice.

Preschool

Applying your child to preschool in Manhattan can be a time of great anxiety, especially if it is your first child. There is a lot of hype about the competition and the need to be well connected and rich. Horror stories make the rounds each year about how you and your children will be arbitrarily judged by sadistic school directors and how failure to get into the best preschool will ruin your child's chances of going to a fine ongoing school as well as label you as a social pariah. You will get advice, solicited or not, from many self-proclaimed experts on planning your strategy. Depending on your personal fortitude, you may stay calm or not rest until notification dates, or experience periodic bouts of both.

It is true that the process can be competitive and that there are certain popular schools (which change from year to year!) that are highly sought after. Particularly for toddler programs, there may be more applicants than places. However, there are many excellent programs in the city, and in due course your child will be happily settled into preschool, the application process a distant memory. With this in mind, the most important thing to remember is to keep the focus on what makes sense for your family and child. Remember, first steps are always awkward but are mastered quickly.

▶ **Is it time for school yet?** This is really a question of your personal preference and what you want for your child. Preschool provides an opportunity to develop socialization and separation skills and, depending on the particular preschool program, varying degrees of more academic skills. Attending preschool, however, is not legally mandated, so the decision to attend, or when to attend, is yours. By law, you are not required to have your child attend school until first grade. Most city kids, however, are school veterans by then, having attended one to three years of preschool and kindergarten. Generally, by age three-and-a-half, many city kids are involved in some kind of preschool program.

In Manhattan, the terms preschool and nursery school are used interchangeably and refer to programs for children between the ages of three and five. Toddler or so-called "two's" programs refer to programs that require that the child be two years old before September of the school year in which the child starts school. The exact date by which the child must have turned two years old will vary among programs, but generally, to be considered a toddler program, the children attending will be less than three years old by December of the year in which they begin school. Many, but certainly not all, preschools offer toddler programs. Many children do not attend toddler programs. Even with respect to the preschools that do offer toddler programs, a child is not required to have attended the toddler program in order to get into a preschool class for an older age group.

Toddler programs are designed to accommodate the developmental needs of the very young child and are best for children who are somewhat verbal and comfortable separating from a parent or caregiver. Toddler groups tend to focus on socialization skills, playing and other activities such as singing and arts and crafts. Nursery schools offer many of the same activities but add in activities for older children and may introduce other academic skills such as work with numbers and letters.

There are two typical entry points for preschool: the child either turns three sometime during the school year or the child has already turned three before the school year starts. Depending on where their birthdays lie, the former group will either be in a toddler program or the youngest class in a preschool program. Your decision about when to apply a child to preschool has to do with what age you determine makes the most sense for your child and family.

Planning for a child just leaving infancy, whose needs are constantly changing and whose personality you are just getting to know, is tricky. Be honest with yourself about what you want, what you think your child can handle and will enjoy, and how your family can accommodate the logistics of getting a young child to school in the morning and home at the end of the school day. Remember, there is no right answer, and not every child goes to a toddler group or even nursery school. No matter what you may hear, you need only do what you believe is best for your particular set of circumstances.

▶ **When do I have to start thinking about applying to schools?** The general rule of thumb is that you must apply to a preschool the autumn before the September you want your child to begin school. For example, if you want your child to begin school in September 1999, you start the application process in September 1998. So if you want to apply your child to a toddler program, you will need to start thinking about this when your child is between 12 and 18 months old. To people outside of New York City, it seems ludicrous to have to plan a year ahead for a toddler, but for better or worse, that is the system we have here.

In order to gear up for the application season, you need to begin your own information gathering in advance so that when the time comes, you are ready to roll. Applications for preschool are made available in September of each year for the school year commencing the following September. The application scramble begins the day after Labor Day. Literally. To a large extent, it is this mad dash for applications that causes the most craziness in the process.

Each school handles the distribution of applications differently, although many limit the total number of applications given out in a particular year. As unfair as this may appear, it has become a necessary practice to make the process manageable for the schools due to the large number of families who apply to multiple schools. Schools that limit applications have devised different ways of dealing with the situation. Some schools have a lottery system, others distribute to a limited number of first callers and others give out applications only until a certain date. Still others schedule parents for a limited number of parent open houses at which applications will be distributed.

As a result, parents start working the phones the first Tuesday in September to be sure to get applications to the schools they want to see. For this reason, you and every other interested parent will have to block out a period of time that day or that week to make your request for applications. You may well get a busy signal, but be persistent and someone will eventually pick up. Schools will be receiving literally hundreds of phone calls, so do not be surprised if they are curt with you. There will be plenty of opportunities to ask questions, so choose your inquiries for this initial contact thoughtfully.

If you are applying to a particular school for a sibling or other type of legacy (e.g., child of a graduate or a child in a family who belongs to the congregation with which the school is affiliated), the application process may be somewhat different. You should clarify the policy and the timetable for obtaining your application, which may be different from that of people with no relationship to the school.

Consequently, we urge you to prepare for the September frenzy by using the spring and summer before you are planning to apply to start your research and think about where you might want to apply. If you have identified schools, you may want to contact them in the spring or over the summer (some have summer camp programs) to ask how they distribute applications so you can be prepared. You do not need to speak to the director to get this information and it is not appropriate to ask to tour the school or meet the director before September.

▶ **Where to begin.** Figuring out what preschools you may want to apply to involves a fair amount of research on your part. Preschools can vary widely in terms of philosophy and implementation of educational concepts. In investigating schools, you will hear terms such as developmental, Montessori, academic and cooperative to describe a school's approach. Finding out what the different labels mean will help make your search easier. As you begin to think about beginning this project, it is worth paying a visit to the library or bookstore to do some basic reading on the subject to get yourself comfortable with what is available. The Early Childhood Resource and Information Center - Division of New York Public Libraries has an extensive collection of materials on education as well as other topics related to young children and sponsors seminars and other free programs. It is located at 66 Leroy Street, New York, NY 10014, 929-0815.

Having mastered the jargon, or at least having become familiar with what to expect in general, it is time to go shopping. Manhattan offers scores of programs, so your next step is to identify preschools in which you think you might be interested.

Most of the preschool programs in Manhattan are private.

In Manhattan, certain private schools are also referred to as independent schools. An independent school is a not-for-profit, racially nondiscriminatory institution that has its own board of trustees and is chartered by the New York State Board of Regents. Most independent schools in New York City are members of the Independent Schools Admissions Association of Greater New York (ISAAGNY). ISAAGNY is a not-for-profit organization of admissions directors and heads of schools that, among other things, sets guidelines and coordinates dates for notification of admission to member schools. Independent schools may also be accredited by the New York Association of Independent Schools or the Middle-States Association of Colleges and Schools.

The term private school can have several meanings. A private school can refer to an independent school that is or is not a member of ISAAGNY or to a school that is owned and operated by an individual or group and is managed as a business enterprise for profit. Knowing whether a school is run as a for-profit or not-for-profit organization is important for evaluating the basis on which schools will be making decisions on everything from curriculum to operating budget. Finally, the term private school is used by many people to refer generically to any school that is not public school.

There are very few public preschools in Manhattan. To find out whether there is a public preschool or toddler program in the school district in which you reside, you can contact your local school district for information as more fully discussed in the section of this chapter on ongoing public schools.

One of the best places to begin your investigation of private preschool options is with the Parents League of New York, a non-profit organization of parents and independent schools. Each year the Parents League publishes two books, *The Toddler Book* and the *New York Independent Schools Directory*, which list toddler and preschool programs available in Manhattan. *The Toddler Book* lists not only preschool-style toddler programs and nursery schools that offer toddler programs, but other types of individual classes and programs for all children under the age of three. The *Independent Schools Directory* lists all preschools that are members of ISAAGNY, including those that offer toddler programs. The books contain basic information about the programs included, as well as a brief description of the school prepared by the school itself. In order to purchase these books and gain access to a wealth of additional information and services, you must be a member of the Parents League. You can obtain an application by calling 737-7385 or writing The Parents League, 115 East 82nd Street, New York, NY 10028. Annual dues are a very well spent $50. Note that the Parents League is closed during the summer.

Another written source is *The Manhattan Directory of Private Nursery Schools* by Linda Faulhaber (Soho Press, 1995). This book contains a description of each school included as well as other useful general information about schools and the application process. It includes a listing of preschools (which are or are not members of ISAAGNY), and therapeutic and special needs facilities.

The Parents League offers an advisory service to members free of charge. You can meet with a volunteer counselor who can help to focus or narrow your search or sort through information. Advisors are extremely knowledgeable. Although they cannot get your child into a particular school and will not recommend programs, advisors can help you identify schools that address your priorities and needs. The Parents League also offers a number of seminars and lectures on the preschool application process in both the spring and fall, which are enormously valuable for reducing your stress level, providing an opportunity to meet other parents and offering useful information.

The proverbial park bench is always an interesting, albeit unreliable, place to get information on preschools. By keeping your ears open and talking with people who have been through the process, you can gain a great deal of information. But beware. While you might get good tips, you may also get a lot of misinformation, gossip or old news. You simply have to keep in mind that you cannot believe all that you hear. Park bench information is most reliable when it comes from people you know and trust. Even then, however, remember that no matter how much you think you share the same values with another parent, a preschool setting that is terrific for one family can be a disaster for another, or vice versa.

Information you get from other parents is usually subjective, opinionated and often based on hearsay rather than fact. What is specific to one school can be interpreted by the park bench as a general truth for all schools. Conversely, what applies to most schools may not apply to a particular school. As long as you edit what you hear, you will be fine.

What can be useful, however, is to talk to other parents whose children attend a school in which you are interested. Answers to specific questions, such as how many children are in a class, how often parents meet with teachers and how discipline is handled, can typically be relied upon as accurate. If the information is consistent with what you have otherwise learned about the school, then you will have a pretty good idea about how the school operates.

Another source for finding out about schools is the National Association for the Education of Young Children (NAEYC). NAEYC sponsors an independent nationwide accrediting system that has been conducted by the National Academy of Early Childhood Programs since 1985. While toddler programs and nursery schools are not required to be accredited in order to operate, those that undertake this step are making a commitment to maintaining quality standards and are willing to have an outside body come in and review their program against objective criteria. The process of accreditation takes from nine to 12 months to complete, so a relatively new program may not be accredited but still be a very good program. You can get a list of accredited early childhood programs in New York City as well as information on the accreditation process by contacting NAEYC at 1509 16th Street, NW, Washington, DC 20036-1426, 202 232-8777, fax 202 328-1846. NAEYC also publishes materials on what to look for in an early childhood program, which are available free of charge.

There are also a number of private educational consultants who can be hired to help with the application process and advise parents on the various options. Consultants can minimize much of the legwork by supplying information on the different schools and opinions as to their personalities and reputations. The most important service they provide is to help identify the schools that will best meet the family's priorities and the child's needs. The fee for this service can be substantial, but for some families, such as those moving to the city from out of town, it can be the most expedient way to dive into the process. You can obtain a list of consultants in the New York City area by contacting the Independent Educational Consultants Association, 4085 Chain Bridge Road, Suite 401, Fairfax, VA 22030, 703 591-4850 or 800 808-4322. A number of educational consultants also advertise in the various local parent publications referenced in Chapter 2.

You can obtain lists of early childhood programs licensed by the New York City Department of Health Bureau of Day Care by contacting the New York City Department of Health, 2 Lafayette Street, New York, NY 10007, 676-2444. Note that the programs in their list will include both preschool programs and day care centers. The Department of Health will not separate out a list of preschool programs only.

Using these resources should help you to develop a preliminary list of schools that sound interesting. After making your list and checking it twice, you can relax until September.

▶ **The application process.** Once you have made your September calls to obtain applications, there is nothing to do until the applications begin to arrive. There are no uniform application forms, fees or procedures among preschools, so you need to review each application carefully and make a checklist of what you need to do for each school. Included for your reference is a sample checklist at the end of this chapter. Most applications are due by the end of November and require an application fee (on average between $25 and $50) unless you are applying for financial aid.

Each school will provide some opportunity for you to tour the school, usually with a group of other parents. Some schools have open houses or parent tours for interested parents who have not yet decided whether to apply. Other schools will not schedule a parent tour until an application (with a paid fee) has been filed. At first glance this may seem unfair. However, for many schools it is the only way to limit classroom disruptions for their children and limit the number of shoppers who are more curious than actually serious about applying.

Most, but not all, schools will meet with your child as part of the application process. Meetings will not be arranged until you have submitted your application and fee. Some schools arrange playgroups of several applicants, while others will meet with you and your child individually. When you set up your appointment for a child visit, it is worth asking how the time will be organized so that both you and your child can be prepared.

Parents often ask to how many schools should they apply. While there is no magic formula, nursery school directors observe that four to six is the average and recommend applying to no more than six schools. The exercise of whittling down your list is useful in working out your priorities.

For schools that are members of ISAAGNY, the application process is completed in late winter. ISAAGNY schools are required to mail admissions decisions on the same date.

Parents then have a prescribed time in which to return a signed contract to the school. Up until 1996, parents had two weeks in which to make their decisions. In 1997, the time period was reduced to one week, where it is likely to remain. During the response period, as parents make their choices, waiting lists are drawn upon. Parents are urged to notify schools as soon as possible of their decisions so that families on the waiting list can be given a place. Schools that are not members of ISAAGNY each have their own notification procedures, which should be confirmed by parents during the application process.

The key to managing the process is organization. Once you have collected applications, done your homework, cut down your list to a reasonable number, filed your applications and scheduled the necessary appointments with each school, you will feel much better. At least until February, when you will start to wonder if there was anything else you could or should have done and did not.

▶ **The inside scoop.** On its face, the process seems relatively straightforward: you investigate, get applications, send in your paperwork, tour the schools, have your child visit the schools and wait for a decision. Then why does applying to nursery school have such a bad rap?

First of all, people are intimidated by the numbers. A typical toddler class has ten to 15 children. Nursery school classes tend to be between 15 and 24 children (depending on the number of teachers). After accounting for siblings, legacies and, if applicable, congregants, a given school may have very few spaces available.

Second, New Yorkers are competitive by nature. There is a perception that there are certain schools that are better than others. It may be because a school seems to have a lot of celebrity, socialite or wealthy families or to be the first step on the path to elite ongoing schools and even universities. It may be that everyone at the playground you frequent is looking at the same cluster of schools in the neighborhood, which makes it appear that your child is one of multitudes. It may be that people you talk to are bragging about the "ins" they have at various schools, which leaves you feeling like a total outsider.

Third, it may seem that decisions are being made about you and your child on what you may feel is very little information. Your school visit with your child may be less than half an hour in a room with ten other children. You may not have a chance to speak personally to the director for more than a few minutes. You may feel like you have no impact on the outcome of your child's application.

Fourth, you may feel that you are making an important decision based on too little or confusing information. You will hear that certain schools demand a pedigree while others are more inclusive, that some accept only brilliant children while others are little more than day care centers. It may be hard to reconcile what you see at the school with what you read or hear on the street. You may feel unsure about what would be the best environment for your child.

If you get through the process without being intimidated at least once, you are in the minority. Just remember that you are not the only one living through this—there are many who have gone before you and survived. Weeding through the information you are exposed to during the process, separating fact from fiction, is an art. We can give you a head start by setting the record straight on a few key issues.

All toddler and preschool programs must be accredited. False. Toddler and preschool programs must be licensed to do business by the New York City Department of Health Bureau of Day Care but do not have to either be chartered by the State University of New York Board of Regents or accredited by any independent professional organization such as NAEYC or belong to ISAAGNY.

Without the right nursery school director, it is impossible to get into an ongoing private school. False. Nursery school directors are important for a lot of reasons. Most are very helpful when the time comes to apply to another school. However, the degree of involvement of the director in out-placement differs among directors. In nursery schools that are affiliated with ongoing schools, the nursery program director may have a very small role in your search for a new school other than completing a school report that is included in your child's application to another school. At the other end of the spectrum, more proactive directors will actively guide you through the admissions process and school selection.

There is a view that a well-connected director can get your child into the school of your choice. In reality, if a child is not well suited for a particular school but is foisted on that school by the nursery school director, only for the experience to be disastrous later, clearly no one is well served. Certainly the director's recommendation would not hold much credit with future applications. So, despite the appearance that some directors "get" children into certain schools, what you are really seeing is a director who is a good matchmaker. To accomplish that, the director has to know the child and a great deal about the different schools, their philosophies and environments. If hands-on guidance through the application process for ongoing schools is an important issue for you, ask about it during your school tour or interview.

Do feeder schools really exist? No. Feeder schools were at one time an important tool used by ongoing schools to select candidates, but that is no longer the case. Except with respect to some ongoing schools that have preschool or pre-kinder-garten programs that feed directly into the ongoing schools, preschools do not have feeder arrangements. Most preschool programs are represented in ongoing schools all over the city. This is not to say that you will not find that several students from the same nursery school end up in certain schools each year, which may give the appearance that there is a feeder relationship.

Each spring, schools offer admission to candidates who have been selected for a variety of reasons. Families in turn accept the offered spots based on their own priorities. What often happens is that parents are attracted to particular ongoing schools because of the similarities to their preschool or because they know many families from their preschool who have moved on to that school. Such things as the school's location, familiar philosophy and the desire to have siblings and friends attend the same school can influence families from a preschool to attend certain ongoing schools.

Additionally, there are preschool directors who have developed relationships with many of the ongoing schools and can be relied on by admissions directors to identify appropriate candidates for their schools. While nursery school directors do not determine who will be admitted to kindergarten, they can provide a comprehensive picture of an applicant that the ongoing school can assume, based on experience, is an accurate assessment of the child. This historical perspective provided by the nursery school allows the ongoing admissions director better to determine whether or not the child is a good match for the school.

Children are given intelligence tests during their visits. False. There is no end of speculation as to what the school staff could possibly be looking for during a child's visit. Most people are convinced that their child is being administered some version of an IQ test. Each school is different, but basically what really goes on, you will be relieved to hear, has little to do with intelligence testing. Some schools do look for developmental and age-appropriate skill levels, but for the most part the emphasis is on the following: the ability to engage in activities, verbal ability, interaction between parent and child and the general level of comfort of the child when dealing with adults other than a parent.

A disastrous interview means your chances are shot. Not necessarily. You bring your bright, adorable, loquacious child to the interview. He or she drops to the floor, dissolves into screams, refuses to take off his or her coat and spits at the teacher. Alternatively, your otherwise outgoing child holds on to your leg for dear life and does not say a word or lift a crayon. You see your child's opportunity to get into this school evaporate. Do not despair. Whatever your child does, it is probably not the first time the teachers or directors have seen it. They are well trained and can usually read the situation objectively. If there are any extenuating circumstances (ear infection, a parent out of town on a business trip, a sleepless night), be sure to explain them. If possible, ask whether you can try again. You may want to send a note to the director about the incident. Do not be defensive, just be honest. It is sometimes possible to avoid a disaster by preparing your child for the visit by explaining in advance what will happen. Also, if your child is ill, reschedule the interview. Finally, the more relaxed you are, the more relaxed your child will be in a new environment.

You need connections to get into preschool. False. There is no dearth of connected people in Manhattan. But who you know is not necessarily an ace in the hole when it comes to applying to preschool. When using connections, use the ones that matter when they matter. If connections are used well, they can have a positive impact. First, do not ask some VIP who has little relationship to your child or family to write or call on your behalf. In this context, your connection will have little influence, and the effort may do little more than entertain the staff. It is more meaningful to have a person who knows your family well and who is very connected to the school support your application, even if the person is not a luminary. Second, do not ask someone to "put in a good word" for you unless you are really interested in the school. It is awkward for everyone involved if the individual, perhaps a board member, recommends your child and then you decline the offer of a spot.

For those of you without connections, panic not. Nursery schools consider many things when putting together classes.

The next best thing to a connection is a sincere, genuine letter that lets the director know the school is your first choice. Remember though, first choice is first choice. Sending more than one such letter is likely to reduce your options, not secure one.

Chaos is creativity. False. The type of school environment that you find appealing is a matter of personal preference. According to NAEYC, a good program "provides appropriate and sufficient equipment and play material and makes them readily available" and is "spacious enough to accommodate a variety of activities and equipment. Most importantly, the facility should be safe for all children and adults." Many adults have a hard time understanding how children play, so when they see chaos, they interpret it as an expression of free-flowing creativity. While small children are by nature not very neat when they play and while many activities certainly leave their impression behind on faces, hands and clothing, a classroom that appears to be a scene from a natural disaster is probably not a well-organized room. The major task for preschoolers is to make sense of the world around them and learn to get along with others. Without a routine, consistent rules gently applied, a safe environment and nurturing, interested adults around them, it is a difficult task to achieve.

Getting on a waiting list is the same as being rejected. False. If the admissions process was perfect, everyone would get into their first choice school. Since it is not perfect, there will be families who find themselves with limited or perhaps no choices and for whom the result of months of work and worrying is disappointment and despair. The prospect of such an outcome is what creates all of the anxiety in the first place.

So, where do you turn? How do you regroup? Understand that the wait lists exist because there is a lot of movement in the period between the notification date and the date by which parents must return a signed contract. Your first step should be to call and notify schools that have wait listed your child as to whether or not you want to remain on the wait list. If not, your spot can be given to someone else. For those schools where you want to stay on the wait list, discuss with the director your options and how to proceed. Schools will let you know when to call back, the anticipated time-frame for giving you an answer and the likelihood that there will be movement on their list. As crazed as you may feel, make sure to stay calm. This is definitely the time when being a squeaky wheel does not help the situation. An atten-tive, cooperative parent is appreciated. Let the director know, by phone or in writing, your level of interest in the school.

If your child has not been accepted or wait listed by any school, you might consider consulting the Parents League advisory service. Advisors can be very helpful. The Parents League keeps a list of ISAAGNY schools that still have open-ings at the conclusion of the formal admissions process. Parents League advisors can also assist families that move to the city after the admission process has been completed. Keep in mind that you must join the Parents League to use the advisory service and that the Parents League offices are closed during July and August.

Though not every family is offered a spot at their first choice school, very few find themselves without any alterna-tives. For many families, the wait list is the answer to finding a place at their first choice school. You simply have to have patience and nerves of steel.

▶ **On to nursery school you go.** Come that first day, when you and your child head off to school, the memory of the prior year's tribulations will fade. Not to worry though, you will have the opportunity to do it all again when it is time for kindergarten.

Ongoing Private Schools

There are many nonpublic elementary schools from which to choose in Manhattan. There are coeducational and single-sex schools, schools that emphasize foreign languages, schools with religious affiliations, schools that end at sixth, eighth or 12th grades, schools with campuses outside the city, large and small schools, schools for children with disabilities and schools with every imaginable type of philosophy.

If you have already survived preschool applications and your child is attending a preschool program, the process of applying to ongoing schools is somewhat familiar. You probably know many more families with children in different schools and have some ideas, even if only vague ones, about some schools. You also know a lot more about your child and may have some views as to the type of school you think might suit him or her.

Unfortunately, even with a few more years of parenting experience, the process is no less threatening, because for some reason the stakes seem higher. Because private schools require some testing and an interview as part of the admissions procedure, parents often become anxious over their child's performance and worry that the child will not qualify for admission to a school of their choice.

Ongoing school seems much more serious than preschool. The decision feels more monumental—you are making a commitment to a school potentially for 13 years. While your child is there, he or she will be building foundational skills for a lifetime, not to mention developing social skills and friendships and going through adolescence.

It is important to remember throughout the process that while you are making an important decision for your child when you choose a school, it is not an irrevocable one. Many students change schools during the elementary school years; in fact, there is a great deal of movement at middle and upper school entry points (sixth, seventh and ninth grades). If the school your child starts at turns out to be the wrong choice or becomes inappropriate over time, it is more than possible to transfer to another school. So take a deep breath and dive in.

Applying to ongoing schools is a major undertaking, but as with preschool applications, there are three keys to getting through application season intact: do your research early and thoroughly, submit your applications and complete your school visits in a timely fashion, and stay organized. Though the process may seem overwhelming, and your child's future seems to be dependent on how well you perform this task, in the end your efforts will pay off and you will find an acceptance to school in the mail come March.

▶ **Getting started.** Applications for ongoing schools become available in September for admission for the following school year. Happily for Manhattan parents, the post-Labor Day frenzy experienced for getting nursery school applications is not replicated. Ongoing school applications can be requested on a more relaxed timetable during the early autumn. Be aware, however, that schools do have application deadlines, some as early as the end of October, so it is important to pay attention to the calendar.

For parents applying their children for kindergarten, the trickier issue is making sure that your child is eligible to apply under the birthday cutoff for the school. In general, most private schools require that the child be five years old sometime between September 1 and December 1 of the year he or she begins kindergarten. Each school will have an exact cutoff date.

Notwithstanding the official birthday cutoff, some schools hesitate to accept children who will turn five on the eve of the cutoff date, preferring that children with birthdays close to the cutoff wait another year before entering kindergarten. For such children, it is vital to consider the child's developmental readiness for kindergarten in addition to technical cutoff dates before proceeding with an application. This is an area where a good nursery school director can guide you well.

Another wrinkle in the process develops if you are interested in an ongoing school that has a preschool or pre-kindergarten class. Such schools tend to draw their kindergartens primarily from their preschools and so may have very few spaces for children applying from elsewhere. If you think you may be interested in one of these schools, you may want to consider moving your child during preschool so that he or she can continue on at the ongoing school. In such a case, you would have to time your application so that you are applying to the school for the final year(s) of preschool rather than for the kindergarten year.

As a general rule, you will begin looking at ongoing schools in September of the school year in which your child: is four and turns five if he or she will do so after December 1 of the school year (so that your child will begin kindergarten at age five+); or turns four if he or she will do so prior to December 1 of the school year (so that your child will turn five before December 1 of the kindergarten year). Children in the latter group often wait a year before applying to kindergarten so that they will turn six during the first semester of kindergarten.

As with the preschool application process, it is worth spending some time over the spring or summer before you begin applying to gather information about schools so that when September arrives you have some sense of what may interest you. Between September and Thanksgiving, you will have the opportunity to visit schools and submit formal applications. Once applications are in, you will have the opportunity to visit the schools and the schools will have an opportunity to meet or observe your child.

▶ **Reading, writing and research.** To review, a private school can refer to any of the following institutions: an independent school that is not-for-profit, racially nondiscriminatory, has its own board of trustees and is chartered by the New York State Board of Regents; a school with a religious affiliation; or a privately owned for-profit institution. Most, but not all New York City independent schools are members of ISAAGNY. Private schools are not required to be chartered by the New York State Board of Regents to operate.

An easy place to begin your research is with a good book or two. Doing some reading early on will help you get the lay of the land and create a list of schools that are worth further investigation. The *New York Independent Schools Directory* is an annual publication of ISAAGNY with the cooperation of the Parents League and is available from the Parents League. Each member school prepares a brief statement about itself for inclusion in the book, which also contains general information about the application process for ISAAGNY schools.

The Manhattan Family Guide to Private Schools, by Catherine Hausman and Victoria Goldman (Soho Press, 1997), is another guide to private schools. This book contains basic information about the application process, testing, and financial aid, as well as descriptions of more than 70 private schools prepared by the authors. This book looks at ISAAGNY member schools as well as non-ISAAGNY schools. It also discusses educational consultants, lists special needs schools and provides information about certain public school options.

The Parents League is a valuable general resource, hosting an annual forum in the early fall at which the application process is discussed. The Parents League also sponsors Independent School Day at which you will have the opportunity to speak with admissions directors from ISAAGNY schools as well as to pick up brochures and application materials. Although Independent School Day, usually held in a school gymnasium, is hectic and crowded with anxious parents, it is an easy way to pick up literature about different schools, ask basic questions about admissions (deadlines, birthday cutoff, etc.), find out about open houses and arrange to get applications if they are not available at the event.

The Parents League also offers a school advisory service to members free of charge. You can meet privately with a volunteer advisor who can provide unbiased and accurate information about schools and help guide you through the process.

Early Steps, a program whose goal is to promote racial diversity within ISAAGNY schools, can be another resource for learning about schools for families of color. To fulfill its mission, Early Steps offers informational workshops and seminars on issues related to students of color attending independent schools and provides counseling, referrals and assistance to families of color throughout the independent schools admissions process. Each autumn, Early Steps sponsors a school fair at which families can meet admissions directors from participating schools. You can reach Early Steps at 540 East 76th Street, New York, NY 10021, 288-9684.

If your child is in preschool, the preschool director is likely to be a major source of assistance through the process. Most directors are available in the fall to discuss ongoing schools and provide direction and suggestions. Many preschools arrange individual conferences to discuss the application process, help you with your application strategy, review your child's test results and recommend schools where the director feels your child will fare well and has a good shot of getting admitted. The degree of involvement, however, differs from director to director, and especially if your preschool is part of an ongoing school program, the director may not get actively involved in your search.

Whatever his or her approach, the nursery school director will be required to prepare a confidential school report about your child, which will constitute a portion of his or her application to ongoing school. Although a copy of this report is not made available to parents, its contents are relevant to your child's application and accordingly, most directors will discuss its general thrust with parents.

Attending open houses and tours conducted by individual schools is another excellent way to learn about schools. Open houses are often held in the evening and consist of a presentation by admissions directors with a question and answer period. Some schools have parents, principals and/or the headmaster either speak or be available to answer questions at the event. Tours are either conducted in conjunction with an open house or at separate times. Some schools require that an application be filed before you can tour the school. Most schools do not offer opportunities to visit until the autumn.

You can also get a great deal of information from other parents who have first-hand knowledge about particular schools. As we discussed in the context of the preschool application process, you may as well listen to all the park bench talk, but do not take it as gospel. Schools evolve and change over time, but reputations are often slower to change and old stories can remain in circulation long after the facts have changed. More importantly, most families tend to be happy where they are and promote their schools, while families who have had negative personal experiences with a school may be hard pressed to find anything good to say about it.

Some parents elect to use private educational consultants to assist them with the application process. Fees can be hefty, and if you have a good preschool director and no anticipated or unusual problems with your child's application, you may not need this service. The Educational Records Bureau, a not-for-profit organization that administers admissions tests for ISAAGNY schools (see below), can provide you with a list of educational consultants, as can the Independent Educational Consultants Association (4085 Chain Bridge Road, Suite 401,

Fairfax, VA 22030, 703 591-4850 or 800 808-4322). A list of educational consultants can be found in *The Manhattan Family Guide to Private Schools* and a number of consultants advertise in the local parent publications referenced in Chapter 2.

Private consultants can be enormously useful if your child has not attended preschool, if you are applying to schools outside of the mainstream timetable, if you are coming to Manhattan from out of town and do not know where to start or if you are conducting your search from outside the city.

Once you have done your homework you will begin to submit applications and proceed through the process. School directors recommend that you apply to between four and six schools although you may have looked at many more to come down to a list of that size.

▶ **Applications 'R' Us.** Although each school designs its own application process, there are some basic similarities among private schools. Each school will: have a written application and application fee (on average, around $50); require your child to be tested (the infamous ERBs); require either an interview with or observation of your child; give parents an opportunity to visit the school; and require a school report from the preschool(s) attended by your child.

Written Applications. The application may simply require basic data about your child and family such as address, birthdays, parents' educational background and occupations, ages and schools of siblings and names of preschools attended by your child. Some parents ask whether applications should be typed. The answer to this is simple: whatever feels more like you. If you choose not to type, make sure to print clearly. The application fee is typically required in order to proceed with the process unless you are applying for financial aid, in which case the fee may be waived or reduced.

Some schools require you to write essays about your child and/or submit letters of recommendation. If an essay is required, the school is looking for a picture of your child that is consistent with other aspects of his or her application (school report, test results) as well as your personal impressions. It is important to communicate your understanding of the school, its philosophy and why you think it would work for your child. Do not try to fake this. Make sure to read the school brochure or review the notes of your tour or school visit carefully.

Recommendations, when required, should be from someone with who knows you and your family. A letter from the president of the United States is impressive, but unless the letter communicates a relationship with your family and knowledge about your child, it does not serve its purpose. The best letters are well written and present an objective and detailed view of the child. Obviously, it is also helpful if the writer has some connection to the school.

Testing. ERB. How can three letters make so many so nervous? ERB does not actually refer to a test, but to the Educational Records Bureau, a not-for-profit national organization that administers and interprets many types of testing for children in the United States and abroad. Since 1966, ERB has been the testing agency for ISAAGNY. ISAAGNY schools have agreed to use the WPPSI-R (the Wechsler Preschool and Primary Scale of Intelligence test, pronounced "whip-see") for kindergarten and first grade applicants and other specific tests for applicants to higher grades. The cost of the test is $200, although financial aid is available. Non-ISAAGNY schools may require a different or additional test, which may or may not be administered by ERB. Be sure to get exact requirements for testing from each such school to which you apply.

The WPPSI-R is divided into two components, verbal and nonverbal. The former looks at general knowledge, vocabulary, comprehension and simple math skills. The latter looks at block design, assembly, and completion of mazes and pictures. The test takes about one hour and is scored in percentiles against a national sample of children of the same age. Most educators agree that the test is not accurate in predicting long-term academic success but is useful as providing a snapshot in time of development. The test is administered by psychologists, either on-site at certain nursery schools, ERB's offices or other authorized test sites.

While professionals insist that is not necessary to prepare or coach your child for the ERBs, many parents and some nursery schools work with their children in advance of the test. Whatever path you follow, the most important thing is for your child to feel comfortable and natural during the testing period. The more relaxed you are, the more relaxed your child will be. Be careful not to send your child the message that something major is at stake for which you feel he or she is responsible or not prepared. However your child does on the ERB, remember that these scores are not etched in stone and may indeed change substantially over time. If you are anxious, you can schedule a private consultation with ERB to discuss your child's test at a cost of $200. You can contact ERB at 345 East 47th Street, New York, NY 10017, 705-8888.

Interviews. There is no standardized procedure for interviews. Each school has its own system. Some schools meet with your child individually while others have several children together at the same time with more than one school representative, faculty or admissions personnel, in the room. While your child is having his or her interview you may be meeting individually or in a group with other parents with an admissions officer or having a school tour. In some cases, the school will send an admissions officer or teacher to observe your child at his or her nursery school.

To some degree the method chosen may tell you something about what the school thinks is important. For example, a school that meets the parents of each family separately and interviews the children in groups might feel that knowing a bit more about the parents helps round out their picture of the child. On the other hand, some schools are less focused on the parents, touring them in groups and spending quality time with each child. Whatever the case, do not read too much into the system, as it may have more to do with the size of the admissions staff or school tradition than anything else.

Most parents are very curious as to what the school is interested in finding out during the child's interview. Some schools simply observe the child in a social setting. Others provide children with different tasks to complete, and some administer their own skill assessment test. The school also is looking at whether their impression of the child is consistent with other parts of the application, especially the nursery school report and test results. Regardless of what specifically is being looked at, you have to place some faith in the fact that each school is trying to make a successful match between school and student.

Parents tend to become very anxious about interviews. It is crucial to stay calm and not scare your child. Here are some tips to keep in mind. If your child is fussy about clothing, make sure he or she wears something comfortable and that he or she likes. There is no point putting on party clothes if your child will be miserable. Find out what will happen and prepare your child, especially if your child will be required to separate from you. Make the process interesting rather than serious. Depending on what your child can handle, you can let your child understand that you are looking at schools but try not to make him or her feel that you will be angry if he or she does not perform well.

One last thought on the subject. As much as you want to present your family in the best light to the admissions personnel, they truly want you to walk away liking their school. Both sides are under a lot of pressure to make the experience a good one.

Parent visits. Again, there is no formula for how parent visits are handled. Some schools have open houses early in the fall that are open to the public. These are worth attending because the information provided and the atmosphere at an open house can offer you a sense of the school that cannot be conveyed in printed materials. Some schools have full-blown tours for parents who are deciding whether to apply as well as those who have applied. Individual or group tours may be given by admissions personnel or parent volunteers. Finally, aside from tours or open houses, some schools arrange private meetings with parents, which may be informational or more in the nature of an interview. Your child's visit may occur at the same time as your visit or at a totally separate time. We advise that you take every opportunity available to go back to schools in which you are interested. At each visit you may see something different or hear information, or other parents' questions answered, that may help form your opinion about the school.

Nursery school report. The report provided by your nursery school director to ongoing schools will contain a checklist of social, emotional, cognitive and physical achievements of your child. It will also contain information about the parents, such as your tuition payment record, issues that may have arisen while your child was at the school, and your financial support of the school. The report is confidential so as to preserve the director's ability to speak freely. Although you will not get a copy of the report as filed, most directors will review their report in general terms because what the report says about your child is relevant to your choice of schools. Most directors will alert you to issues about your child raised in the report that may affect an application.

▶ **Keeping track.** The application process has a number of steps and deadlines, so it is necessary to keep organized. You may want to carve out some shelf or file space or buy an accordion folder or notebook with pockets to keep your information on each school in order, designating one calendar to be used to note deadlines and appointments. Some suggestions on keeping track:

Important dates. Make sure to note application deadlines. Most schools have deadlines in November or December for filing a written application, which includes the fee and any parent essays. Typically, letters of recommendation, school reports and ERB scores follow under separate cover, with the completion of the entire package, including any requisite interviews, required by the end of January or early February. Make sure to consult each school's materials to confirm all deadlines.

ERBs and interviews. If the ERB is administered at your nursery school, consult the director about any scheduling or timing issues. You will not need to schedule the appointment but you will have to send in your check to ERB before the test can be administered. If your school does not arrange testing on-site, contact ERB to schedule an appointment.

You will need to call each school to which you have applied to arrange tours and interviews as required by that school. Be sure to confirm the time and date and who is expected to attend (one or both parents). If you need to send your child to an appointment with a caregiver, make sure that this will not be a problem as schools expect to see parents whenever possible. As soon as you become aware of a scheduling conflict, call to reschedule. Changing your appointment on a whim is not recommended, but if you must reschedule, do it as early as possible as appointments get filled very quickly.

There is some debate about how to time ERBs and school interviews. By and large, strategies are not terribly meaningful, absent extenuating circumstances. For example, you would not want to schedule for the week you expect to bring home a new baby or are settling into a new apartment. It is best not to pick a week when you or your spouse will be out of town or returning from a trip (if this is upsetting to your child), have house guests or expect any other life-disrupting event to occur. If at all possible, try to arrange appointments for times of day when your child is at his or her best, even if it means missing a day of preschool, and try to avoid scheduling during an activity your child loves and will resent missing (such as a favorite gym class). If an appointment is scheduled for a meal or nap time, try to feed your child or carve out rest time before the appointment.

A complete application. A completed application consists of the written application, recommendations if required, ERB scores, school report, and interviews. For your files, you should retain a photocopy of all materials you send to each school so that anything lost in the mail or at a school is easily replaced. It is also wise not to leave any piece of the application sent independently of the written form to chance. Give the nursery school a list of the schools to which you are applying and make sure to confirm that reports have been sent to each school. You will need to provide a written list to ERB as to where to send scores. There is no charge for sending out scores to five schools. There is a $3 charge for each additional report. You should then confirm with each ongoing school that it has received a school report and ERB report as well as anything else they are to receive from third parties.

In advance of the final application deadline, be sure to call the school to confirm that there is nothing outstanding. You may want to consider writing a thank you note to the admissions person with whom you met during your visit to the school. A note provides an opportunity to reflect on what you saw and your impressions. If you really have one, you may also want to write a sincere letter to your first choice school indicating that it is your first choice. Such letters are taken seriously by the schools and are best when written from the heart, expressing your reasons for making such a decision.

The waiting game. Once you have reviewed your checklist not once, but twice, you can take a deep breath and know that you have done all that could have been done. ISAAGNY schools must mail out admissions decisions on the same date. Families receiving an acceptance have a certain period (previously two weeks, reduced to one week in the 1996-1997 school year) to return a signed contract to the school. During this period, the wait lists move and many spaces open up. We urge parents who receive multiple acceptances to contact schools as early as possible so that other families have an opportunity to get a place before the end of the decision period. You should confirm notification dates with non-ISAAGNY schools.

If you have the good fortune to have several choices of schools, you may well find yourself in a quandary when it comes time to pick. Most schools have an open house for parents whose children have been accepted right after the notification date. At these events you will have a chance to meet other parents and school personnel. At some schools the kindergarten teachers are available to answer questions. If you are still unsure, you can usually arrange to meet with an admissions officer and visit kindergarten classes. This is the time to rely on your instincts about what you think will be the best match.

While you are waiting to find out where your child will be going the next school year, your anxiety level may rise. Keep in mind the following. No one piece of the application is inherently more important than the others. Schools are looking for a consistent picture of your child. If the school report, ERB and interview all present the same story, so much the better. If one piece of the picture is out of whack, do not panic. Many outstanding students had meltdowns on their interviews or ERBs that were not up to their usual levels of performance and still got into their first choice schools. With the myriad choices in Manhattan, there is almost always a place for every child whose family is looking for one.

▶ **Other stuff.** There are a few other items worthy of mention regarding the admissions process. Some may apply to you, others will not. Keep in mind that if you have questions during the process, you should contact admissions personnel at the schools directly. The admissions office should not be considered untouchable. If you have a question, call. More often than not you will be addressed by a warm and approachable individual. If you have the misfortune to reach someone within the department who is less than enthusiastic, basically uninformative or otherwise seems bothered by you, keep in mind that they are fielding many calls, are not superhuman and can have a bad day too.

Siblings and legacy applicants. Siblings of current students and legacies (relatives of an alumnus or persons with another relationship to the school) may have different application procedures. ISAAGNY schools have an early notification policy for legacies under which families will be notified about a month in advance of the regular notification date. If you accept a place under the early notification policy, you are required to withdraw applications pending at other ISAAGNY schools. Participation in the early notification program is optional.

Transferring schools. The decision to transfer your child from one school to another can be very smooth or very rough, depending on the situation. Where the decision was reached by mutual agreement on the best course of action for the child, school administrators at the school the child currently attends can be helpful in selecting a school that would be more appropriate.

If you have initiated the move because of problems with the school, the situation may be awkward. Because the current school must send a school report to other schools to which you are applying, your search cannot be kept secret for very long. If the school has initiated the move, you may feel angry, frustrated and resentful. However, in order for you to find another school for your child you need to be as objective as possible while remaining your child's advocate.

Whatever the impetus for a transfer, you can make it less complicated by maintaining a professional relationship with your child's current school and taking advantage of whatever resources—principal, faculty, psychologist, admissions office—the school can offer you in finding the right place for your child.

If you are applying to transfer to a new school where your child will attend first grade, ISAAGNY schools follow the same procedures as for kindergarten admissions, including a common notification date and response period. For transfers into second grade and up, ISAAGNY schools will use tests administered by ERB but notification dates are at the schools' discretion, with a common outside date for responses. Many schools have rolling admissions for transfers. Because available spaces in higher grades may be filled quickly, it is advisable to begin the process as soon as possible in the school year.

Applying to schools on a different timetable. If you find yourself scheduled to move to New York City without sufficient notice to go through the standard admissions process timetable, do not fear. You will still be able to find a place for your children to go to school. Though to a certain extent there is something to be said for bypassing the six-month admissions experience and finding a school on an abbreviated schedule, not having an acceptance in hand can make a big move more stressful.

How to proceed is dependent on several factors: where schools are in the admissions process when you begin your search, when you will actually be moving into the city (midyear is the hardest); and how easily you can bring your children into town for interviews and/or testing. Your knowledge of the schools is important, so if you are unfamiliar with New York City schools, it is wise to get the books describing the different schools so you have an idea of where you want to focus your efforts. You can contact the Parents League for assistance and advisory services. The Parents League can usually tell you which ISAAGNY schools have open spaces.

You may want to call upon a professional consultant, who

can often be very helpful in directing your search, finding out which schools have places available and making all of the calls and appointments for you. These services can be well worth the money, particularly when you are under a time constraint and out of town. In some situations, your employer may pick up the fees of a school consultant as part of a relocation benefits package. Before you hire a consultant, clarify what services are included in the fee. Remember, no one can legitimately promise you a spot in an independent school.

If you elect to proceed on your own, contact any school to which you want to apply. The admissions director can tell you whether there are any spaces and how to proceed with an application. It is essential to keep accurate notes because each school will have a different procedure. This task is not impossible, but it is hard work.

Financial Aid. Admission to independent school is made without regard to a family's financial situation. However, an admission is not automatically accompanied by a financial aid package. You must separately apply to each school for assistance where decisions will be made by a scholarship committee.

If you are applying for financial aid in connection with an application to an independent school, the school will send you a Parent Financial Statement (PFS), which is prepared by the School and Student Service (SSS), a organization that is affiliated with the National Association of Independent Schools and administered by the Educational Testing Service (ETS) in Princeton, New Jersey. Although you will receive a PFS from each school, you need only complete one. The PFS is comprehensive and requires you to submit certain backup information, so follow directions carefully. You will need to provide ETS with a list of schools to which your report should be sent. Be sure to include yourself on the list of recipients as this will be your only opportunity to review the information for accuracy.

The SSS will process your PFS according to national guidelines for families sending children to independent schools. The report will include a recommendation as to what SSS determines the family can pay in tuition. Schools receiving the report may adjust the recommendation to account for the local cost of living. The SSS may see your financial situation very differently from how you do. You may consider sending a personal account of your circumstances to individual schools to assist them in evaluating your situation and how you expect your needs to change over time (e.g., a parent who expects to return to work).

Although the financial aid application process is somewhat simplified by use of the PFS, individual schools may ask for additional information and each will have its own deadlines. A school will also have its own philosophy for awarding scholarships and allocation of funds available for this purpose. There may appear to be little rhyme or reason to a school's decision process, but if your efforts pay off and you receive a much-needed scholarship, consider the sacrifices you make for your child to receive a private education well rewarded.

Connections. Connections can be of significance or they may not have any influence on an application. There is no denying that if a school board member has a niece or nephew applying to the school, a call to the admissions director will be meaningful. In some cases children will be admitted on this basis. However, when the school does not select a child on the basis of the criteria it has established to ensure a good match between school and child, no one is well served. For this reason, few schools allow connections to be the paramount determining factor. This is not to say that if there are two candidates of equal merit and one has a letter or call supporting the application from a person important to the school that that child will not have an advantage. So what kind of connection is a good one? A family member, alumnus, teacher, board member or anyone else affiliated with the school who knows you and your child well. A letter or call from such a person can make a difference.

◪

Ongoing Public School

The New York City public school system serves in excess of one million children. Unfortunately, within the system there are individual schools where children pass through metal detectors to be taught in overcrowded classrooms by under-qualified teachers. But that is only part of the story. In addition to many fine, clean and decently equipped neighborhood schools, the public school system also contains schools and programs that are on the cutting edge of what is exciting and modern in education. You may be among the lucky families zoned for one of the better schools or you may have to do some digging to find one, but in either case, public school is certainly a viable educational alternative. And you cannot beat the price.

▶ **The basics.** There are six school districts in Manhattan. Each district contains approximately 15 to 20 schools on the elementary and junior high school levels. Each school serves a specifically bounded geographical area called a zone or catchment area. By law you are entitled to send your child to the school closest to your home that is in your school zone. On occasion, the school most near to your home may not actually be in the school zone in which you live. If the school for which you are zoned does not have space for your child, the City Board of Education is responsible for finding a place in another school that is within an acceptable distance from your home.

Students typically enroll for school the spring before the September that they will begin attending school. If your child will be attending the school in your zone, there is no application process, you simply register your child. The birthday cutoff for kindergarten in public schools is December 31. In other words, your child must turn five by December 31 of the year he or she is in kindergarten.

Under a school choice policy (sometimes referred to as the parent choice policy) initiated by the Board of Education, parents have the opportunity to select a school that is either outside of their zone but within the same district or outside of their district altogether. You can get specific information about the parent choice policy (and a copy of Regulation A-180, which sets forth the policy) by calling the Board of Education Office of Parent Advocacy at 718 935-5202.

In order to take advantage of the school choice policy, you must apply to the school (or program within a particular school) or schools in which you are interested. Depending on the school or particular program within a school to which you are applying, the application process can range from filing the right paperwork to requiring the testing of your child and/or an interview with you and/or your child.

This is where things get complicated. Because New York City has a decentralized school system, the application and admission process is not uniform. Worse still, there is no handbook or other publication that lists all of the schools that accept students from outside the zone or district or explains their application procedures or admissions policies, although some districts do have written material about programs within the district. Each district, and in many cases, each school, has its own rules, deadlines, procedures and admissions criteria. Unlike the admissions process for ISAAGNY schools, public schools have no common notification dates and response periods for acceptances, although programs for gifted and talented students often time their notification to that of ISAAGNY schools. Because there are no citywide timetables for admissions, and a great deal happens on a first come, first served basis, it is wise to begin your investigations early in September of the year before your child will begin kindergarten.

If you have opted to apply to a school outside of your zone, once your child has been accepted, you need to effect the "transfer" out of the school for which your child was zoned (even if your child never attended the zoned school) and into the school of choice. For a transfer to another school within your district or to a school in another district, you must obtain a "variance." If your child attends a public school outside of your school zone, the city does not provide transportation, although your child is entitled to a city bus pass that will allow him or her to ride New York City buses for free during certain hours. Therefore, factor into your decision to apply out of your school zone your logistics for getting your child to and from school.

▶ **The alternatives.** Before embarking on a search for a public school, it helps to become familiar with the alternatives. There are option/alternative schools, gifted programs (also known as TAG for "talented and gifted"), and magnet programs that implement special projects such as bilingual education, liaison with cultural institutions and development of new curricula.

An option/alternative school is a specialized program that has a distinctive philosophy and vision. Such programs tend to be educationally progressive and may be supported in part by private sector grants. Option/alternative schools are often housed within another school's building, sometimes on a designated floor, but they operate totally independently of their immediate neighbors. While each program is unique, they typically have small classes, teachers hired directly by the program administrator and a high level of parent involvement. To be successful, these programs require a serious commitment by families to the school. Option/alternative programs are not considered gifted programs and so do not require entrance testing, but many do require a meeting with the child and/or parents.

Every district has programs for gifted and talented

children. Generally, such programs operate within a public school open to all children. There are, however, a few schools operated solely for gifted children, Hunter Elementary School probably being the most well-known. As a prerequisite to admission, most gifted programs require the applicant to have a minimum score on a standardized IQ test. Unlike the ERB, which is accepted by all ISAAGNY schools, there is no single test that is accepted by all public school gifted programs. When applying to programs for gifted children, it is necessary to clarify the specific test used and obtain a list of authorized test centers.

There is no common theme to magnet programs built around special projects. On the contrary, these programs are one-of-a-kind and are intended to implement a particular educational philosophy or pursue a curriculum built around certain academic subjects (such as science or the arts) and to draw families interested in the program. Such schools are often, but not always, progressive.

▶ **Getting educated about public education.** The first order of business is to find out for which school you are zoned. This can be accomplished by calling the Board of Education Zoning Unit at 718 935-3566 or your district office. A list of the Manhattan school districts can be found at the end of this chapter. If you want to look beyond your zoned school, you will need to do a lot of legwork, make scores of phone calls and be prepared to spend a lot of time on hold. Stamina, patience and organization will keep you going through this process.

Because the public school system is decentralized and each district develops its own guidelines regarding transfers, the Board of Education is not the best place to begin your research. The better place to start is to call the community school district office for districts in which you are interested and ask for the superintendent or deputy superintendent's office. Do not call the community school board as they will not have the information you require. Request from the district office a list of the schools, including the names of the individuals in charge of gifted, option/alternative, magnet or special programs. Some districts have compiled this information in a single source book, but most likely you will receive a list of numbers and addresses. Depending on the detail provided to you by the district office, you will probably have to call individual schools to obtain program details and admissions and tour information.

Though there is no way to avoid the laborious step of calling schools directly, there are additional sources of information worth tapping. The Public Education Association (PEA) is an organization chartered by the New York State Board of Regents. The PEA is dedicated to ensuring a quality public education for every child in the system. The PEA offers an advisory service and files full of materials on schools. To access their files, you must visit their offices at 39 West 32nd Street, 15th Floor, New York, NY 10001, 868-1640. It is advisable to call ahead to make sure someone will be available to assist you. The PEA also publishes various pamphlets regarding public education in New York City that can be extremely helpful in your search.

The 92nd Street Y has historically sponsored an informative discussion and school fair series each fall. At these events, parents have the opportunity to meet teachers and principals of different public schools to learn about curriculum and educational programs and to get answers to other questions. In the past, the series occurred over two different evenings at a cost of $15 for both sessions. Advance registration is required so call Y-Charge at 996-1100 early in September for details.

The Yorkville Civic Council has compiled *A Parent's Guide to the Public Schools on the Upper East Side,* an informative booklet about the public schools located between 59th to 96th Streets on the East Side of Manhattan. The information in the booklet is supplied by the principals of the schools covered. You can get this publication by sending your request with a $6 check or money order to The Yorkville Civic Council, 110 East 59th Street, 5th Floor, New York, NY 10022 or calling 909-0364.

You can also contact the New York Networks for School Reform at 369-1288 to obtain a directory of the schools that receive funds from various programs supported by the Annenberg Foundation, which awards grants to innovative school programs.

The Parents' Guide to New York City's Best Public Elementary Schools, by Clara Hemphill (Soho Press, 1997) is an excellent guide to over 140 public school programs in the five boroughs. The author reviews and describes the various programs and provides a great deal of information on learning about public school programs and the admissions process.

As you develop your list of schools, keep in mind that public schools do not have uniform admissions procedures, so deadlines for applications and timing of admissions decisions will vary. Your best strategy is to call schools as early in the fall as possible to clarify application procedures and to schedule appointments for school tours, testing for your child if necessary, and interviews with school officials if required. If you are applying to more than one program for gifted children and your child will be required to take several tests in connection with those applications, remember that testing can become expensive, so balance the decision to apply to multiple schools against the prospect of putting your child through multiple evaluations.

▶ **Evaluating public schools.** The PEA recommends that when you look at a public school, you should look for the following characteristics: schools that are small or are subdivided into small units; collaborative schools administered with the participation of staff, students and parents; schools that have interactive, challenging, activity-based methods and curricula to engage students fully in their learning; and schools that reach out to the community to provide necessary social supports for students and their families.

To assess how effective a school is at teaching its curriculum, you can review the scores received on city-administered reading and math tests (higher grades evaluate additional subjects) in an annual report published by the Board of Education, which appears in most city newspapers. When analyzing test scores be aware that the scores of the students in gifted programs within individual schools are not reported separately, so these scores will bring up the school average. Test scores also may reflect the energy the school has devoted to preparing students for the test and not necessarily the totality of academic achievement.

The Board of Education Division of Assessment and Accountability can also provide certain specific information about schools, in the form of Annual School Report Cards, which can assist you in evaluating them. The Annual School Report Card provides information about student/teacher ratios, expenditure per pupil and the number of hours available for enrichment activities such as gym, computer lab, art, music and other specialties, and information on the building, programs and staff. You must make your request for a School Report Card directly to the Division of Assessment and Accountability by calling 718 935-5252.

If you are interested in a school, you may want to contact the head of its Parents Association to discuss particular issues about the school that may be of concern to you. Some possibilities: opportunity for parent participation, how effective the school is in implementing the curriculum, quality of teaching, amount of school work and so forth.

▶ **The waiting game.** Once you have selected schools and programs of interest, submitted the necessary paperwork, taken your child to required interviews, and for programs where testing for eligibility is part of the admission procedure, had your child's scores forwarded to the relevant schools, you are left with nothing more to do than sit and wait. The schools and programs for gifted children, including Hunter, tend to follow the ISAAGNY schedule for notification of admission since the independent schools are their biggest competitors for talented students. Other public schools follow the notification policy set by that school. Some schools notify parents on a rolling admissions basis while others do not make decisions until the spring.

It is important to be aware of the context in which public school admissions decisions are made. For citywide school budget allocations, all public schools must submit pupil projections for the following year by May of the current school year. With the exception of last minute enrollments within the school zone, once projections are submitted, the school cannot readily increase the student population above the budgeted enrollment. While choice is surely a reality and not simply propaganda, in most districts your choice can be effectively limited due to overcrowding and the lack of optional schools. In addition, students who are zoned for a school must be given first priority, followed by students who do not live in the zone but do live in the same district.

▶ **What is a "variance" and how do you get one?** Once your child has been accepted by a school or program, there is still a bit more work to do before you can congratulate yourself on a job well done. A variance is the documentation required to permit your child to attend a school other than the one for which he or she is zoned. It is the piece of paper generated by the district office in the district where the school to which your child has been accepted that allows the accepting school to place your child on its register.

As with many aspects of this process, very little is standard. Make sure that all necessary transferring procedures have been satisfied for the districts involved and, if applicable, those of the school itself.

Transfers within a district are governed by the rules and the procedures set by that district and tend to be less complicated than transfers between districts. If your child is transferring within the district, contact your district office, the school your child will be attending and the school for which you are zoned for specific instructions on effecting the transfer.

Transfers to another district are handled according to procedures set by the Board of Education. Districts are required to accept students who apply from out of the district, provided that there is room in the chosen school. Districts cannot set requirements for out-of-district students that are different from those they set for district students. Students living within the school zone or district are given priority over out-of-district applicants. If a school does not have specific admissions requirements, such as test scores required by gifted programs, then after students from within the zone and district are placed, admission is determined by random lottery.

Once you are notified that your child has been accepted into a school, you must take the written acceptance to the district office for the accepting school and apply for the variance. You must then bring the letter of acceptance and the variance to your home district office and request that records for your child be transferred to the accepting school. This is required even for children entering kindergarten who have never attended school in their own district. Be sure that your child is indeed on the register in the accepting school or he or she will not be officially discharged from the home district school.

A district cannot refuse to allow a student to transfer to a school in another district, and the superintendent from the home district is responsible for forwarding records once a variance has been granted. Note that a transferring student is required to stay in the new district for at least a year and a student cannot be sent back to his or her home district for truancy or disciplinary reasons.

▶ **If your application for a variance is denied.** If you are denied a variance, you can appeal first to the district superintendent for the district in which the accepting school is located. If unsuccessful, you can further appeal to the community school board president for the accepting district. The forum of last resort is the Office of the Chancellor of the New York City school system. If you have exhausted all other options, you can direct your request for a transfer directly to the Office of the Chancellor, Board of Education, 110 Livingston Street, Brooklyn, NY 11201, 718 935-2794.

◤

In Conclusion

Gone are the days when you simply sent your child to school with the secure feeling that by graduation, somehow, some way, your child would have acquired the knowledge and skills necessary to succeed in life. The plethora of available options, both public and private, compel us to investigate as many alternatives as we can before committing to a particular school. The bad news is that it is a time-consuming, complicated project for parents who are already juggling family and professional lives. The good news is that by going through the process, we are more likely to make the kind of informed and reasoned choices that will best support our children. At least we hope so.

Resources

General Resources

Independent Schools Admissions
Association of Greater New York
(ISAAGNY)
Does not maintain an office, but
can be reached by contacting
either co-chair of the organization
as noted in the *Independent Schools
Directory* (see below)

Independent Educational
Consultants Association
4085 Chain Bridge Road
Suite 401
Fairfax, VA 22030
800 808-4322

Parents League of New York, Inc.
115 East 82nd Street
New York, NY 10028
737-7385

Preschool

Early Childhood Resource and
Information Center
Division of New York Public
Libraries
66 Leroy Street
New York, NY 10014
929-0815

*The Manhattan Directory of Private
Nursery Schools* by Linda Faulhaber
(Soho Press, 1995)

National Association for the
Education of Young Children
(NAEYC)
1509 16th Street NW
Washington, DC 20036
202 232-8777

New York City Department of
Health
Bureau of Day Care
2 Lafayette Street
New York, NY 10007
676-2444

The Toddler Book, published annually by the Parents League

Ongoing Independent/ Private School

Early Steps
540 East 76th Street
New York, NY 10021
288-9684

Educational Records Bureau (ERB)
345 East 47th Street
New York, NY 10017
705-8888.

*The Manhattan Family Guide to
Private Schools*, by Catherine
Hausman and Victoria Goldman
(Soho Press, 1997)

*New York Independent School
Directory*, published annually by
ISAAGNY and the Parents League

Ongoing Public School

Board of Education of the City of
New York
110 Livingston Street
Brooklyn, NY 11201
718 935-2000

Chancellor's Committee for
Parents' Complaints 718 935-4321
Division of Assessment and
Accountability 718 935-5252
Office of Parent Advocacy
718 935-5202
Zoning Unit 718 935-3566

Community School Districts:

District 1
80 Montgomery Street
New York, NY 10002
District Office: 602-9700
School Board: 602-9765

District 2
333 Seventh Avenue
New York, NY 10001
District Office: 330-9400
School Board: 330-9418

District 3
300 West 96th Street
New York, NY 10025
District Office: 678-2880
School Board: 678-2845

District 4
319 East 117th Street
New York, NY 10035
District Office: 828-3500
School Board: 828-3572

District 5
433 West 123rd Street
New York, NY 10027
District Office: 769-7500
School Board: 769-7600

District 6
4360 Broadway
4th Floor
New York, NY 10033
District Office: 795-4111
School Board: 795-9549

New York Networks for School
Reform at 369-1288

92nd Street Y (school fair series)
1395 Lexington Avenue
New York, NY 10128
Y-Charge 996-1100

*The Parents' Guide to New York
City's Best Public Elementary Schools,*
by Clara Hemphill (Soho Press,
1997)

Public Education Association
39 West 32nd Street
15th Floor
New York, NY 10001
868-1640

The Yorkville Civic Council
110 East 59th Street
5th Floor
New York, NY 10022
909-0364
Publishes *A Parent's Guide to the
Public Schools on the Upper East Side*

Sample Checklist for Nursery School Applications
(one per school)

 School name
 Call to obtain application
 Application due date
 Submit Application:
 Return completed application
  form
 Fee
 References if required
 Schedule Appointments:
 Open house or tour
 Parent appointment (note who
  is required to attend)
 Child appointment (who has to
  bring child)
 Thank you note to admissions
  officer or director (optional)
 Recommendation if requested
 If applicable, first choice letter

Sample Checklist for Ongoing School Applications
(one per school)

School name
Call to obtain application
Application due date
Schedule ERB on-site at nursery
  school or at a testing center
Pay ERB fee
Submit Application:
  Return completed application
    form
  Fee
  References if required
  Arrange for ERB report to be sent
    to school
  Arrange for nursery school report
    to be sent to school
Schedule Appointments:
  Open house or tour
  Parent appointment (note who is
    required to attend)
  Child appointment (who has to
    bring child)
Financial aid: Obtain and complete
  all required forms including PFS
Confirm that school has received
  application, ERBs, nursery school
  report, PFS (if applicable), refer-
  ences
Thank you note to admissions
  officer or director (optional)
Recommendation if requested
If applicable, first choice letter

Sample Checklist for Ongoing Public School Applications
(one per school)

School name
Register in home district
Contact districts for lists of schools
Contact each school for its applica-
  tion materials, procedures and
  information
Contact district for
  information/procedures on
  applying to school within the
  district and obtaining a variance
Application due date
Submit application
Schedule testing if required
Schedule appointments if required:
  Open house or tour
  Meeting with principal, director
    or admissions officer
  Parent appointment (note who is
    required to attend)
  Child appointment (who has to
    bring child)
Confirm that school has received
  all necessary paperwork and test
  scores
Confirm decision date, process for
  notification and amount of time
  you have to make a decision
  whether to accept a place if
  offered
Apply for variance
Effect transfer from home zone or
  district

Chapter 9

CHALLENGES ALONG THE WAY

Our responsibility to the children in our lives is to assist them in achieving their full potential. This does not mean we must push them to the point of perfection, but it does mean that we should provide them with the opportunity to enhance their strengths and develop strategies to deal with their weaknesses.

Children develop on their own timetables. Over time, milestones will be reached and aptitudes will emerge. From time to time, any child may experience setbacks, have difficulty mastering a skill or be unable to advance with his or her usual alacrity in a particular area. In some cases the problem will be temporary and will resolve in due course with your support and aid. Other times, the situation may be more complicated and require more than the passage of time and your help to work through. Unfortunately, on occasion, despite your concern, you might not be able to isolate a problem, find a solution or help your child to find his or her own solutions.

Few things are as difficult and ambiguous as identifying and addressing special needs or mental health issues. When a child is first observed as having trouble reaching a developmental milestone or performing tasks, exhibiting unusual behavior or otherwise facing intellectual, emotional and/or physical challenges, a parent's reaction can range from denial to panic. In some households, conflicting reactions to the situation can complicate the issue still further.

Facing such challenges requires energy and determination on the part of parents to work through the problem and if necessary find appropriate professionals to conduct evaluations, diagnose the problem and create an intervention plan. For most, it involves diving into uncharted waters where discrete or even consistent answers may not be forthcoming.

Many parents dealing with these issues feel like the conductor of an orchestra who does not know how to read music. The learning curve associated with tackling most special needs issues can be overwhelming at first, but once you have a handle on the problem and begin to address it, you can get some perspective on matters and focus on being the best possible advocate for your child. There is a great deal of information and support out there—you simply have to seek it out.

It would be impossible, and it is not our intention, to provide a "how to" manual for evaluating, diagnosing or treating your child's issues because each situation is totally unique and we are not qualified professionals. Our goal in this chapter is to offer some guidance in: finding your way to professionals who can help your child, networking with other parents, understanding the role your child's school may play in the process, becoming aware of your legal rights vis-a-vis the public school system and acting as an advocate for your child. At the end of this chapter, you will find a list of resources that we hope you will find helpful in your search for answers and assistance.

◤

Putting the Pieces Together

How do you know when there is a problem that needs special attention? Children go through many stages in childhood. Many issues noticed by parents are manifestations of developmental phases that resolve over time. When a problem persists, gets worse or begins to interfere with other aspects of your child's or your family's life, it may be time to investigate further.

A first step is for you to begin to observe your child closely and, if appropriate, alert other adults in your child's life (such as caregivers, relatives, teachers, pediatrician) to your concerns to see whether their observations are consistent with yours. It is important to be honest with yourself about what you think might be going on with your child and follow your instincts.

Dr. Dale Hirsch, founder of The Learning Adventure in Manhattan, notes that most parents sense something is wrong early on. Generally speaking, issues that have not been specifically identified earlier tend to reveal themselves around the age of three. At this age it becomes more obvious if various developmental milestones have not been met because the child is involved in more complex activities and interactions. Learning-related issues tend to be identified in school by teachers or learning specialists and brought to the attention of parents, although it can certainly happen the other way around. Many issues can, however, appear to arise out of the blue, requiring a parent to do more than simply peruse the current child development literature for answers.

▶ **Where to start.** While there is no perfect time to act on a concern, ignoring an issue of which you have become aware can have serious consequences. The significance of early intervention truly depends on the nature and severity of the issue in question. A professional's guidance can be extremely important. Keep in mind that the longer a child's issues are ignored, the more behavior he or she will organize around the issue (such as avoidance of situations, loss of self-esteem, overcompensation, aggression, etc.) and the more intervention the child may ultimately require.

Some issues, like ADD, are multidimensional, while others, like nearsightedness, are not. Yet very different causes can create similar behavioral manifestations. Do not feel as though you need to diagnose what the disability or problem is. You are probably not qualified to do so. What you can do is bring your concerns to people who can help you figure out what is going on with your child and how best to help him or her.

It is helpful to try to put together a picture of the child's behavior including cognitive and motor skill abilities and social skills, noting when milestones were achieved and when difficulties appeared. A detailed profile can greatly assist a professional in determining what diagnostic tools are appropriate and at what point intervention would be beneficial, as well as the potential ramifications of postponing intervention.

Take your observations and any other relevant information to an individual you feel confident can help direct your inquiry. Such individuals might include: your pediatrician or another health care provider; teacher or school administrator; school psychologist; or session leader from a parenting class. If you start with your pediatrician, even if the problem is not medical in nature, your pediatrician can refer you to specialists in different fields or to a developmental pediatrician, who is a pediatrician who has additional training in developmental issues. If your pediatrician is not in tune with issues that are not purely medical in nature or you feel that he or she is not giving your concerns sufficient attention, you may need to seek guidance elsewhere.

Depending on the type of problem that is suspected, you may need to consult one or several types of professionals to conduct evaluations or for opinions on diagnosis and treatment. It is fair to say that in general, if the source of the problem is not immediately evident, it is useful to rule out medical conditions such as vision, hearing, allergy and other physical and neurological problems before focusing on non-medical conditions. You must also consider environmental factors such as family stress or school pressure, both of which can have a dramatic impact on performance, behavior and health. As you begin to explore what might be at the root of a problem, remember that some diagnoses are more elusive than others and require more patience to be properly identified.

Depending on the age of your child, he or she may be very sensitive to your discussing details of his or her life with your friends or professionals. As best as you can, respect your child's privacy and make sure that the individuals with whom you discuss his or her situation treat the information as privileged. It is a good idea to discuss the issue with your child in an age-appropriate way, perhaps with the advice of the professional you are consulting, emphasizing that you love him or her no matter what. Each family will cope with the situation its own way. Some families are more open and others are more private. Finding the right balance between publicly and privately acknowledging your child's situation is up to the individuals involved.

◢

Getting Professional Help

▶ **Finding a professional.** Having decided to seek the services of a professional, you must find your way to a practi-

tioner in the appropriate field. While this may sound obvious, many problems are multidimensional and your first step
may involve exploring the possibilities. Do you need to consult with a psychiatrist or psychologist, a psychopharmacolo-
gist, a learning specialist, an occupational therapist, a speech
therapist or some combination of specialists? Depending on
your child's diagnosis and how you got to that diagnosis, he
or she may need various types of intervention, either con-
temporaneously or over time, to tackle the situation.

New York City is filled with specialists of every ilk and
school of thought. One of the most anxiety-producing tasks
for parents is to find the right type of intervention and the
right person, or people, to work with their child. Your first
line of attack is to talk about your situation both with professionals whose opinion you value and other parents facing a
similar issue. Your pediatrician, mental health professionals,
therapists, physicians, and, if your child is in school, professionals at your child's school can frequently provide important information and referrals and in some cases help you
put together a team.

There are many wonderful parent support groups for specific conditions that can offer both excellent and current
information about treatment and referrals as well as emotional support for you. There are also numerous local and
national organizations and foundations created to address
various problems and illnesses, which offer information,
access to research findings and lists of practitioners to contact. The Internet is fast becoming a tremendous resource for
sharing information and helping parents sort out complex
problems and competing treatment plans. The list at the end
of this chapter can help you get started.

Parents of school-age children are often unclear as to
whether to involve the school in their inquiry. The answer to
this question is: it depends. In both private and public
schools, school psychologists, administrators and teachers
often have good insights and resources to offer and can

arrange for evaluations and services to be delivered to your child at school or refer you to a network of specialists with whom they have worked. If your child is in school and you want your child to receive the evaluations and services the public school districts have the legal obligation to provide at no cost to you (as detailed below), you will need to involve the school.

Your decision will depend on your confidence in the school to be of help to your family and protective of your child. While the school does not need to know everything about your child and family, do remember that depending on the nature, severity and extent of the problem, it is quite possible that the school is already aware that there is a problem.

▶ **Interviewing and selecting professionals to work with your child.** Once you have gotten names of specific practitioners, whether in one field of practice or in several, the process of choosing the right person, or people, begins. The individual you consult for an evaluation may or may not be the person who conducts the intervention. The person you choose to work with your child will do so over a period of time on what may be very emotionally charged issues. To get the most from the work done together, the intervention requires a positive and (ultimately) trusting relationship between professional and client. This is true for all types of intervention—psychotherapy, speech therapy, work with learning specialists, and even physical therapy.

It is important to keep in mind that the most esteemed authority in a particular field may not necessarily be the right person to work with your child. No matter how fabulous the professional's credentials, if he or she does not establish a good rapport with your child, the value of the therapy may be meaningfully diluted.

When considering therapists and other practitioners, it is worth thinking about the proximity of their offices to your home or your child's school. Particularly if your child will be working with more than one specialist, it is important to look at the kind of schedule you will be creating for your child. You do not want your child's whole life to be about intervention. Children need down time, the opportunity to pursue personal interests, the chance to build friendships and participate in extracurricular activities and time to do homework. Fitting everything into the week can be difficult and so the logistics of getting to an office is a relevant concern.

You will probably have several people you want to talk to before settling on a person to work with your child. Before making an appointment to meet with any practitioner you will want to make sure that he or she has available appointment hours at appropriate times to work with your child, and discuss rates. If the person will not actually be able to work with your child, you may still want a consultation in order to get a professional opinion about the case. You may be able to do some initial screening on the telephone, but in general, you should be prepared to have a meeting with any professional you are seriously considering, for which you will probably be charged, to go into detail about your child.

It is important for parents to meet the professional before bringing in their child. This gives you an opportunity to tell your story, get an initial read on a possible course of action or explanation of alternatives, ask questions about the nature of the work to be done with the child and give the professional a case history without the child being present. You can also use the time to ask questions about the professional's training, credentials, and approach.

Because selecting a professional to work with your child is such an important decision and likely to be complicated, you should feel free to ask whatever questions you have to get you comfortable with the person to whose care you may be entrusting your child. Intervention works best when the parents and child feel comfortable, confident and clear about the process and goals of the intervention.

Michelle Ascher Dunn, C.S.W., a Manhattan psychoanalyst and child therapist, suggests that you inquire into the professional's: training, school of thought (if any in particular) behind the therapeutic approach, technique and philosophy. She advises discussing how he or she plans to deal with parents. Does the therapist meet with parents together with the child, separately from the child or not at all? How will progress be evaluated and communicated to parents? Does the therapist work only with children or does he or she treat adults? What type of general time frame should parents expect for the intervention? Dunn stresses that not only must the child trust the professional, but the parents must as well. Parents need to feel secure that the information they provide will be private and confidential and that they are free to discuss anything relevant without fear of being criticized or feeling threatened.

Once you have decided to have your child work with a particular person, he or she will probably want to take an extensive case history from you and, if appropriate, other relevant adults. Depending on the situation and type of intervention, this may be accomplished at the initial meeting or in one or more subsequent meetings. In some situations, it is sometimes possible for the therapist to guide the parents in conducting the intervention without ever working directly with the child. In such cases, the therapist will meet with the parents at scheduled intervals to review progress and adjust the strategy.

When a child works directly with a professional (either for an evaluation or for ongoing intervention), it becomes necessary to make introductions. While you will probably want to discuss with the professional how he or she should be introduced to your child, Michelle Ascher Dunn offers these basic guidelines. In general, children under the age of four do not need much advance preparation. Simply telling them that they are going to play with a new adult may suffice. Children between the ages of four and six will probably need more of an explanation. In this age group, you may want to tell the child that he or she is going to meet a person who can help with his or her feelings or specific issue (e.g., speech, coordination, reading).

A child between the ages of six and eight can handle more specific information and can be told that he or she is meeting an expert who can help solve a problem. A child between the ages of eight and 12 is more likely to be aware that he or she has an issue that needs to be addressed and about which his or her parents are concerned. A child of this age may be either relieved to see a specialist who can help or reluctant or embarrassed to go. He or she may need to be told more definitively that meeting with a specialist is necessary.

If your child will be working with more than one professional, you may want to give some thought as to how to coordinate their efforts. Some therapists have a developed network of practitioners with whom your child can work that will facilitate communication. If the people with whom your child will be working do not have any relationship, it can sometimes be very difficult to get them to talk to each other about your child's case. This leaves you as the parent in the middle, communicating with each specialist and trying to put the information together yourself. In this situation, you may want to propose having them meet, at your expense, for a conference or conference call in which you can participate at various intervals or on an as-needed basis.

Addressing a child's disabilities or facing a mental health issue requires your energy, commitment, and financial resources. Certain types of therapy will be covered in whole or in part by health insurance and others will not. Dr. Dale Hirsch recommends that while it is optimal to create a multidisciplinary team for complex issues, if for financial or other reasons you must limit the intervention, you should prioritize the remediation tools with the help of a qualified professional.

A final important point on working with specialists. It is crucial to assess your child's progress several times a year to determine if the intervention is in fact producing maximum remediation and help for your child. If at all possible, your child's abilities should be quantitatively measured against age-appropriate norms. It is not always easy to tell if the program is working, but you should be able to determine if some progress, however subtle, is being made over a reasonable time period.

If the intervention is not producing results, you must be prepared to modify the intervention and where necessary change practitioners or reconfigure the remediation team or types of intervention being provided. It is not only reasonable to arrange for periodic reevaluation but vital to getting the most effective help for your child.

◤

Your Child's Legal Rights

There are two important federal statutes that create legal rights for children with various disabilities: Section 504 of the Rehabilitation Act and the Individuals with Disabilities Education Act (IDEA).

Section 504 requires that schools that receive federal funds not discriminate against students with disabilities. Under Section 504 schools must undergo self-evaluations for compliance with the law and have a local compliance coordinator. Schools need to notify the public of a general right to nondiscrimination in an effort to identify children with disabilities in the district and specifically notify children known to be disabled about the responsibilities of the school district to: provide evaluation, educational and related services free of charge; put disabled children in the least restrictive environment possible; and provide the most appropriate education possible together with the services necessary to do so. To be eligible for Section 504 services, a student must have a mental or physical impairment that substantially limits one or more major life activities as defined by the statute.

IDEA also requires a general notice of rights to parents as well as a specific notice if the school intends to take some action with respect to a child. The kind of rights afforded by IDEA include rights to: free, full and independent evaluation of the child's needs; explanation and justification for any proposed action to be taken and options rejected by the school; an Individual Education Program (IEP); services to support the IEP and have the child mainstreamed to the extent possible. The statute also addresses parental consent, confidentiality of information in the child's records, and the right of parents to an impartial due process hearing to challenge the services to be provided to or withheld from a child. To be eligible for IDEA services, the child must fall into one of the statutory eligibility categories, each of which has its own diagnostic criteria.

In compliance with these and other federal laws, New York State has developed law and policy implemented through various agencies and the public school system to provide the services necessary to students with special needs. The law is extensive and complicated, but for parents of children who may qualify for services, it is important to become acquainted with your rights in greater detail. The resources listed at the end of this chapter can help you work your way through the system as it applies in New York City.

◤

Special Programs for Children from Birth to Five

New York State has established 15 Early Childhood Direction Centers (ECDC) throughout the state. ECDCs are funded by the State Education Department and administered by the State Office of Vocational and Educational Services for Individuals with Disabilities (VESID). The ECDC in Manhattan is sponsored by New York and Presbyterian

Hospital, New York-Cornell Campus (formerly New York Hospital Cornell Medical Center). The family of any child who has a suspected or diagnosed physical, mental, and/or emotional disability can receive, at no cost, confidential information and referrals with respect to diagnostic and evaluation services; medical, educational and social services; support group; counseling; and entitlements. The ECDC can refer infants and toddlers to the Early Intervention Program and children between the ages of three and five to the Committee on Preschool Special Education (CPSE).

The Early Intervention Program is a statewide program administered by the New York State Department of Health. Children under the age of three who have developmental or physical delays, mental conditions likely to cause a developmental delay, including cognitive, physical, visual, hearing, communication, social/emotional or adaptive impairment, are eligible for the Early Intervention Program. The program will provide, at no cost to the family, and depending on the child's needs, services such as evaluation and diagnostic testing, coordination of services, support groups, home visits, and various types of therapy and social services.

Children between the ages of three and five are eligible for evaluation by the CPSE in the school district in which they reside (or if they are attending a public preschool, in the district in which that school is located). The local CPSE will arrange for an evaluation at no cost to the family and if a disability is found, the child will be recommended for preschool special education services to be delivered free of charge.

The evaluations conducted in connection with the Early Intervention Program or directed by the CPSE are provided by the Board of Education or private practitioners who are under contract with, or otherwise approved by, the state. If services are not being provided within a public school (as may be the case with preschoolers receiving services), the services will also be delivered by private providers. It is often comforting to parents to know that the same individual authorized by a publicly supported program to service specific disabilities or limitations might have been the same individual they could have found after networking on their own.

◤

Special Needs at School

If your child is attending ongoing school, the evaluation, diagnostic and intervention process may very well involve the school, at least to some degree if not exclusively. Parents are often reluctant to bring their concerns to the school or advise the school of an ongoing intervention because of their fear that their child will be stigmatized and that confidentiality will not be maintained. Consider, however, that school is where a child will spend the bulk of the day and that support and cooperation from the school can really help. It is to everyone's advantage when parents and schools can work in partnership.

There are two ways that issues are addressed once a child is in school. Parents either bring concerns to the attention of the teacher or the school approaches the parents with their observations and discusses how the situation should be pursued. If the problem was brought to your attention by, or was otherwise evident in school, then the school already is aware of the issue and can probably assist you.

If your child is truly symptom free at school, your decision to advise the school is a function of your confidence in the school. If your child is working with a professional to address the problem, you should discuss with that person whether and when to raise it with the school and how much information is appropriate to give to the school under the circumstances. If you feel that the school cannot be made a partner in the evaluation process and cooperate in providing the necessary support, then you should consider if your child is in the right school.

▶ **Nonpublic schools.** Private schools do not have the legal obligation to provide the types of services or facilities for special needs students that are provided as of right in the public school system. Nonpublic preschools and ongoing schools may or may not have, or may not have the inclination, to allocate resources to special education programs or address the issues of particular students. Some schools are simply ill-equipped to be of much assistance when a child is experiencing difficulty. Each school will have its own level of dedication and expertise with respect to meeting the specific needs of each student, procedures for identifying issues and determining and executing the appropriate intervention.

Many of the private schools are very supportive and will work with a child on-site as well as with outside support services to ensure that a child is receiving optimal intervention. There are also quite a few schools that have developed extensive programs for intervention and remediation. There is, however, no standard protocol. It is very much up to each school to determine what it can and will do.

For parents in the throes of dealing with a child's issues it can be a time of great confusion and anxiety. Parents of private school students who may be accustomed to an intimate, nurturing and personalized support network at school may be disappointed and feel abandoned when their child's issues become involved to a degree that the school is not prepared to support. Your child needs you to become his or her advocate and make sure that everything that can be done is being done. If that does not prove to be the case, be prepared to move on to a better environment.

At the same time, you must also realize that every individual and every resource has its limitations and it is up to *you*, not the school, to seek out professionals to help you make decisions and implement interventions that are beyond what the school can offer. If you are not happy with what the school can provide, do not waste time being offended or dissatisfied. Consult with an outside professional and keep searching until you find the assistance and services you need. Remember, this is about getting your child appropriate help and it is you who must protect and advocate for your child.

One last point for parents of private school students. By law, and depending on the nature of your child's issues, your child may be eligible for an evaluation and various forms of intervention at no cost and expense to you through your school district, even though your child does not attend public school. Consult your local school district office for information as to eligibility and available services.

▶ **Public schools.** The Board of Education has established guidelines, in compliance with applicable law (such as IDEA), to govern the evaluation, diagnosis of and intervention management for students with various disabilities. Each local school district has a Committee on Special Education (CSE) which coordinates and conducts evaluations and recommends programs, services and placements for students living or attending school in the district. The Board of Education's booklet, *A Parent's Guide to Special Education for Children Ages 5-21*, available from your school district or the Board of Education, outlines these guidelines. A list of school districts can be found in Chapter 8.

The formal review process. Pursuant to the federal statutory rights afforded to students with disabilities as implemented under New York law, schools must follow certain formal procedures in identifying, evaluating and arranging for and delivering services to qualifying students. Dr. Richard Curci, a Manhattan learning specialist, explains that the formal evaluation process in New York City public schools generally (but not always) operates as follows:

◢ The teacher or other school professional approaches the appropriate school official (i.e., the principal) to discuss a child's issue, whether raised by the parents or suspected by the school personnel. The teacher and school official then meet with a School Based Support Team, also referred to as a Child Study Team, consisting of a psychologist, social worker, and educational evaluator. A meeting is then arranged with parents to discuss the situation. If warranted, a written request to the CSE for an evaluation will be made. Parents may initiate a request directly to the district CSE for evaluation. Referral of the child for evaluation and diagnostic testing cannot proceed without the written consent of the parents.

◪ A battery of psychoeducational testing is conducted and a social history of the child is outlined by the social worker in conjunction with the parents. All areas relating to the disabilities suspected must be explored. By law, this evaluation is conducted at the school's expense. A standard private evaluation can cost $1000 and upward, although the cost can be more or less depending on the nature of the suspected disability and the depth of testing. Parents have the right to provide the CSE with outside evaluations conducted at the parents' expense although the CSE is not bound by the findings of such private evaluations.

◪ Evaluations (whether done at the school or district office or by private testers at the school's cost) must be completed, and a recommendation made by the School Based Support Team, based on the diagnosis resulting from evaluation, to the school district's CSE within 90 days. If you disagree with the findings of the CSE, you can request an independent evaluation. The CSE can either pay for the independent evaluation or request an impartial hearing to approve the CSE findings.

◪ Based on the diagnosis of the disabilities and determination of eligibility for services, an IEP is established, which outlines the services to be provided. Be aware that the school is not required to provide remediation unless the child is performing below his or her grade level as measured against standard norms. The determination may be based on either quantitative measures (such as reading scores) or a profile of the child's ability to function within the mainstream population at his or her grade level in his or her school.

■ The IEP must include a detailed description of the child's current level of educational performance, goals and the anticipated time frame for achievement, services to be delivered (e.g., counseling, speech, occupational or physical therapy) for how long it is anticipated that services will be necessary, and the child's class placement. By law, students must be placed in the least restrictive environment. Parents have the right to participate in formulating the goals and the structuring of the IEP and must consent to it being implemented. The IEP must be reviewed annually and modified to incorporate updated goals and strategies. It is required that the child be retested periodically. Under a flexible assessment program, retesting of the child can be done upon request if it is determined to be necessary or at specified intervals. At the very least, retesting must be done triannually.

■ Throughout the process, there are specific notices to be sent to parents and opportunities for parents to participate in the process, including the right to protest the action taken (or not taken) and call for a due process hearing.

Informal actions to make extra help available. Throughout the city, many dedicated educators are doing their utmost in the face of budget constraints and the growing number of students needing intervention to make services available to children in whatever way they can. As a result, there are many innovative programs taking place in the public schools.

Most public schools have a Pupil Personnel Committee, organized by the principal, to discuss children at risk and possible intervention techniques. If the school has volunteer service providers, temporary services may sometimes be delivered by a school volunteer association, which can provide valuable short-term intervention. If there is space available, the principal can provide a child with extra help at the on-site Resource Room, which is a classroom staffed with learning specialists.

Children identified by the School Based Support Team and the CSE as requiring support services from the Resource Room will either leave the classroom (so-called pull out services) for supplemental help or work with the Resource Room service provider within the classroom (so-called push in services) for a scheduled period of time each week. If this type of temporary intervention is not doing the job, the child will be referred for the full formal evaluation.

City public schools are each supposed to have a Consultant Teacher Program, under which students can receive direct (pull out or push in) or indirect (modification of the classroom curriculum for the child) service in the classroom. This program benefits children designated to receive in-class assistance as well as those requiring a little extra help. This program is relatively new to New York City schools although it has been well established in other parts of the state.

▶ **The special education experience is for most a positive one.** If you trust in the professionals guiding you through the identification, evaluation and diagnostic process, and those individuals are worthy of that trust, the result will be genuine help for your child. Due in part to the legislation passed in recent years, labels cannot be given to children at the whim of a teacher or principal. Documentation must validate any label applied to a child's disability. Your consent must be obtained for an evaluation, an IEP and at the annual review.

On the other hand, you need to be aware that the public schools are faced with the obligation to provide services to a growing population in the face of budget cuts and increased class size. Does this mean your child is not getting quality intervention? Not necessarily, but it is a reason to stay on top of your child's progress to be sure optimal intervention is being made available.

Parents must realize as well that there is a difference between not getting what your child is entitled to and not having your expectations met. Most disabilities are not cured. Rather, the child is taught strategies to compensate for and, when possible, overcome obstacles. It is important to understand the distinction between what remediation is available for the identified disability and what the school is required by law to provide. This will enable you to determine if you have grounds to challenge any decisions by the school system. If the therapy you seek is beyond what the school must give your child, you may want to consider supplementing the school-provided remediation with private therapy.

To be your child's advocate and part of his or her educational team, you need to maintain a dialogue with those handling your child's education and intervention. The need to communicate with service providers is key to your child's success. As a parent, you are free to bring private consultants (learning specialists, psychologists or even a lawyer) to your meetings with public school officials. If your concerns or requests have not been addressed to your satisfaction, do not be intimidated by the system. Follow up at the school, and if that does not produce results, move up the hierarchy until you have the answers you need. It is not always easy to challenge the system, but the potential rewards for your child outweigh the burdens of fighting City Hall.

Resources

General Resources

American Association for Home-
Based Early Intervention
6500 University Blvd.
Logan, UT 84322
800 396-6144

American Self-Help Clearinghouse
Northwest Covenant Medical
Center
25 Pocono Road
Denville, NJ 07834
973-625-7101
Information on self-help groups.
Publishes the *Self-Help Sourcebook*.

Boys Town National Hotline
800 448-3000
Referral and support for a variety of
behavioral and learning issues.

Child Study Center
New York University Medical
Center
550 First Avenue
New York, NY 10016
Clinical care, research, educational
outreach, prevention and advanced
training for professionals. AD/HD,
developmental delays and behavioral difficulties, learning disabilities and gifted programs, research
unit for Pediatric
Psychopharmacology and clinical
trials.

Early Childhood Direction Center
(ECDC)
New York and Presbyterian
Hospital
New York Hospital-Cornell
Campus
435 East 70th Street #2A
New York, NY 10021
746-6175

Free confidential information and
referral for services for young children (five years old or under) with
diagnosed or suspected special
needs. Funded in part by the New
York State Department of
Education and sponsored by New
York and Presbyterian Hospital.

Federation for Children with
Special Needs
800 331-0688
Information and referral services.
www.fcsn.org

Internet Resources for Special
Children
www.irsc.org

Jewish Board of Family and
Children's Services, Inc.
888 JBFCS-New York
Community-based, residential and
day treatment programs and referrals

Manhattan Parent Resource Center
22 East 28th Street
7th Floor
New York, NY 10016
481-5584
Information, referrals, support
groups, telephone helpline and
other services. Designed and run
by parents.

March of Dimes Birth Defects
Foundation
Resource Center
888 663-4637

National Easter Seal Society
800 221-6827

National Information Center for
Children and Youth with
Disabilities (NICHCY)
PO Box 1492
Washington, DC 20013
800 695-0285
www.nichcy.org
Information clearinghouse. Also
provides list of state resources for
all states.

National Maternal and Child
Health Clearinghouse
2070 Chain Bridge Road
Suite 450
Vienna, VA 22182
703 821-8955
www.circsol.com/mch

National Organization for Rare
Disorders
PO Box 8923
New Fairfield, CT 06812
800 999-NORD (800 999-6673)

New York City Self-Help Center
120 West 57th Street
New York, NY 10019
586-5770
Information and referral to support
and self-help groups.

New York Easter Seal Society
845 Central Avenue
Albany, NY 12206
518 438-8785

New York Foundling Hospital
Pediatric Center
590 Sixth Avenue
New York, NY 10011
633-9300
Therapeutic inpatient rehabilitative
facility for children 0 to 5 years
old, emergency diagnostic reception centers and community-based
prevention programs. Services
geared toward families in crisis.

Parent to Parent of New York State
500 Balltown Road
Schenectady, NY 12304
800 305-8817
New York City office 741-5545
www.parenttoparentnys.org
Information and referrals by parents.

Parents Helping Parents
www.php.com

Resources for Children with Special
Needs
200 Park Avenue South
New York, NY 10003
677-4650

St. Vincent's Hospital and Medical
Center
Brian Wert C.H.I.L.D. Center
75 Morton Street
7th Floor
New York, NY 10014
929-7003

The Parents' Resource Almanac by
Beth DeFrancis (Bob Adams, Inc.,
1994)
Lists many national organizations
on topics relating to special needs.

Toys R Us Toy Guide for
Differently Abled Kids
Catalogue free at Toys R Us stores.

Governmental Resources

Board of Education of the City of
New York
Division of Special Education
110 Livingston Street
Room 310
Brooklyn, NY 11202
718 935-5213
718-935-4042 Division of Student
Services
Publishes *A Parent's Guide to Special
Education for Children Ages 5-21*

New York City Department of Health
Physically Handicapped Children's Programs
2 Lafayette Street
Box 34, 11th Floor
New York, NY 10007
676-2948
Provides services for chronically ill and disabled children.

New York City Department of Mental Health, Mental Retardation and Alcoholism Services
93 Worth Street
New York, NY 10013
219-5400
Early Intervention Program 219-5580 (this office implements the statewide Early Intervention Program in New York City).
TOT Line 800 577-BABY (2229)
Information and referral services.

New York State Commission on Quality of Care
99 Washington Avenue
Suite 1002
Albany, NY 12210
518 473-7378
New York City office
270 Broadway
Room 2808
New York, NY 10007
417-5096
Protection and advocacy agency for mentally and physically disabled.

New York State Commission for the Blind and Visually Handicapped
Department of Social Services
40 North Pearl Street
Albany, NY 12243
518 473-1801
New York City office
270 Broadway
New York, NY 10007
417-4629

New York State Department of Education
Office for Special Education Services
One Commerce Plaza
16th Floor
Albany, NY 12234
Preschool Unit (ages 3 to 5) 518 473-6108
Special Education Unit (ages 5 to 21) 518 486-9592
New York City office 718 722-4544

New York State Department of Health
Early Intervention Program
Bureau of Child and Adolescent Health
Corning Tower
Room 208
Empire State Plaza
Albany, NY 12237
518 473-7016
Publishes *A Family Guide for the New York State Early Intervention Program for Infants and Toddlers with Disabilities,* Early Intervention Coordinating Councils (state and regional)
Central New York City office
219-5580
Manhattan Borough office
487-3920
Growing Up Healthy Hotline
800 522-5006
To access services and information regarding physically handicapped children's programs and Early Intervention Programs.
Child Health Plus (insurance program) 800 698-4543

New York State Department of Health
Bureau of Child and Adolescent Health
Family Professional Training Institute
Corning Tower
Room 208

Empire State Plaza
Albany, NY 12237
518 474-6781
Publishes *New York State Directory of
Self-Help/Mutual Support for Children
with Special Health Needs and Their
Families,* which lists self-help clear-
inghouses and national organizations and support networks for
more than 50 conditions and illnesses.

New York State Developmental
Disabilities Planning Council
155 Washington Avenue
2nd Floor
Albany, NY 12210
518 432-8233

New York State Office of the
Advocate for Persons with
Disabilities
Technology Related Assistance for
Individuals with Disabilities
(TRAID) Project
1 Empire State Plaza
Suite 1001
Albany, NY 12223
518 474-2825 or 800 522-4369
SATIRN 800 522-4369 Database of
services.
www.state.ny.us/disabledadvocate
Helps individuals access assistive
technology services and devices.
Links with SATIRN II (resource
directory of assistive technology
devices), HyperAble Data (directory
of devices) and TRAID-IN
Equipment Exchange Program.

New York State Office of Mental
Health
44 Holland Avenue
Albany, NY 12229
518 473-6902 State mental health
representative for children and
youth.

New York State Office of Mental
Retardation and Developmental
Disability
44 Holland Avenue
Albany, NY 12229
518 473-1997
Bureau of Consumer and Family
Supports 518 473-1890
"Care at Home" Program 518 474-
5647
New York City regional office 229-
3230/1
Metro New York Developmental
Disabilities Services Office 229-
3216

New York State Office of
Vocational and Educational
Services for Individuals with
Disabilities
One Commerce Plaza
Room 1613
Albany, NY 12234
800 222-5627
For information about Early
Childhood Direction Centers
Resource on Deafness 518 474-
5652

**Learning and Educational
Issues**

Advocates for Children of New
York
105 Court Street
4th Floor
Brooklyn, NY 11201
718 624-8450

Dial-a-Teacher (tutors)
United Federation of Teachers and
Board of Education
777-3380

ERIC Clearinghouse on Disabilities
and Gifted Education
Council for Exceptional Children
800 328-0272

Learning Disabilities Association of New York
27 West 20th Street
New York, NY 10011
645-6730

National Center for Learning Disabilities
381 Park Ave South
Suite 1401
New York, NY 10016
545-7510

New York Branch of the Orton Dyslexia Society
71 West 23rd Street
New York, NY 10010
691-1930

Parents Educational Resource Center
1660 South Amphlett Blvd.
Suite 200
San Mateo, CA 94402
650 655-2410
Support for learning differences.

Parents League of New York, Inc.
115 East 82nd Street
New York, N Y 10028
737-7389

What Schools Forget to Tell Parents About Their Rights by Reed Martin, JD. This book describes students rights to special services under Federal law and can be purchased from Future Horizons Inc, 720 North Fielder, Arlington TX 76012, 800 489-0727.

Mental Health

Ackerman Institute for the Family
149 East 78th Street
New York, NY 10021
879-4900

Alliance for the Mentally Ill of New York State
260 Washington Avenue
Albany, NY 12210
800 950-3228
www.crisny.or/not-for-profit/aminys

American Psychiatric Association
1400 K Street NW
Washington, DC 20005
202 682-6000
New York County District Office
150 East 58th Street
31st Floor
New York, NY 10022
421 4732

American Psychological Association
750 First Street NE
Washington, DC 20002
202 336-5700

Child Psychiatry Research Center at Columbia University
722 West 168th Street
New York, NY 10032
543-2383

Columbia-Presbyterian Child Anxiety Research Program
722 West 168th Street
New York, NY
543-6072

Institute for Contemporary Psychotherapy
1841 Broadway
4th Floor
New York, NY 10023
595-3444

LifeNet
800 LIFENET (800 543-3638)
Information and referral network for emotional and substance abuse problems. LifeNet is a service of the Mental Health Association of New York City, Inc. in collaboration with New York City Department of

Mental Health, Mental Retardation
and Alcoholism Services.

Mental Health Association of New
York City
666 Broadway
Suite 200
New York, NY 10012
254-0333
Advocacy, information and educa-
tion, direct services and referrals.

Mental Health Association of New
York State
169 Central Avenue
Albany, NY 12206
800 766-6177

National Alliance for the Mentally
Ill (NAMI)
200 North Glebe Road
Suite 1015
Arlington, VA 22203
703 524-7600
Information, list of family support
groups, education, support, advocacy, support for research.

National Alliance for the Mentally
Ill (NAMI) New York City Metro
432 Park Avenue South
New York, N Y 10016
684-3365

National Mental Health
Association
800 969-6642

New York Psychoanalytic Institute
and Society
247 East 82nd Street
New York, NY 10028
879-6900

Post Graduate Center for Mental
Health
Child, Adolescent and Family
Services
124 East 28th Street
New York, NY 10016
576-4150

St Vincent's Hospital and Medical
Center
Child and Adolescent Psychiatry
Service
203 West 12th Street
3rd Floor
New York, NY 10011
604-8211

**Specific Conditions, Illnesses,
etc.**

ADD Resource Center
215 West 75th Street
New York, NY 10023
724-9699

American Lung Association of New
York
Family Asthma Program
432 Park Avenue South
New York, N Y 10016
889-3370

American Speech-Language-
Hearing Association
Information Resource Center
800 638-8255

Association for the Help of
Retarded Children
200 Park Ave South
New York, N Y 10003
780-2500

Autism Society of America
800 3-AUTISM (800 328-8476)
www.autism-society.org

Brain Injury Association of New
York State
10 Colvin Avenue
Albany, NY 12206
518 459-7911
800 228-8201

Children and Adults with
Attention Deficit Disorders
(CHADD) 800 233-4050
954 587-3700
www.chadd.org

Children's Advocacy Center of Manhattan
333 East 70th Street
New York, NY 10021
517-3012
Intervention and treatment program for child victims of sexual and physical abuse.

Epilepsy Foundation of New York City
305 Seventh Avenue
12th Floor
New York, NY 10001
633-2930

Food Allergy Network
10400 Eaton Place
Suite 107
Fairfax, VA 22030
703 691-3179
www.foodallergy.org

Gay Men's Health Crisis
807-6655 hotline
Child Life Program for children and families dealing with AIDS
367-1268
www.gmhc.org

Genetics Services Program
New York State Department of Health
Wadsworth Center
PO Box 509
Empire State Plaza
Room E275
Albany, N Y 12201
518 474-7148

Hospital for Joint Diseases
Attention Deficit Disorder Clinic
301 East 17th Street
New York, NY 10003
598-6490

Lyme Disease Foundation
Lyme Disease Hotline
860 525-5963

National Attention Deficit Disorder Association (ADDA)
800 487-2282
www.add.org

National Cancer Institute
Cancer Information Service
800 4CANCER (800 422-6237)
www.cancerlit

National Heart, Lung and Blood Institute
Information Center
301 251-1222

New York State Speech-Language-Hearing Association
25 Chamberlain Street
PO Box 997
Glenmont, NY 12077
518 463-5272

NYSARC, Inc. (New York State Association for Retarded Children)
393 Delaware Avenue
Delmar, NY 12054
518 439-8311

Stuttering Foundation of America
800 992-9392

United Cerebral Palsy Associations (National)
800 872-5827

United Cerebral Palsy Associations of New York State
330 West 34th Street
New York, NY 10001
947-5770

Chapter 10

SHOP TIL YOU DROP

Manhattan is a mecca for shoppers. From bargain to bespoke, you can find it, have it made, or order it from, here. Depending on whether you are a born consumer or hate to shop, the scope and variety of merchandise available in New York City is either a blessing or a curse. Wherever you may fall on the buying spectrum, there is no question that if you want it, in all likelihood you can have it without ever leaving the borough.

Shopping for children in Manhattan is a unique experience. The vast selection of clothing, shoes, toys and other children's products and services can unnerve even the hardiest of shoppers. Our goal is to help you find your way to the products you want, both in terms of price and location of the shops convenient to you. In this chapter, you will find a list of stores specializing in children's clothing, shoes, books, toys and supplies.

Please note that we do not attempt to chronicle every shop that sells something for or related to children. In a city with an ever-changing landscape of hundreds of thousands of square feet of retail space, to do so would be virtually impossible. Therefore, we have not included every neighborhood candy, pharmacy or stationery store that carries some children's items, adult clothing or gift stores that carry a few items of children's clothing, accessories or baby paraphernalia, bookstores that carry a small selection of children's books, furniture stores that carry a few pieces either designed or suitable for children's rooms or sporting goods stores that carry a few items for kids. Rather, we have focused on those businesses that are primarily devoted to children's goods and/or carry a significant inventory of products for children.

Each entry in this chapter contains information about what is carried in the store, the general price range of merchandise and where exactly the store is located. At the end of the chapter, you will find the stores indexed by the type of goods sold together with a neighborhood locator notation. Happy shopping!

◪

The Shopping Landscape

There are basically three categories of stores in Manhattan: department stores, multi-unit stores and boutique/specialty stores. Department stores are large institutions that carry many types of goods for men, women, children and the home. Multi-unit stores are those that are individual locations of larger businesses, whether regional, national or even international in scope. Finally are the boutique or specialty stores that are usually single-location businesses, although there occasionally may be an additional location in the city or in the tri-state area. Boutique and specialty stores, big or small, carry unique merchandise individually selected by the store's management.

▶ **Department Stores.** There are several department stores in Manhattan that carry children's merchandise. Department stores at the higher end of the spectrum, such as Bergdorf Goodman and Barney's, tend to carry exclusive, imported and expensive items for infants and young children as well as luxury accessories for the layette and nursery. Stores such as Bloomingdale's, Saks Fifth Avenue, Macy's and Lord & Taylor have much more extensive children's departments, typically going up to pre-teen or teen sizes, stocking both premium or designer (i.e., more expensive) labels as well as more moderately priced labels and a respectable selection of accessories, stuffed animals and perhaps dolls. The discount department stores such as Kmart carry nationally known clothing labels as well as toys and baby supplies.

▶ **Multi-unit Stores**. Multi-unit stores range from the discount to luxury categories. Included within this group would be moderately priced stores you are likely to find in shopping malls, such as the Gap, Talbots Kids or Gymboree or national chains such as Toys R Us, as well as stores (in both the moderate or expensive price ranges) that have boutiques in various other cities in the U.S. or even around the world. For example, Manhattan is home to a number of higher-end European chains such as Jacadi, Catimini and Oilily. For us, these stores feel more like the boutique or specialty category by virtue of the unique merchandise they carry, but in fact they are not stand-alone stores. Also in this group are discount stores such as Daffy's.

▶ **Boutiques and Specialty Stores.** The plethora and variety of boutique and specialty shops are, to many, what New York shopping is all about. It is in these individually owned and operated stores that one can often find amazing merchandise. Some are big and well known while others are tiny retail spaces crammed full of goodies and good ideas. These stores can carry anything from antique toys to environmentally correct products to everything you could possibly need for your new baby or older child, from luxury layette to funky downtown clothes, from handmade playthings to science fiction toys. Prices range from bargain to the stratosphere, depending on the nature of the merchandise carried. Some boutiques are known only to neighborhood cognescenti while others are magnets for shoppers from all over. The boutiques and specialty stores of Manhattan truly offer something for everyone.

▶ **What you will find in this chapter.** We confess that putting together this listing of stores was not an entirely scientific process. Our list was culled from advertising sources, word of mouth and pounding the pavement. We have endeavored to be as current as possible keeping in mind that small businesses tend not to advertise and to open and close without much fanfare, all of which makes it difficult to be totally comprehensive. The goal is to provide you with a broad range of shopping options, both in terms of price, location and type of merchandise, to assist you in finding what you need when and where you need it. To be sure, there will be stores that we may have missed or that you think should have been included, but we think you will agree that this list, containing over 275 establishments, is by far the most comprehensive list of its type to date.

Please remember that we do not list every store that carries some children's items. We have focused on those businesses that either cater entirely to the younger set, carry a meaningful selection (in our subjective opinion!) of children's merchandise, or offer merchandise so unique or special (even if only in a limited quantity) that we thought you would want to be aware of them.

▶ **How to use this chapter.** All entries are listed in alphabetical order together with their addresses and cross streets and a brief description of what is carried in the store. The intention is to give you an objective listing of the merchandise carried and a general indication of the price point at which the majority of the goods in the store are sold. In compiling this information we developed a list of categories of children's merchandise, which we share with you.

Please remember that these are the broadest descriptions of each category and not every store listed as carrying a certain type of merchandise will have each item we included in our definition. Additionally, even if a store does carry most of the items on our list for a particular category, quantities of particular items will vary among stores. The definitions are here mainly to serve as a *very general* guideline as to what you can expect, not an inventory of each individual store. Therefore, if you are shopping for a very specific item in a certain category, we urge you to call first and make sure that the store carries it.

■ Activewear—clothes and accessories for sports and dance, leotards, bathing suits, sports shorts, warmups and sweats.

■ Books—all types of books for children, hard and soft cover, board and/or fabric books for infants. Larger bookstores will also carry books for young readers (chapter books, series, classics, etc.).

■ Clothing and accessories—all types of children's clothing, which generally also includes undergarments, pajamas, seasonal clothing (e.g., snowsuits and bathing suits) and outerwear. Stores that carry clothing also typically carry a variety of accessories such as hats, gloves, scarves, socks and tights, slippers, hair ornaments (bows, headbands), belts, ties, suspenders, bags (backpacks, children's purses), and sometimes water shoes (jellies, flip-flops). Stores that carry baby clothes often carry some stuffed animals and crib toys (and sometimes even a few baby books) to package with baby gifts. Most clothing stores carry clothing up to sizes 12-16 children's (fitting children between the ages of ten and 12). Most stores organize merchandise by numerical sizes, while others categorize their merchandise by the age of the child it is meant to fit. For our purposes, if an entry does not contain a size or an age range, you can assume that the store carries items for infants up to ten- or 12-year-olds. If a particular store carries a more limited range of sizes (or only fits up to a certain age range), it is specifically indicated.

■ Decorative accessories—accessories for the nursery or older child's room, such as toyboxes, grow sticks, hat/coat racks, easels, child-sized furniture (tables, chairs, miniature sofas), rocking toys, bulletin boards, decorative storage boxes and units, baskets, step stools, storage cabinets, hampers, decorative pillows, wall hangings and throws. Many of these items are hand wrought, handpainted/decorated or personalized.

■ Equipment—merchandise for infants and toddlers (typically up to preschoolers) such as strollers, baby carriers, prams, car seats, playpens and portable cribs, swings, cloth diapers and burp clothes, crib sheets and accessories, toddler bedding, crib toys and mobiles, baby bathtubs, diaper bags, nursery monitors, gadgets, child-proofing and child safety items, bottles, first cups, cutlery and dishes.

■ Furniture—cribs, rockers, kid-sized tables and chairs, beds, changing tables, bureaus, armoires. Some stores carrying furniture may also include lamps and decorative accessories, and floor coverings (area rugs) for the nursery or child's room.

■ Layette—bedding for cribs, cradles and bassinettes, newborn clothing, hats, booties, receiving blankets, bibs, crib toys and stuffed animals, decorative pillows, quilts and blankets and accessories for the newborn. Bedding can consist of basic sheets and blankets or can include bumpers, bed skirts, wall hangings and coordinating window treatments.

◪ Linens—a number of higher-end imported fine linen stores carry some bedding and bath accessories (towels, robes) for children.

◪ Outerwear—coats, jackets and foul weather gear.

◪ Shoes—casual shoes, dress shoes, sandals, sneakers and athletic shoes and watershoes.

◪ Sporting goods—sports equipment, rackets, balls, skates, rollerblades, helmets, bats, gloves and gear for water sports. Sporting goods stores usually also carry athletic shoes and activewear.

◪ Toys—anything kids play with, including games, puzzles, dolls, stuffed animals, educational toys, building toys, arts and crafts supplies, models, cars and trucks, ride-on toys (which may include bicycles and tricycles), project kits, puppets, action figures, character figures (Sesame Street, Pooh), classic toys, handmade toys, some sports toys, models, dress-up, crib and baby toys, etc. Some toy stores carry some computer software, electronic toys, some audio and/or video tapes and a few books.

▶ **A word about price.** Indicating the price range of merchandise carried in a store is extremely complicated. While it is easy to identify stores in the discount and luxury categories, the vast majority of stores sell somewhere in the middle or sell merchandise at multiple price points. To attempt to quantify price points specifically is an exercise in futility. As a result, we came up with a not-quite-perfect three-point system for looking at prices: $ for discount or value-priced goods; $$ for moderately priced goods and $$$ for expensive or luxury goods. It is best to think of these valuations as relative rather than as absolutes—a way of distinguishing among choices when you are faced with a shopping expedition. For example, you may want to seek stores in the $ or $$ category for playclothes and the $$$ category for party clothes and baby gifts.

In addition, it is our experience that many of the stores in the $$ category stock inventory at the top and bottom of the range, or even into the next range. It is, for example, quite common to find a clothing store that carries great value leggings and T-shirts next to $200 hand-knit sweaters and $95 imported jeans. In such cases, we have indicated the store's price range as $$ to $$$. Also, even stores at the top of the $$$ category may have incredible blow-out sales for which you should be on the lookout.

Toystores and bookstores are also difficult to differentiate in terms of price. Most toystores carry an assortment of toys, small to large, inexpensive to expensive. Bookstores too may carry an array of inexpensive paperback books as well as full-price hardbound books. For that reason, we have not noted price ranges for toystores and bookstores unless the products are discounted.

In order to help you figure out where toystores and bookstores fall in the spectrum, here are some general rules. Boutique toystores carrying unique, specialty, educational, imported and handmade toys will generally have a selection of more expensive merchandise than those carrying more commercial brands (such as Fisher Price) or national chains such as Toys R Us or Kmart. Books at the smaller specialty bookstores or neighborhood stores will likely be higher priced than what is available at either the discounters or the chain superstores.

Remember, prices are relative and identifying the prices of goods is a highly subjective process. A bargain to one family can be a luxury to another, while for other families price is not the top priority in making a purchase. The system we have used is neither foolproof nor perfect, but we hope it will help you identify, at least generally, the stores you want to start with when you need or want to shop.

Let's Go Shopping

■ ABC Carpet and Home $$ to $$$
888 Broadway at 19th Street
473-3000
A full-service home furnishings emporium that also carries clothes, toys and books for children up to age 6, layette, furniture (new and antique) and linens. Design services available.

■ A Bear's Place Inc. $$ to $$$
789 Lexington Avenue between 61st and 62nd Streets
826-6465
A varied selection of unique toys as well as decorative accessories and some children's furniture.

■ Aida & Jimmy's $
41 West 28th Street between Sixth Avenue and Broadway, 2nd Floor
689-2415
Discount fine children's clothing.

■ Albee's $ to $$
715 Amsterdam Avenue between 94th and 95th Streets
662-8902
Everything you need for the new baby and young child including clothes (ages 0-12 months), equipment, layette, furniture, toys and books.

■ Alphabets $
115 Avenue A between Seventh and Eighth Streets, 475-7250
2284 Broadway between 82nd and 83rd Streets, 579-5702
47 Greenwich Avenue between Perry and Charles Streets, 229-2966
Unique retro toys, novelties and reproductions of goodies from yesteryear.

■ American Museum of Natural History Store
Central Park West between 77th and 81st Streets
769-5100
Educational toys and books, many relating to current exhibits, souvenirs and T-shirts.

- America's Hobby Center
146 West 22nd Street between Sixth and Seventh Avenues
675-8922
Toys and hobbies for children ages 10+.

- Anime Crash $$
13 East Fourth Street between Broadway and Lafayette Street
254-4670
Toys and accessories based on popular Japanese cartoon characters
(pochacco, keroppi, hello kitty, etc.).
For children ages 2+.

- April Cornell $$ to $$$
860 Lexington Avenue between 64th and 65th Streets,
570-2775
487 Columbus Avenue between 83rd and 84th Streets,
799-4342
Quality classic clothing for girls from ages 1-10 and women.

- Art & Tapisserie $$ to $$$
1242 Madison Avenue between 89th and 90th Streets
722-3222
Unique selection of decorative accessories and some furniture,
much of which can be personalized, toys and books.

- Astor Place Hair Designers
2 Astor Place at Broadway
475-9854
Downtown's own trendy, but basic, barbershop.

- Au Chat Botte $$$
1192 Madison Avenue between 87th and 88th Streets
722-6474
Fine imported, classic layette, imported equipment and furniture
and clothing for girls up to size 8 and boys up to size 6.

- B. Dalton Bookseller
396 Sixth Avenue between Sixth and Eighth Streets
674-8780
Books for all ages.

■ B. Shackman & Co. $ to $$
85 Fifth Avenue at 16th Street
989-5162
Old-fashioned, Victorian collectibles and reproductions, miniatures,
dollhouse accessories, toys, books and stuffed animals.

■ Baballoon
22 Eighth Avenue at 12th Street
463-9647
Party supplies and party favors for kids of all ages.

■ Baby Collection, Inc. $$$
1384 Lexington Avenue between 90th and 91st Streets
828-8633
Fine classic imported layette and clothing up to size 7.

■ Baby Depot at Burlington Coat Factory $
707 Sixth Avenue at 23rd Street
229-1300
Discount department store. The children's department carries
clothing, equipment, layette, and furniture for the nursery.

■ Baby Guess $$
775 Madison Avenue at 66th Street
628-2229
All-cotton casual clothing under the Baby Guess label up to size 6x
as well as a selection of contemporary bed linens.

■ Baby Palace $$
1410 Lexington Avenue between 92nd and 93rd Streets
426-4544
Everything for the new baby and young child including equipment,
layette, furniture, toys, books and clothing up to size 6.

■ Bambini $$$
1367 Third Avenue at 78th Street
717-6742
Classic imported clothes, layette and unique imported shoes.

■ Bank Street Bookstore
610 West 112th Street at Broadway
678-1654
Extensive selection of children's books, educational toys/games as
well as books on education, learning and parenting.

■ Barnes & Noble Jr.
120 East 86th Street between Park and Lexington Avenues 427-0686
Extensive selection of children's books for infants to teens, many
discounted.

■ Barnes & Noble Superstores
105 Fifth Avenue at 18th Street, 807-0099
675 Sixth Avenue at 22nd Street, 727-1227
Citicorp Building, 160 East 54th at Third Avenue, 750-8033
4 Astor Place at Broadway, 420-1322
1280 Lexington at 86th Street, 423-9900
600 Fifth Avenue at 48th Street, 765-0590
1960 Broadway between 66th and 67th Streets, 595-6859
33 East 17th Street at Union Square North, 253-0810
2289 Broadway between 82nd and 83rd Streets, 362-8835
Check your phone book for smaller Barnes & Noble stores.
Books for all ages, many discounted.

■ Barney's New York $$$
660 Madison Avenue between 60th and 61st Streets
826-8900
High-end department store with a charming children's department
that carries unique, mostly imported clothing (up to size 6),
decorative accessories and some nursery furniture and linens.

■ Bear Hugs & Baby Dolls $$ to $$$
311 East 81st between First and Second Avenues
717-1514
Collectible dolls (including Mme. Alexander) and stuffed animals
(including Steiff) and unique (including handmade) toys.

■ Bebe Thompson $$ to $$$
1216 Lexington Avenue between 82nd and 83rd Streets
249-4740
Unique selection of clothing, contemporary to classic, much
imported, layette, some toys and handmade items.

■ Bed Bath & Beyond $
620 Sixth Avenue between 18th and 19th Streets
255-3550
Discount department store for all things for the bed, bath and
kitchen. For children, there is bedding, bath accessories (towels,
robes, accessories for the sink and tub), toys, some books, dishes,
storage units and closet organizers, decorative accessories and
gadgets galore.

■ Bellini Juvenile Designer Furniture $$ to $$$
110 West 86th Street between Columbus and Amsterdam Avenues
580-3801
Everything for the new baby and young child, including
equipment, layette, furniture, toys, books and clothing for sizes 0-
12 months.

■ Bellini Juvenile Designer Furniture $$ to $$$
1305 Second Avenue between 68th and 69th Streets
517-9233
Everything for the new baby and preschooler, including equipment,
layette and furniture. The East Side store does not carry clothing or
toys.

■ Benetton $$
542 Fifth Avenue between 48th and 49th Streets
593-0290
Contemporary clothing with the Benetton label. From size 2
(toddler) to adult.

■ Ben's For Kids $$ to $$$
1380 Third Avenue between 78th and 79th Streets
794-2330
Everything for the new baby and young child, including
equipment, layette, furniture, toys (for babies to age 7/8), books, art
supplies and clothing for ages 0-2.

■ Bergdorf Goodman $$$
754 Fifth Avenue at 57th Street
753-7300
High-end department store with a lovely children's department that
carries classic imported layette, furniture for the nursery, linens and
clothing for ages 0-2.

- Big City Kite Company
1210 Lexington Avenue at 82nd Street
472-2623
A store specializing in all types of kites and other airborne toys.

- Bloomingdale's $$ to $$$
1000 Third Avenue at 59th Street
705-2000
Full-service department store with a large children's department
that carries clothes, layette, lots of stuffed animals and Barbies.

- Bombalulu's $$ to $$$
332 Columbus Avenue between 75th and 76th Streets,
501-8248
101 West Tenth Street at Sixth Avenue, 463-0897
Unique contemporary clothing up to size 7, shoes, toys and
wonderful handmade quilts.

- Bonne Nuit $$$
551 Fifth Avenue at 45th Street (inside New York Look Store)
681-1100
30 Lincoln Plaza at 62nd Street and Broadway
489-9730
Fine imported classic clothing up to size 6 as well as some crib and
baby toys.

- Bonpoint $$$
811 Madison Avenue at 68th Street, 879-0900
1269 Madison Avenue at 91st Street, 722-7720
Fine imported classic clothing, shoes and layette. The 68th Street
store carries up to size 12 for girls, up to size 8 for boys. The 91st
Street store carries up to size 16 for girls, up to size 12 for boys.

- Bookberries
983 Lexington Avenue between 71st and 72nd Streets
794-9400
Neighborhood bookstore with a selection of children's books and
toys.

■ Books of Wonder
16 West 18th Street between Fifth and Sixth Avenues
989-3270
Extensive selection of children's books and related items such as
dolls and puzzles.

■ Borders Books and Music
5 World Trade Center between Church and Vesey Streets, 839-8037
461 Park Avenue at 57th Street, 980-6785
Books for all ages, many discounted.

■ Boston & Winthrop $$$
by appointment, 410-6388
Custom, handpainted furniture.

■ Bradlees $
40 East 14th Street between University Place and Broadway
673-5814
Discount department store. Children's department carries clothing,
shoes, equipment, layette, furniture, toys, books and sporting
goods.

■ Brooks Brothers $$ to $$$
346 Madison Avenue at 44th Street
682-8800
Traditional clothing for boys sizes 6-20.

■ Bunnies Children's Department Store $
100 Delancey Street between Essex and Ludlow Streets, 529-7567
116 West 14th Street between Sixth and Seventh Avenues, 989-9011
Discount children's department store that carries clothing up to size
12, equipment, layette and furniture.

■ Canal Jean Co. $
504 Broadway between Spring and Broome Streets
226-1130
Discount casual clothing for children and adults starting at size 12
months.

- Capezio $$
1650 Broadway at 51st Street, 2nd Floor, 245-2130
1776 Broadway at 57th Street, 586-5140
136 East 61st Street between Lexington and Park Avenues, 758-8833
1651 Third Avenue between 92nd and 93rd Streets, 3rd Floor, 348-7210
Dance and activewear for dancers of all ages.

- Catimini $$$
1284 Madison Avenue between 91st and 92nd Streets
987-0688
European (mostly casual) clothing and layette with the Catimini label.

- Century 21 $
22 Cortlandt Street between Broadway and Church Street
227-9092
Discount department store. The children's department carries discounted major brand and designer label clothing, shoes and layette.

- Charl's Layette $$$
920 Park Avenue between Madison and Park Avenues
861-1113
Fine imported classic layette and clothing for ages 0-2.

- Children's General Store
2473 Broadway at 92nd Street
580-2723
Housed within Playspace (an indoor play area), this store features a good selection of unique and many educational toys.

- Children's Museum of Manhattan Store
212 West 83rd Street between Amsterdam and Broadway
721-1223
A good selection of unique and educational toys and books, many tied in to current exhibitions.

■ Children's Place $ to $$
901 Sixth Avenue between 32nd and 33rd Streets, 268-7696
400 World Trade Center in the Main Concourse, Lower Level, 432-6100
173 East 86th Street between Lexington and Third Avenues, 831-5100
A good selection of basics for school and play as well as some trendier items.

■ Children's Room $$ to $$$
140 Varick Street at Spring Street
627-2006
Quality wood furniture for decorating your older child's room (i.e., no cribs).

■ Chocks $
74 Orchard Street between Broome and Grand Streets
473-1929
Discount layette, sleepwear, underwear and hosiery for children and adults as well as some wooden toys.

■ Chocolate Soup $$ to $$$
946 Madison Avenue between 74th and 75th Streets
861-2210
Fun, contemporary clothing, handpainted tops, custom-dyed basics (leggings, T-shirts, overalls), handknits as well as unique small toys and stuffed animals/dolls and some books for younger children.

■ Citykids NY $$ to $$$
37 West 20th Street, Suite 604, between Fifth and Sixth Avenues
620-0906
You can order from the catalogue (800 435-8339) or visit the showroom for quality toys, stuffed animals, layette items, handknits, handpainted decorative accessories and gift baskets. Visit the website at www.gift-baskets.com.

■ Classic Toys
218 Sullivan Street between Bleecker and West Third Streets
674-4434
Classic toys for children and adults.

- CO2 $$
284 Columbus Avenue between 73rd and 74th Streets
721-4966
Trendy, retro and contemporary clothing for sizes 7 to 16.

- CoCo & Z $$ to $$$
222 Columbus Avenue between 70th and 71st Streets
721-0415
Fine layette and clothing, from contemporary to classic up to size 8.

- Coliseum Books
1771 Broadway at 57th Street
757-8381
Discounted books for all ages.

- Compleat Strategist
11 East 33rd Street between Fifth and Madison Avenues,
685-3880
630 Fifth Avenue between 50th and 51st Streets, 265-7449
342 West 57th Street between Eighth and Ninth Avenues, 582-1272
Games and toys for children ages 3+ and adults.

- Conway Stores $
general information, 967-5300
225 West 34th Street between Seventh and Eighth Avenues
967-7390
11 West 34th Street between Sixth and Seventh Avenues, 967-1370
1333 Broadway at 35th Street, 967-3460
201 East 42nd Street at Third Avenue, 922-5030
450 Seventh Avenue between 34th and 35th Streets, 967-1371
45 Broad Street at Exchange Place, 943-8900
151 William Street at Fulton Street, 374-1072
Discount department store. The children's department carries
clothing and layette. Some stores may have a modest selection of
toys.

- Corner Bookstore
1313 Madison Avenue at 93rd Street
831-3554
Books for all ages.

- Cozy's Cuts for Kids

1125 Madison Avenue between 84th and 85th Streets, 744-1716
448 Amsterdam Avenue at 81st Street, 579-2600
Haircuts for children up to age 12 in a totally child-friendly and fun
setting. The store also carries a good selection of hair accessories
and unique toys.

- Daffy's $
111 Fifth Avenue at 18th Street, 529-4477
135 East 57th Street between Park and Lexington Avenues, 376-
4477
335 Madison Avenue at 44th Street, 557-4422
1311 Broadway at 34th Street, 736-4477
Discount department store. The children's department carries major
brand clothing, shoes, layette and some toys.

- Danskin $$
159 Columbus Avenue between 67th and 68th Streets
724-2992
Not just for dancing, this store carries dance and activewear.

- Darrow's Fun Antiques
1101 First Avenue between 60th and 61st Streets
838-0730
Collectible antique and reproduction toys.

- Dave's Army & Navy Store $
779 Sixth Avenue between 26th and 27th Streets
989-6444
Playclothes and Levis for adults and children.

- Dinosaur Hill $$ to $$$
302 East Ninth Street between First and Second Avenues
473-5850
Quality educational toys (many handmade or handfinished) and
casual clothes.

- Disney Store $$
711 Fifth Avenue at 55th Street, 702-0702
39 West 34th Street between Fifth and Sixth Avenues, 279-9890
147 Columbus Avenue at 66th Street, 362-2386
210 West 42nd Street at Seventh Avenue, 221-0430
Clothing, toys, books and gift and novelty items with Disney
themes for the whole family.

- Dollhouse Antics
1343 Madison Avenue at 94th Street
876-2288
Dollhouses and dollhouse accessories.

- E.A.T. Gifts $$ to $$$
1062 Madison Avenue between 81st and 82nd Streets
861-2544
Unique, eclectic selection of toys, books, decorative accessories,
some furniture, party goods and dishes.

- E. Braun & Co, Inc. $$$
717 Madison Avenue between 63rd and 64th Streets
838-0650
Imported luxury linens.

- East Side Kids $$ to $$$
1298 Madison Avenue at 92nd Street
360-5000
Full selection of children's shoes from classic to trendy.

- Eastern Mountain Sports $$ to $$$
611 Broadway at Houston, 505-9860
20 West 61st Street between Columbus Avenue and Broadway,
397-4860
Outerwear for children and everything for outdoors for
all ages.

- Economy Handicrafts $
50-21 69th Street, Woodside, off Queens Blvd.
800 216-1601
Everything you could possibly need for arts and crafts projects, all
at a discount. Mail/telephone ordering available.

- Enchanted Forest
85 Mercer Street between Spring and Broome Streets
925-6677
Unique nostalgic toys and books in an incredible setting.

- F.A.O. Schwarz
767 Fifth Avenue at 58th Street
644-9400
An extensive selection of toys (from commercial brands to unique items), stuffed animals, dolls, art supplies, party goods, books, costumes and an entire Barbie department, accessories and some clothing all in an amazing setting.

- Farmers Daughter and Son $$ to $$$
1001 First Avenue at 55th Street
421-0484
Unique fine clothing for ages 0-3.

- First & Second Cousin $$
142 Seventh Avenue South between Tenth and Charles Streets
929-8048
Mostly new and some resale clothing, shoes and toys.

- Forbidden Planet
821 Broadway at 12th Street
473-1576
The store for science fiction toys, books and even accessories and T-shirts. For ages 3+.

- Freed of London $$
922 Seventh Avenue at 58th Street
489-1055
Dancewear and supplies for dancers ages 2 to adult.

- Frette $$$
799 Madison Avenue between 67th and 68th Streets
988-5221
Imported luxury linens.

■ Fun by the Basket $$ to $$$
1349 Lexington Avenue between 89th and 90th Streets
289-5960
Personalized toys, decorative accessories, some books and unique
gift baskets.

■ Funcut Salon
1567 York Avenue between 83rd and 84th Streets
288-0602
Haircuts in a child-friendly and fun environment.

■ G.C. William $$$
1137 Madison Avenue between 84th and 85th Streets
396-3400
Classic and contemporary European clothing for children ages 6-16.

■ Game Show
1240 Lexington Avenue between 83rd and 84th Streets,
472-8011
474 Sixth Avenue between 11th and 12th Streets, 633-6328
Games for adults and children ages 4+.

■ Gap Kids $$
various locations
Call 800 GAP-STYLE to locate the store nearest to you
Stylish, contemporary basics for babies to adults.

■ Geppetto's Toybox
161 Seventh Avenue South between Perry and Charles Streets
620-7511
Higher-end quality and educational toys (some handmade) and
books.

■ Gloria's KidsBeds $$
33 West 17th Street between Fifth and Sixth Avenues
888 600-5437
Wood furniture, decorative accessories and some linens for older
children's rooms (i.e., no cribs). Some custom furniture available.

■ Good Byes Children's Resale Shop $
230 East 78th Street between Second and Third Avenues
794-2301
Resale clothing, equipment, toys and books.

■ Gracious Home $$$
1217 Third Avenue between 70th and 71st Streets
988-8990
This housewares store carries everything from hardware and home
appliances to home furnishings and now a high-end baby
department too. The baby department carries furniture for the
nursery, layette, linens, decorative accessories, as well as wall and
window coverings. Custom design services available.

■ Granny Made $$ to $$$
381 Amsterdam Avenue between 78th and 79th Streets
496-1222
Quality clothing (including handmade items), for children and
adults.

■ Great Feet $$
1241 Lexington Avenue at 84th Street
249-0551
Full selection of shoes, from classic to trendy.

■ Greenstone's $$ to $$$
442 Columbus Avenue between 81st and 82nd Streets, 580-4322
Greenstone's, too, 1184 Madison Avenue between 86th and 87th
Streets, 427-1665
Fun, contemporary and unique clothing.

■ Guggenheim (Solomon R.) Museum
1071 Fifth Avenue at 89th Street, 423-3500
Guggenheim Museum Soho, 575 Broadway at Prince Street, 423-
3500
Educational toys and books and some decorative accessories.

■ Gymboree Store $$
1120 Madison Avenue between 83rd and 84th Streets, 717-6702
1332 Third Avenue between 76th and 77th Streets, 517-5548
1049 Third Avenue at 62nd Street, 688-4044
2271 Broadway between 81st and 82nd Streets, 595-9071
2015 Broadway at 69th Street, 595-7662
Colorful basics and shoes up to age 7.

■ Harry's Shoes $$
2299 Broadway at 83rd Street
874-2035
Full-service shoe store for children and adults. Children's
department carries everything from basics to party shoes.

■ Homboms Toy & Craft Emporium
1500 First Avenue between 78th and 79th Streets
717-5300
Toys, crafts and art supplies.

■ Ibiza Boutique $$ to $$$
42 & 46 University Place between Ninth and Tenth Streets
533-4614
European and eclectic clothing, handmade and unique goods, toys
and books.

■ Infinity $$
1116 Madison Avenue at 83rd Street
517-4232
Trendy clothing, small toys and novelties for children and adults.

■ Iris Brown's Victorian Doll Shop
253 East 57th Street between Second and Third Avenues
593-2882
Vintage and collectible dolls and dollhouse accessories.

■ JB Toys
379 Grand Street between Essex and Clinton Streets
673-7160
Toys, crafts, art supplies and some books.

• Jacadi $$$
1281 Madison Avenue at 91st Street, 369-1616
787 Madison Avenue between 66th and 67th Streets, 535-3200
Fine imported classic clothing, equipment, layette, furniture for the
nursery and linens.

• Jewish Museum Store
1109 Fifth Avenue at 92nd Street
423-3200
Educational toys and books.

• Jodi's Gymwear $$
244 East 84th Street between Second and Third Avenues
772-7633
Housed within Jodi's Gym, this shop carries dance, gymnastics and
activewear.

• Judy's Fancies $$ to $$$
249 East 45th Street between Second and Third Avenues
681-8115
Classic handmade layette and clothing up to size 6/8.

• Julian & Sara $$$
103 Mercer Street between Prince and Spring Streets
226-1989
Fine European clothing, layette (including some handmade items)
and shoes.

• Just Jake
40 Hudson Street between Duane and Thomas Streets
267-1716
Educational toys, books, art supplies, decorative accessories, some
handmade items and some linens.

• Kay-Bee Toys
901 Sixth Avenue in the Manhattan Mall at 32nd Street
629-5386
Commercial toys and art supplies.

■ Kidding Around
60 West 15th Street between Fifth and Sixth Avenues,
645-6337
68 Bleecker Street between Broadway and Lafayette Street, 598-0228
Educational toys, books and fun and unique clothing (up to size 8
in the 15th Street store, up to size 24 months in the Bleecker Street
store).

■ Kids are Magic $
2293 Broadway between 82nd and 83rd Streets
875-9240
Discounted basic major brand clothing, layette, and toys.

■ Kids Cuts
201 East 31st Street between Second and Third Avenues
684-5252
Haircuts for children in a totally child-friendly and fun setting. The
store also carries a good selection of hair accessories and unique
toys. Haircuts available for adults too.

■ Kids R Us $
1293 Broadway at 34th Street
643-0714
Major brand clothing.

■ Kids Supply Co. $$ to $$$
1325 Madison Avenue between 93rd and 94th Streets, 2nd Floor
426-1200
Children's furniture, some decorative accessories and linens.
Custom design services available.

■ Kidstown $
10 East 14th Street between Fifth Avenue and University Place
243-1301
Value-priced clothing, layette, furniture and toys.

■ Kmart Stores $
One Penn Plaza at 34th Street between Seventh and Eighth
Avenues, 760-1188
770 Broadway at Astor Place,
673-1540
Discount department store. The children's department carries major
brand name clothing, shoes, equipment, toys and books.

■ Koh's Kids $$ to $$$
311 Greenwich Street between Chambers and Reade Streets
791-6915
Sophisticated downtown clothing (up to size 8), shoes, layette and
toys.

■ La Layette et Plus $$$
170 East 61st Street between Lexington and Third Avenues
688-7072
Fine imported layette and clothing (up to size 2) and handpainted
and carved furniture.

■ La Petite Etoile $$$
746 Madison Avenue between 64th and 65th Streets
744-0975
Fine imported classic clothing, layette and equipment.

■ Lapin $$$
968 Third Avenue at 58th Street
826-7159
Casual European clothing for girls up to size 10, boys up to size 8.

■ Laura Ashley $$ to $$$
398 Columbus Avenue at 79th Street
496-5110
Classic clothes for girls and layette.

■ Leron $$$
750 Madison Avenue at 65th Street
753-6700
Imported luxury linens.

■ Lester's $$
1522 Second Avenue at 79th Street
734-9292
Contemporary to classic clothing, shoes, layette, many items
discounted, as well as some toys and books.

■ Lilliput $$ to $$$
265 Lafayette Street between Prince and Spring Streets
965-9567
Contemporary imported clothes clothing, shoes, layette and
specialty toys.

■ Little Eric $$ to $$$
1118 Madison Avenue between 83rd and 84th Streets, 717-1513
1331 Third Avenue between 76th and 77th Streets, 288-8987
High-fashion shoes for the younger set.

■ Little Extras $$ to $$$
550 Amsterdam Avenue between 86th and 87th Streets
721-6161
Unique decorative accessories and some furniture and toys, many
of which can be personalized.

■ Little Folks $
123 East 23rd Street between Park and Lexington Avenues
982-9669
Discount children's department store that carries clothing, shoes,
equipment, layette, furniture and toys.

■ Little Rickie
49 First Avenue at Third Street
505-6467
Unique, retro, reproduction and classic toys as well as some
clothing (T-shirts, boxers) and a selection of handmade global folk
art pieces. For all ages.

■ Logos
1575 York Avenue between 83rd and 84th Streets
517-7292
Neighborhood bookstore carrying books for all ages.

■ Lolli Pop $$$
241 Third Avenue between 19th and 20th Streets
995-0977
European imported clothing for ages 0-8.

■ Lord & Taylor $$
424 Fifth Avenue between 38th and 39th Streets
391-3344
Full-service department store. The large children's department
carries clothing, layette, and some toys.

- M & J Trimmings
1008 Sixth Avenue between 37th and 38th Streets
391-9072
Trimmings and sewing supplies for all types of craft projects.

- M. Kreinen & Co. $
301 Grand Street at Allen Street
925-0239
Discounted better clothing and layette.

- MacKenzie-Childs, Ltd. $$$
824 Madison Avenue at 69th Street
570-6050
This high-end home accessories emporium carries a unique
selection of goods (many of them handmade, handpainted or
handfinished), some of which are appropriate for children's rooms,
baby gifts or for children.

- Macy's Herald Square $$
151 West 34th Street at Herald Square
695-4400
Full-service department store. The large children's department
carries clothing, shoes, layette and toys.

- Madison Avenue Maternity & Baby $$$
1043 Madison Avenue between 79th and 80th Streets,
2nd Floor
988-8686
Fine imported layette and clothing for ages 0-1.

- Magic Windows $$$
1186 Madison Avenue at 87th Street
289-0028
Classic imported clothing, layette and nursery furniture. The Magic
Windows store includes M.W. Baby and M.W. Teens.

- Manhattan Dollhouse
236 Third Avenue between 19th and 20th Streets
253-9549
New and vintage dollhouses and dollhouse accessories.

■ Manny's Music
156 West 48th Street between Sixth and Seventh Avenues
819-0576
Musical instruments for all ages.

■ Maraolo $$ to $$$
782 Lexington Avenue at 61st Street, 832-8182
551 Madison Avenue between 55th and 56th Streets, 308-8793
835 Madison Avenue between 69th and 70th Streets, 628-5080
Outlet Store, 131 West 72nd Street between Columbus Avenue and
Broadway, 787-6550
This adult shoe store carries a selection of fashion shoes for children
in European sizes 25-34.

■ Marsha D.D. $$
1324 Lexington Avenue between 88th and 89th Streets
534-8700 (girl's store), 876-9922 (boy's and unisex jeans)
On the cutting edge. Clothing, shoes, small toys, novelties and
costume jewelry for ages 7-preteen and some adult sizes.

■ Mary Arnold Toys
1010 Lexington Avenue between 72nd and 73rd Streets
744-8510
Extensive selection of toys, dolls (Mme. Alexander and Carroll),
Steiff animals, books, clothing for ages 0-2 and some layette items.

■ Metropolitan Museum of Art Store
Fifth Avenue between 81st and 84th Streets
535-7710
Large selection of educational toys and books.

■ Michael's Children's Haircutting Salon
263 Madison Avenue between 90th and 91st Streets
289-9612
This barbershop for children and adults is a Manhattan tradition.

■ Monkeys & Bears $$ to $$$
506 Amsterdam Avenue between 84th and 85th Streets
873-2673
Unique contemporary clothing, handknit sweaters, layette and
some toys and books. For children ages 0-8.

■ Morris Bros. $ to $$
2322 Broadway at 84th Street
724-9000
Large selection of casual clothes for children and teens (which
includes some adult sizes) and some layette. Morris Brothers also
makes name tags (sew-in or iron-on) and is an official camp
outfitter.

■ Moschino $$$
803 Madison Avenue between 67th and 68th Streets
639-9600
Tucked within the Moschino store for adults are unique designer
clothing and shoes for children.

■ Museum of Modern Art Store
11 West 53rd Street between Fifth and Sixth Avenues
708-9400
Large selection of educational books and toys. Remember to visit
the Design Store across the street from the Museum.

■ My Favorite Place
265 West 87th Street between Broadway and West End Avenue
362-5320
Housed within this indoor playspace is a store filled with toys and
books.

■ New York Exchange for Women's Work $ to $$$
149 East 60th Street between Lexington and Third Avenues
753-2330
This not-for-profit store sells handmade items, including children's
clothing, toys, blankets, quilts and dolls.

■ New York Firefighter's Friend
263 Lafayette Street between Prince and Spring Streets
226-3142
Your little firefighter will love this store filled with firefighter motif
clothing, toys and official-looking boots. For children and adults.

■ Niketown $$
6 East 57th Street between Fifth and Madison Avenues
891-6453
For the athlete, all types of Nike activewear and athletic shoes for
children and adults.

- Nocturne $$$
698 Madison Avenue between 62nd and 63rd Streets
750-2951
Fine sleepwear, mostly for girls, up to size 12.

- Noodle Kidoodle
112 East 86th Street between Park and Lexington Avenues
427-6611
An extensive selection of educational toys, craft kits and art supplies.

- Nursery Lines $$$
1034 Lexington Avenue at 74th Street
396-4445
Fine imported classic clothing and linens and unique handpainted furniture. Custom linens and design services available.

- O'givee $ to $$
901 Sixth Avenue in the Manhattan Mall at 32nd Street
947-1667
Contemporary clothing and some baby toys.

- Oilily $$$
870 Madison Avenue between 70th and 71st Streets
628-0100
Signature multicolor and patterned clothing from this Dutch label for children up to age 12 and some adult sizes.

- Old Navy Clothing $
610 Sixth Avenue at 18th Street
645-0663
Well-priced basic clothing and shoes.

- Once Upon a Time $
171 East 92nd Street between Lexington and Third Avenues
831-7619
Primarily resale, but some new clothing and shoes. New clothes include baby items and special occasion clothing up to size 8 for girls and 6 for boys.

■ Osh Kosh B'Gosh $$
586 Fifth Avenue between 47th and 48th Streets
827-0098
Name brand clothing (up to size 16) and shoes (up to age 5).

■ Paragon Athletic Goods $$
867 Broadway at 18th Street
255-8036
Sporting goods emporium for all ages, carrying a large selection of
sporting goods and activewear for children.

■ Patagonia $$ to $$$
101 Wooster Street between Prince and Spring Streets
343-1776
This outdoor specialist for adults also carries a line of outerwear for
children.

■ Paul Mole
1031 Lexington Avenue at 74th Street, 2nd Floor
535-8461
This barbershop for adults also specializes in children's haircuts.

■ Peanut Butter & Jane $$ to $$$
617 Hudson Street between Jane and 12th Streets
620-7952
Cool clothing, shoes and toys.

■ Penny Whistle Toys
1283 Madison Avenue between 91st and 92nd Streets,
369-3868
448 Columbus Avenue between 81st and 82nd Streets,
873-9090
Unique toys, art supplies and some books for younger children.

■ Plain Jane $$ to $$$
525 Amsterdam Avenue between 85th and 86th Streets
595-6916
Unique vintage and retro decorative accessories, layette, antique
furniture and clothes for babies 0-6 months.

■ Polo/Ralph Lauren $$$
867 Madison Avenue at 72nd Street
606-2100
Classic clothing for girls up to age 4, boys up to age 14.

■ Pop Shop
292 Lafayette Street between Houston and Prince Streets
219-2784
This not-for-profit store for adults and children carries all things
Keith Haring, including clothing and toys.

■ Porthault Linens $$$
18 East 69th Street between Fifth and Madison Avenues
688-1660
Imported luxury linens, custom infant bedding and clothing for
ages 0-4.

■ Pratesi $$$
829 Madison Avenue between 69th and 70th Streets
288-2315
Imported luxury linens.

■ Prince & Princess $$$
33 East 68th Street between Madison and Park Avenues
879-8989
Fine classic imported clothing, layette and some shoes.

■ Promises Fulfilled $$ to $$$
1592 Second Avenue between 82nd and 83rd Streets
472-1600
Personalized decorative accessories, furniture and toys.

■ Quest Toys
Two World Financial Center at 225 Liberty Street
945-9330
Unique, educational toys and some books.

■ Rand-McNally Map Store
150 East 52nd Street between Lexington and Third Avenues
758-7488
Maps and books for all ages.

■ Red Caboose
23 West 45th Street between Fifth and Sixth Avenues
575-0155
Train sets and accessories.

■ Regine Kids $
2688 Broadway between 102nd and 103rd Streets
864-8705
Value-priced major brand clothing, equipment, layette, nursery
furniture and toys.

■ Replay $$$
109 Prince Street at Greene Street
800 250-6972
Imported Italian casual and basic clothing and shoes.

■ Richie's Shoes $
183 Avenue B between 11th and 12th Streets
228-5442
Discounted children's shoes.

■ Rizzoli Bookstores
31 West 57th Street between Fifth and Sixth Avenues, 759-2424
454 West Broadway between Houston and Prince Streets, 674-1616
3 World Financial Center in the Winter Garden, 385-1400
Books for all ages.

■ Robin's Nest $$ to $$$
1168 Lexington Avenue between 80th and 81st Streets
737-2004
Contemporary clothing and layette.

■ Ruby's Book Sale
119 Chambers Street at West Broadway
732-8676
Discounted books for all ages.

■ Saks Fifth Avenue $$ to $$$
611 Fifth Avenue at 49th Street
753-4000
Full-service department store. The large children's department
carries clothing, layette and stuffed animals.

- San Francisco
975 Lexington Avenue between 70th and 71st Streets
472-8740
Nostalgic classic clothing and some toys for girls up to size 8/10, boys up to size 4/6.

- Schneider's Juvenile Furniture $$
20 Avenue A at Second Street
228-3540
Everything for the new baby and young child including equipment, layette, furniture and toys.

- Second Act $
1046 Madison Avenue between 79th and 80th Streets, 2nd Floor
988-2440
Resale clothing, shoes and toys.

- Shakespeare & Co. Booksellers
716 Broadway at Washington Place, 529-1330
939 Lexington Avenue between 68th and 69th Streets, 580-7800
1 Whitehall Street at Bridge Street, 742-7025
Books for all ages.

- Shoofly $$
465 Amsterdam Avenue between 82nd and 83rd Streets
580-4390
Unique selection of fashionable shoes, hats and accessories.

- Small Change $$$
964 Lexington Avenue between 70th and 71st Streets
772-6455
Fine clothing, from contemporary to classic.

- Space Kiddets $$
46 East 21st Street between Broadway and Park Avenue South
420-9878
Contemporary clothing, shoes, layette, toys and some vintage furniture.

■ Speedo Authentic Fitness $$
5 World Trade Center, 775-0977
50 Columbus Avenue between 66th and 67th Streets, 501-8140
90 Park Avenue at 39th Street, 682-3830
721 Lexington Avenue between 58th and 59th Streets,
688-4595
40 East 57th Street between Madison and Park Avenues,
838-5988
Swimwear and swimming gear for adults and children
ages 4+.

■ Spring Flowers $$$
1050 Third Avenue at 62nd Street, 758-2669
905 Madison Avenue between 72nd and 73rd Streets,
717-8182
Classic imported clothing, layette and shoes.

■ Star Magic
745 Broadway at Eighth Street, 228-7770
275 Amsterdam Avenue at 73rd Street, 769-2020
1256 Lexington Avenue between 84th and 85th Streets,
988-0300
A store dedicated to science and stars—toys, books, objects.

■ Sterns $$
899 Sixth Avenue at 33rd Street
244-6060
Full-service department store. The children's department carries
clothing and layette.

■ Strand Book Store
828 Broadway at 12th Street, 473-1452
95 Fulton Street between Gold and William Streets, 732-6070
Discounted books for all ages.

■ Strawberry $
14 West 34th Street between Fifth and Sixth Avenues,
279-8696
901 Sixth Avenue in the Manhattan Mall at 32nd Street,
268-7855
Value-priced clothing for girls up to size 14, boys up to size 7.

■ Stuyvesant Trains & Hobbies
345 West 14th Street between Eighth and Ninth Avenues, 2nd Floor
675-2160
Train sets and accessories and specialty models.

■ SuperCuts
Call 800 SUPERCUT to locate the nearest salon
Well-priced haircuts for all ages.

■ Swatch Timeship $$
5 East 57th Street between Fifth and Madison Avenues
317-1100
Flagship store for Swatch and FlikFlak watches, complete with a
children's playroom.

■ Syms $
400 Park Avenue at 54th Street, 317-8200
42 Trinity Place at Rector Street, 797-1199
Discount department store. The children's department carries
discounted major brand and designer label clothing, shoes, layette
and some toys and books.

■ T.J. Maxx $
620 Sixth Avenue between 18th and 19th Streets
229-0875
Discount clothing and some toys and books.

■ Takashimaya $$$
603 Fifth Avenue between 54th and 55th Streets
350-0100
This high-end department store carries luxury layette, clothing
(0-24 months), unique toys and vintage items such as silver cups
and infant jewelry.

■ Talbots Kids & Babies $$
1523 Second Avenue at 79th Street
570-1630
Large selection of contemporary basic clothing.

■ Teachers College Bookstore
1224 Amsterdam Avenue at 120th Street
678-3920
Good selection of children's books as well as books on education
and learning.

■ Terra Verde $$$
120 Wooster Street between Prince and Spring Streets
925-4533
Environmentally sensitive, all-natural clothing (0-24 months),
layette and furniture as well as other products for adults and the
home. Some custom furniture available.

■ Timberland $$ to $$$
709 Madison Avenue between 62nd and 63rd Streets
754-0436
This outdoor specialist for adults also carries boy's and unisex
clothing and shoes for children.

■ Tiny Doll House
1146 Lexington Avenue between 79th and 80th Streets
744-3719
Dollhouses and dollhouse accessories.

■ Tootsies Children's Books
554 Hudson Street between Perry and 11th Streets
242-0182
Extensive selection of books and quality toys and games for infants
to teens.

■ Tortoise and the Hare
1470 York Avenue at 78th Street
472-3399
Haircuts for children in a totally child-friendly and fun setting. The
store also carries a good selection of unique toys.

■ Tower Books
383 Lafayette Street at Fourth Street
228-5100
Books for all ages, some discounted.

• Toys R Us
1293 Broadway at 34th Street, 594-8697
24-32 Union Square East at 15th Street, 674-8697
Commercial toys and equipment.

• Tutti Bambini $$ to $$$
1490 First Avenue between 77th and 78th Streets
472-4238
Contemporary clothing for girls up to size 12, boys to size 8/10.

• Village Kidz $$ to $$$
3 Charles Street between Seventh and Greenwich Avenues
807-8542
Contemporary clothing, shoes, layette and specialty toys.

• WNET Store of Knowledge
1091 Third Avenue at 64th Street   223-0018
The public television store carries educational toys and books (a
good source for science items) and many items related to public
television's children's programming, such as Sesame Street, Barney,
Arthur, etc.

• Waldenbooks
57 Broadway between Rector Street and Exchange Place
269-1139
Books for all ages.

• Warner Bros. Studio Store $$
1 East 57th Street at Fifth Avenue, 754-0300
1 Times Square between Broadway and Seventh Avenues, 840-4040
Clothing, toys, books and gift and novelty items with Warner Bros.
themes for the whole family.

• Wee Bee Kids $$
285 Broadway at Chambers Street, 766-2147
93 Nassau Street at Fulton Street, 766-1494
Everything for the new baby and young child, including
equipment, layette, furniture and clothing up to size 14.

• West Side Kids
498 Amsterdam Avenue at 84th Street
496-7282
Unique and educational toys and books.

■ Whitney Museum of American Art Store
943 Madison Avenue between 74th and 75th Streets
606-0200
Unique toys and books and some decorative accessories.

■ Wicker Garden Stores $$$
1327 Madison Avenue between 93rd and 94th Streets
410-7001
Classic imported layette, nursery furniture and clothing up to
size 6.

■ Wings for Kids $
1519 Third Avenue between 85th and 86th Streets
879-1710
Name brand casual clothing and sneakers.

■ Wynken, Blynken & Nod's $$ to $$$
306 East 55th Street between First and Second Avenues
308-9299
Unique clothes (for ages 0-6), layette, educational toys, decorative
accessories and furniture.

■ Youngworld $
1915 Third Avenue at 106th Street
423-0600
Discount children's department store that carries clothing,
equipment, layette and furniture.

■ Z'Baby Company $$ to $$$
100 West 72nd Street between Columbus Avenue and Broadway
579-2229
Charming clothing, layette and many handmade items up to size
16 for girls, up to size 7 for boys.

■ Zitomer and Zittles $$ to $$$
969 Madison Avenue between 75th and 76th Streets
737-4480
Unique pharmacy and department store with a large selection of
layette and children's clothing, from basics to imported to designer
and from classic to trendy. The Zittles toy store carries both
commercial and unique and educational toys and books.

Neighborhood Locator

es	East Side, East 23rd Street through and including East 60th Street
lm	Lower Manhattan, below 23rd Street
ues	Upper East Side, East 61st Street up to 110th Street
um	Upper Manhattan, 110th Street and above
uws	Upper West Side, West 61st Street up to 110th Street
ws	West Side, West 23rd Street through and including West 60th Street

Activewear, Dancewear, Outerwear, Sporting Goods and Swimwear

Capezio various locations
Danskin uws
Eastern Mountain Sports lm and uws
Freed of London ws
Jodi's Gymwear ues
Niketown es
Paragon Athletic Goods lm
Patagonia lm
Speedo Authentic Fitness various locations

Clothing and Accessories

ABC Carpet and Home lm
Aida & Jimmy's ws
Albee's uws
April Cornell ues and uws
Au Chat Botte ues
Baby Collection, Inc. ues
Baby Depot at Burlington Coat Factory lm
Baby Guess ues
Baby Palace ues
Bambini ues
Barney's New York ues

Bebe Thompson ues
Bellini Juvenile Designer Furniture uws
Benetton es
Ben's For Kids ues
Bergdorf Goodman ws
Bloomingdale's ues
Bombalulu's lm and uws
Bonne Nuit es and uws
Bonpoint ues
Bradlees lm
Brooks Brothers es
Bunnies Children's Dept. Store lm
Canal Jean Co lm
Catimini ues
Century 21 lm
Charl's Layette ues
Children's Place various locations
Chocks lm
Chocolate Soup ues
Citykids NY lm
CO_2 uws
CoCo & Z uws
Conway Stores various locations
Daffy's various locations
Dave's Army & Navy Store lm
Dinosour Hill lm
Disney Store various locations
F.A.O. Schwarz es
Farmers Daughter and Son es
First & Second Cousin lm
G.C. William ues

Gap various locations
Good Byes Children's Resale Shop
   ues
Granny Made uws
Greenstone's uws
Greenstone's, too ues
Gymboree Store various locations
Ibiza Boutique lm
Infinity ues
Jacadi ues
Judy's Fancies es
Julian & Sara lm
Kidding Around lm
Kids are Magic uws
Kids R Us ws
Kidstown lm
Kmart Stores lm and ws
Koh's Kids lm
La Layette et Plus ues
La Petite Etoile ues
Lapin es
Laura Ashley uws
Lester's ues
Lilliput lm
Little Folks es
Lolli Pop es
Lord & Taylor ws
M. Kreinen & Co. lm
Macy's Herald Square ws
Madison Avenue Maternity & Baby
   ues
Magic Windows ues
Marsha D.D. ues
Mary Arnold Toys ues
Monkeys & Bears uws
Morris Bros. uws
Moschino ues
New York Exchange for Women's
   Work ues
New York Firefighter's Friend lm
Nocturne ues
Nursery Lines ues
O'givee ws
Oilily ues
Old Navy Clothing lm
Once Upon a Time ues
Osh Kosh B'Gosh ws
Peanut Butter & Jane lm
Plain Jane uws
Polo/Ralph Lauren ues

Pop Shop lm
Porthault Linens ues
Prince & Princess ues
Regine Kids uws
Replay lm
Robin's Nest ues
Saks Fifth Avenue es
San Francisco ues
Second Act ues
Small Change ues
Space Kiddets lm
Spring Flowers ues
Sterns ws
Strawberry ws
Syms es and lm
T.J. Maxx lm
Takashimaya es
Talbots Kids & Babies ues
Terra Verde lm
Timberland ues
Tutti Bambini ues
Village Kidz lm
Warner Bros. Studio Store es and
   ws
Wee Bee Kids lm
Wicker Garden Stores ues
Wings for Kids ues
Wynken, Blynken & Nod's es
Youngworld ues
Z'Baby Company uws
Zitomer and Zittles ues

Crafts

Economy Handicrafts Queens
M & J Trimmings ws

Dollhouses and Dollhouse Accessories

B. Shackman & Co. lm
Dollhouse Antics ues
Iris Brown's Victorian Doll Shop es
Manhattan Dollhouse lm
Tiny Dollhouse ues

Equipment

Albee's uws
Au Chat Botte ues
Baby Depot at Burlington Coat
    Factory lm
Baby Palace ues
Bellini Juvenile Designer Furniture
    ues and uws
Ben's For Kids ues
Bradlees lm
Bunnies Children's Dept. Store lm
Good Byes Childrens Resale Shop
    ues
Jacadi ues
Kmart Stores lm and ws
La Petite Etoile ues
Little Folks es
Regine Kids uws
Schneider's Juvenile Furniture lm
Toys R Us lm and ws
Wee Bee Kids lm
Youngworld ues

Furniture and/or Decorative Accessories

A Bear's Place Inc. ues
ABC Carpet and Home lm
Albee's uws
Art & Tapisserie ues
Au Chat Botte ues
Baby Depot at Burlington Coat
    Factory lm
Baby Palace ues
Barney's New York ues
Bed Bath and Beyond lm
Bellini Juvenile Designer Furniture
    ues and uws
Ben's For Kids ues
Bergdorf Goodman ws
Boston & Winthrop
Bradlees lm
Bunnies Children's Dept. Store lm
Children's Room lm
Citykids N Y lm
E.A.T. Gifts ues
Fun by the Basket ues
Gloria's KidsBeds lm
Gracious Home ues
Guggenheim Museum ues

Guggenheim Museum Soho lm
Jacadi ues
Just Jake lm
Kids Supply Co. ues
Kidstown lm
La Layette et Plus ues
Little Extras uws
Little Folks es
MacKenzie-Childs, Ltd ues
Magic Windows ues
Nursery Lines ues
Plain Jane uws
Promises Fulfilled ues
Regine Kids uws
Schneider's Juvenile Furniture lm
Space Kiddets lm
Terra Verde lm
Wee Bee Kids lm
Whitney Museum of American Art
    Store ues
Wicker Garden Stores ues
Wynken, Blynken & Nod's es
Youngworld ues

Haircuts

Astor Place Hair Designers lm
Cozy's Cuts for Kids ues and uws
Funcut Salon ues
Kids Cuts es
Michael's Childrens' Haircutting
    Salon ues
Paul Mole ues
SuperCuts various locations
Tortoise and the Hare ues

Layette

ABC Carpet and Home lm
Albee's uws
Au Chat Botte ues
Baby Collection, Inc. ues
Baby Depot at Burlington Coat
    Factory lm
Baby Palace ues
Bambini ues
Bebe Thompson ues
Bellini Juvenile Designer Furniture
    ues and uws
Ben's For Kids ues
Bergdorf Goodman ws

Bloomingdale's ues
Bonpoint ues
Bradlees lm
Bunnies Children's Dept. Store lm
Catimini ues
Century 21 lm
Charl's Layette ues
Chocks lm
Citykids New York lm
CoCo & Z uws
Conway Stores various locations
Daffy's various locations
Gracious Home ues
Jacadi ues
Judy's Fancies es
Julian & Sara lm
Kids are Magic uws
Kidstown lm
Kmart Stores lm and ws
Koh's Kids lm
La Layette et Plus ues
La Petite Etoile ues
Laura Ashley uws
Lester's ues
Lilliput lm
Little Folks es
Lord & Taylor ws
M. Kreinen & Co. lm
Macy's Herald Square ws
Madison Avenue Maternity & Baby
  ues
Magic Windows ues
Mary Arnold Toys ues
Monkeys & Bears uws
Morris Bros. Uws
Nursery Lines ues
Plain Jane uws
Prince & Princess ues
Regine Kids ws
Robin's Nest ues
Saks Fifth Avenue es
Schneider's Juvenile Furniture lm
Space Kiddets lm
Spring Flowers ues
Sterns ws
Strawberry ws
Syms es and lm
Takashimaya es
Terra Verde lm
Village Kidz lm

Wee Bee Kids lm
Wicker Garden Stores ues
Wynken, Blynken & Nod's es
Youngworld ues
Z'Baby Company uws
Zitomer and Zittles ues

Linens

ABC Carpet and Home lm
Baby Guess ues
Barney's New York ues
Bed Bath and Beyond lm
Bergdorf Goodman ws
E. Braun & Co, Inc. ues
Frette ues
Gloria's KidsBeds lm
Gracious Home ues
Jacadi ues
Just Jake lm
Kids Supply Co. ues
Leron ues
Nursery Lines ues
Porthault Linens ues
Pratesi ues

Music

Manny's Music ws

Party Goods

Baballoon lm
E.A.T. Gifts ues
F.A.O Schwarz es

Resale

First & Second Cousin lm
Good Byes Children's Resale Shop
  ues
Once Upon a Time ies
Second Act ues

Shoes

Bambini ues
Bombalulu's lm and uws
Bonpoint ues
Bradlees lm
Century 21 lm
Daffy's various locations

East Side Kids ues
First & Second Cousin lm
Great Feet ues
Gymboree Store various locations
Harry's Shoes uws
Julian & Sara lm
Kmart Stores lm and ws
Koh's Kids lm
Lester's ues
Lilliput lm
Little Eric ues
Little Folks es
Macy's Herald Square ws
Maraolo various locations
Marsha D.D. ues
Moschino ues
Old Navy Clothing lm
Once Upon a Time ues
Osh Kosh B'Gosh ws
Peanut Butter & Jane lm
Prince & Princess ues
Replay lm
Richie's Shoes lm
Second Act ues
Shoofly ues
Space Kiddets lm
Spring Flowers ues
Syms es
Timberland ues
Village Kidz lm
Wings for Kids ues

Toys and/or Books

A Bear's Place Inc ues
ABC Carpet and Home lm
Albee's uws
Alphabets lm and uws
American Museum of Natural
    History Store uws
America's Hobby Center lm
Anime Crash lm
Art & Tapisserie ues
B. Shackman & Co. lm
Baby Palace ues
Bank Street Bookstore uws
Barnes & Noble various locations
Barney's New York ues
Bear Hugs & Baby Dolls ues
Bebe Thompson ues
Bed Bath & Beyond ws

Bellini Juvenile Designer Furniture
    uws
Ben's For Kids ues
Big City Kite Company ues
Bloomingdale's es
Bombalulu's lm and uws
Bookberries ues
Books of Wonder lm
Borders Books and Music es and
    lm
Bradlees lm
Children's General Store uws
Childrens Museum of Manhattan
    Store uws
Chocolate Soup ues
Citykids NY lm
Classic Toys lm
Coliseum Books ws
Compleat Strategist various
    locations
Conway Stores lm
Corner Bookstore ues
Cozy's Cuts for Kids ues and uws
Daffy's various locations
Darrow's Fun Antiques ues
Dinosour Hill lm
Disney Store various locations
E.A.T. Gifts ues
Enchanted Forest lm
F.A.O. Schwarz es
First & Second Cousin lm
Forbidden Planet lm
Fun by the Basket ues
Game Show lm and ues
Geppetto's Toybox lm
Good Byes Childrens Resale Shop
    ues
Guggenheim Museum Store ues
Guggenheim Museum Soho Store
    lm
Homboms Toy & Craft Emporium
    ues
Ibiza Boutique lm
JB Toys lm
Jewish Museum Store ues
Just Jake lm
Kay-Bee Toys ws
Kidding Around lm
Kids are Magic uws
Kids Cuts es

Kidstown lm
Kmart Stores lm and ws
Koh's Kids lm
Lester's ues
Lilliput lm
Little Extras uws
Little Folks es
Little Rickie lm
Logos ues
Lord & Taylor ws
Macy's Herald Square ws
Mary Arnold Toys ues
Metropolitan Museum of Art Store
    ues
Monkeys & Bears uws
Museum of Modern Art Store ws
My Favorite Place uws
New York Exchange for Women's
    Work ues
New York Firefighter's Friend lm
Noodle Kidoodle uws
Peanut Butter & Jane lm
Penny Whistle Toys ues and uws
Pop Shop lm
Promises Fulfilled ues
Quest Toys lm
Rand-McNally Map Store es
Red Caboose ws
Regine Kids uws
Rizzoli Bookstores various
    locations
Ruby's Book Sale lm
San Francisco ues
Schneider's Juvenile Furniture lm
Second Act ues
Shakespeare & Co. Booksellers
    various locations
Space Kiddets lm
Star Magic various locations
Strand Book Store lm
Stuyvesant Trains & Hobbies lm
Syms es and lm
T.J. Maxx lm
Takashimaya es
Teachers College Bookstore um
Tootsies Childrens Books lm
Tortoise and the Hare ues
Tower Books lm
Toys R Us lm and ws

Village Kidz lm
WNET Store of Knowledge ues
Waldenbooks lm
Warner Bros. Studio Store es and
    ws
West Side Kids uws
Whitney Museum of American Art
    Store ues
Wynken, Blynken & Nod's es
Zitomer and Zittles ues

Watches

Swatch Timeship es

Chapter 11

ABOUT BIRTHDAYS

Making a birthday party for a child is like putting an exclamation point after the words "I love you." It is an opportunity to let your child know what a very important person he or she is. Birthdays are special events no matter how big or small, simple or elaborate the party may be. It is a time designated to celebrate the birthday child. It is no wonder children love birthdays. It is great to feel special, and if cake and presents are involved, all the better. Even a rough childhood can be sprinkled with happy birthday memories.

In the proverbial olden days, birthday parties used to follow a fairly predictable formula. Parties were typically held in the home of the birthday child. The guests arrived, party games were played, cake and ice cream were served, gifts were opened, loot bags were given out and good-byes were said. Parties rarely lasted more than an hour and a half. It was easy to stick to the golden birthday rule: keep it small, short, simple and moving.

Much has changed since the days when we had our own birthday parties. Parties have become bigger, grander and more sophisticated. Not only are there facilities solely dedicated to housing children's parties, but almost all children's activity establishments will organize or accommodate a birthday party. Manhattan birthday parties have become big business and with that has come an increase in both the expectations and requirements of children and parents for ever better birthdays.

Unfortunately, it is not always easy to avoid the temptation to keep pace with the level and type of birthday parties to which your child may have been exposed. On the other hand, it is more important for the birthday party you plan for your child to reflect your own family values than those of other families. It is up to you to set the tone and make the birthday special in the most appropriate way for your family.

The demands of busy schedules can make it hard to plan and organize birthday parties. There are many books on planning parties and there are even party planners for the younger set. Parties can be organized at any number of out-of-home locations, many of which will even supply you with invitations and order the cake.

What is the best party in town? Who is the hottest entertainer? The answers to questions like these depend on the age of your child, what time of year the party will take place, and your own personal preferences. We will direct you to some wonderful resources for making your child's birthday special as well as give you some tips on getting it together. Whether you do arrange it yourself or have someone else do it for you, getting it right starts with understanding what your child has in mind, exercising your own good judgment and planning with care.

► **Whose party is it?** Let your child and his or her interests provide the initial direction for the party. Planning a party can be a wonderful shared experience and your child may enjoy planning as much as attending the party. Consider the interests, age and abilities of the guests as well as the personality and sociability of the birthday child. Be realistic about what the birthday child and the children attending can do. No one will have any fun if the activity is frustrating or not age appropriate or the entertainment is incomprehensible or frightening to the audience. If your child has chosen a party that you know will not work for the age group, gently guide your child in another direction.

Do remember that a first birthday is really for the parents. Second birthdays create a great deal of excitement but are rarely remembered by the child. By the age of three, a child can anticipate and enjoy a birthday party, which can be the source of conversation for weeks. With each year thereafter, children take great pleasure in planning and hosting birthday parties, and become, as they mature and with your guidance, good hosts and hostesses.

► **Picking the date and time of the party should be made with the child in mind.** Too often, this detail of the party is determined by the schedules of busy entertainers and the availability of party spaces. It is important, however, to choose the timing of the party carefully. For younger children, many of whom nap, the time of day can be critical. A tired child, regardless of age, may rally for a party initially but is likely to fall apart long before the birthday candles are lit. Timing is also relevant for older children who have busy after-school schedules and homework.

There is no perfect time to have a party, but here are some things to think about when you make your plans:

☑ Many children leave the city on weekends.

☑ Parties on school nights that go into the evening may interfere with homework or after-school commitments.

✔ If your party will be occurring during mealtime hours, be prepared to serve the children a meal or you may end up with a group of hungry, cranky children. On the other hand, if you do not want to serve a meal, schedule the party for a reasonable time after the meal hour and before the next one.

✔ If your guests will have to travel across town, consider potential travel problems. There is nothing like trying to get to Rockefeller Center for a skating party on December 20 at 4:00 p.m.

✔ If the party is of the drop-off variety, consider the logistics of pickup for the parents of your guests. If pickup would be very complicated, such as after a Friday night performance of a Broadway show, it may be thoughtful to arrange to bring the children home rather than asking parents to pick them up. Also, if you want to have a party at an out-of-the-way location, such as an afternoon party at your country home, consider inviting the other children's parents and siblings too.

✔ Pay attention to the school calendar. If you schedule a party during the winter or spring holidays or over a holiday weekend, you may have very few guests.

✔ If your child is in a school class where the birthdays tend to cluster, you may want to coordinate with other parents so birthday party dates can be spread out among the class.

▶ **Birthday magic can start with a theme.** A brainstorming session with your child will generate many possibilities. Some children are set on a Barbie party or a sports party while others simply want a party at a gym with a favorite instructor. A theme can give you a focus and help direct you in making certain decisions about the party. The decision to have a theme, however, does not have to limit your party planning. You can have a ballet party with an Aladdin theme or a party in the park with a tools theme.

The activity of the party does not necessarily drive or reflect the theme. A theme can be carried out in the accoutrements—everything from the invitations, paper goods, music, games (old favorites like "hot potato" and "musical chairs" can be modified to fit the theme), decorations, cake decorations, activities and even party favors. We do not mean to suggest that if you are without a theme the party will not be a success. Rather, having a theme can make putting the pieces of the party together a little easier and a lot more fun and creative for you.

▶ **At the gym, in a restaurant, a picnic in the park or is there no place like home?** Deciding where to have the party can be difficult indeed. For many Manhattanites, physical living space limits the option of a home party. Even for those with the space, the idea of a home party can be more than they are willing to take on. Happily, there are many options for having a party elsewhere and more likely than not, it will be your budget, not your imagination, which will be the limiting factor in your planning.

Some excellent resources for location ideas include: *New York Family Magazine*, *PARENTGUIDE*, and *Big Apple Parent*, each of which produces an annual birthday guide listing location and entertainment options. The *Parents League Guide to New York and Calendar* contains a comprehensive list of birthday party locations and entertainers. In addition, the Parents League maintains a birthday file that contains information provided by other parents on a variety of birthday topics. In Chapter 12 of this book, you can find listings of facilities that offer birthday parties. You will also find that places that do not specifically advertise birthday party services may, with the right incentive or for the right price, create one for you. Simply review what is around the city and if something looks interesting, give the place a call to see whether a birthday party can be accommodated.

Out-of-home parties can be simple and inexpensive or

elaborate and requiring very deep pockets. Some involve more work on your part than others, but at least someone else shares in the job of making the party a success. There are an impressive assortment of locations and facilities that organize parties. Some places do the whole party and you have little more to do than show up with the birthday child and a loaded camera. At the other end of the spectrum, there are empty party spaces that you can rent, in which case you must provide your own entertainment, activities, supplies, decorations, refreshments and labor and hopefully live to tell about it. There are many places that fall in between and will provide some, but not all, birthday services.

Make sure when you book an out-of-home party that you are very clear about what the facility will provide and what you are responsible for handling. You will also want to confirm the deposit requirement, payment methods, the date by which a final head count is necessary, the activities included in the fee, the maximum number of children that can attend the party, whether siblings of guests can be accommodated and the cancellation policy in case the party must be postponed. Be aware that on-site party coordinators and staff are generally tipped for a job well done.

An in-home party is great fun for the children when you can pull it off. The first order of business is to determine the number of children you and your apartment can comfortably tolerate and pick an activity or entertainer that is appropriate for the space you have. Planning is essential, so make certain you have a realistic activity schedule. Flexibility and a sense of humor are key factors in the success of the party. Do not feel compelled to get through every game you have planned and in fact, be prepared with a backup in case things go faster than you planned or an activity turns out to be a dud.

As you move through your in-home party, consider moving children from one room to another for different parts of the party (games, entertainer, cake) rather than trying to set up different activities in the same room with the children present. Also, do not bother to go all-out cleaning your apartment before the party as your small guests will neither notice nor appreciate your efforts and you will be doing it again when your guests leave. If the party is a drop-off party, be sure to have some extra adults available to help. Although the in-home party may be a lot more work than one where you do not have to do the work yourself, it can be very satisfying for you and exciting for the birthday child, and you do not have to schlep any stuff to the party or the gifts home.

Whether the party is in-home or outside your home, if you are planning to hire an entertainer, there are some things to check out in advance of the party. Make sure the entertainment is age appropriate by watching a video of the show or observing another party (believe it or not, this is a reasonable request). Ask how a lack of attention or overly enthusiastic group is handled. Confirm the length of the show, dates, times, deposit and payment method. Find out what will happen during the show so that your child can be somewhat prepared (without giving away surprises). Make special issues known prior to the show such as whether your child is shy, has a handicap or fear or enjoys or does not enjoy coming up to the "stage."

▶ **The slumber party, do you dare?** Slumber parties take on a wonderful fascination for children around the age of seven or eight. The idea of having a group of children spend the night is as attractive to this age group as the all-night prom is to high school seniors. In fact, some slumber parties are all-nighters for everyone, including the parents.

Before agreeing to a slumber party, consider: do you have the energy and patience to handle however many children and all of their situations for an extended period of time; have the prospective guests gone on sleepovers before (if not you may be dealing with middle of the night dropouts); can you accommodate your child's immediate circle of friends? Or, if the guest list needs to be trimmed, will there be repercussions from the friends left out?

A common birthday dilemma is whether to invite a few children to sleep over after the birthday party. While it can work for some, for many children it is way too much birthday, and issues such as playing with the new toys are inevitable, not to mention that those not invited to sleep over may leave the party with hurt feelings.

All things considered, a well-planned slumber party can be the source of great birthday memories and an experience for the whole family.

▶ **Guess who's coming to my party.** Kids often want everyone with whom they have ever played to come to their birthday parties. While this is not practical or advisable, you may find that keeping the party too small can exclude key friends in your child's life. To address this issue, most birthday sages suggest this rule of thumb: the ideal number of guests equals the age of the child plus one. Clearly, this rule was not developed by a Manhattan parent.

The truth is that with more and more children entering organized programs earlier and earlier, children and their parents have more social connections than in generations past. This fact, coupled with the uniquely Manhattan trend of having dozens of children to even a second birthday, makes creating a reasonable guest list a challenge. Are Manhattan parents sabotaging their children's birthdays by going overboard on the guests? Sometimes. Smart mothers and fathers do their best to keep the numbers down, and when they cannot, select an activity that engages the crowd and enlist a lot of helpers.

Here are some thoughts on developing your guest list and determining how many people are appropriate for the party you have in mind:

The nature of the activity can limit or expand the guest list. Some activities lend themselves to large groups (e.g., sports parties) while others work best for small gatherings (e.g., crafts parties). Once you get to the age of drop-off parties, large numbers of children become hard to manage and monitor, particularly if the party is in a place that is open to the public or does not have a separate party room. If you are taking responsibility for a lot of kids, make sure you can maintain security and have enough other adults around to keep track of everyone. If the group is very large, plan an activity, such as a gym party, that will engage children of different skill levels and attention spans and have backup for kids who do not want to participate.

Offer your child options. Older children can be given the choice of different types of parties that would accommodate different numbers of children. For example, the child can choose between a gym party for a lot of children, a museum party for 12, five kids to a sporting event or three for a sleepover. A young birthday boy we know happily reduced the number of guests he wanted to invite when he was reminded that he would have to send a handwritten thank-you note for each gift he received.

Set a reasonable budget. Parties in Manhattan are not cheap. When you add up the cost of everything from invitations to party favors, you can easily run up a birthday bill beyond your wildest dreams. Making your child feel special on his or her birthday does not require you to give him or her the moon and take out a second mortgage on your co-op.

Be aware of school birthday party policies. Many schools have a specific policy regarding birthday invitations, the goal of which is to promote a sense of community and minimize the quotient of hurt feelings. If your school has a policy, by all means honor it. If it does not, you may want to consider following a typical policy, which is to either invite the whole class, keep the party single sex or invite less than half of the class.

Be prepared to deal with the siblings of your guests. Many parents find themselves with more guests than they bargained for when their guests show up at the party with siblings. It is often difficult for some of your guests, whose parents work or who may not have a babysitter to watch a sibling during the party, to avoid bringing older or younger brothers or sisters. Depending on when and where the party is, this may or may not be a problem. Keep in mind that some facilities do charge for siblings, adding to the cost of the party.

Sometimes you can avoid the situation by timing the party to when siblings will be in school or specifying that the party is a drop-off one. You may want to clarify with the parents of guests you know may have an issue whether they intend to bring siblings or that bringing siblings may not be feasible. In the latter case, you may want to arrange transportation to and from the party for the child to make it easier for the family. However you want to deal with the issue, know that you may potentially have additional guests of assorted ages, have a plan, communicate with the parents of guests with siblings and bring an extra favor or two just in case.

Be alert to the composition of the group. Many times we find ourselves in awkward party situations. Some examples: your daughter is having an all-girl ballet party but you feel funny not inviting the sons of your two close friends; everyone at your son's party is from his school except one friend from camp with whom he likes to play occasionally; or your daughter is having the whole class and some friends from last year's class, but wants to omit a friend from last year with whose parents you have become friendly. There are endless permutations of complicated situations and unfortunately, there are no official rules.

What to do? First and foremost, it is your child's birthday and within the bounds of good manners, his or her wishes should prevail. Sometimes, however, birthday desires have to bend so as not to hurt the feelings of schoolmates or otherwise good friends. Your decision may depend in part on the personality of the child in question and the nature of the relationship you have with the family. In some cases it is best to err on the side of inclusiveness rather than exclusiveness and use the experience to talk to your child about empathy and kindness. If you do invite someone who will not know anyone at the party, be sure to introduce the child to the others and make sure that he or she is included in activities.

In other cases it may make sense not to invite a particular child or children. If you choose not to invite a child because, for instance, she would be the only girl at an all-boy hockey party, you can arrange for your child to have a separate birthday celebration, perhaps lunch or a special playdate, to mark the occasion. Whatever you choose, if your child is old enough to understand the issue, discuss the decision and its ramifications with your child. It may offer a useful opportunity to talk about your family values.

▶ **Repondez, s'il vous plait.** Invitations should include instructions for the RSVP, including a date by which you want a response. This will allow you to get enough of whatever you will need for the party. Also, many party places require a head count in advance of the party so that they have enough staff on hand to run the party.

When parents call you about the party, it is a good time to inquire about any issues such as food allergies, special situations (such as how to handle a child with a fear of animals at a zoo party) and whether they intend, or are invited, to bring siblings. You may want to assist in organizing transportation, particularly if it is a drop-off party or at a distant location. You may be asked to give gift suggestions so be prepared and be careful not to give the same idea out too many times. Most importantly, if you have not heard from a guest, call. Invitations have been known to be lost in the mail or thrown away by mistake.

▶ **Snacks, meals and birthday treats.** If you plan to serve a meal, keep it small and simple, because most kids simply do not eat much at a party. If you expect parents to stick around during the party, have some grown-up refreshments on hand. As for cakes, some of the best looking ones do not cut it when it comes to taste, at least as rated by kids. Simple is better, with lots of icing. Keep in mind, too, that those festive birthday candles can be dangerous when too close to loose hair or clothing.

Food allergies have become more and more common among children. For some children, even the most traditional birthday treats can be forbidden. It certainly is not necessary to create a menu to address every guest's sensitivities, but it is a good idea to eliminate some of the most common problem foods like nuts, which also happen to be a choking hazard. If you are aware of the allergies of a particular child, be sure to contact the parents about what you are serving. You can either have special food on hand that the child can eat or ask the parents to send specially prepared safe food for the child, which you will serve when the children are eating.

▶ **Birthday presents.** It used to be customary to open gifts at the party. Most parties today do not include gift opening as an activity. Some disadvantages to opening presents during the party: perceived and actual differing gift values that create a sense of competition among the guests; receipt of duplicate gifts; uncensored remarks among the children; comments from the birthday child that may hurt the gift giver's feelings.

If you decide that these issues can be managed and want to make opening presents part of the event, set some ground rules ahead of time to ensure that all moves smoothly. Such rules might include: asking your child to say something nice about, and say thank you for, each gift; letting the children know that only positive comments are appropriate; and announcing whether the children can play with the gifts once they are opened. Whenever you open the presents, remember to make a list of who gave each gift for the thank-you notes.

▶ **A word on thanks.** No matter how old your child may be, thank-you notes will require some effort on your part. You will either have to write them yourself or nag your older child to get them done. The trick is to make them as painless as possible while still making them meaningful. If your child is too young to write the note, he or she can decorate your note or a printed form note (with crayons, markers, stamps or stickers), write his or her name or put stamps on the envelope. If you use a computer, your child can participate in designing the note by choosing clip art or typing with your assistance. Older children can create their own notes on the computer or hand write a simple thank you.

▶ **Preserving your memories.** It seems like a silly thing to have to remind parents, but people do forget. Sometimes, even when parents remember the camera, they run out of film or battery power at the crucial moment. Whether you take pictures or video yourself, delegate the job to a friend or hire a professional, be clear about the images you want (e.g., candids or staged shots). If you want to hire a professional photographer or video service, check the parents' papers and with friends for referrals. Do not hesitate to ask for references and make sure that the assignment does not turn into a major movie production. The only lights you want shining on your child's face are those of the candles.

If you want to remember the way things looked before the festivities began, make sure to tell the photographer. It can be fun to photograph or video the different stages of the party. Planning, selecting items, set up, the party and the aftermath can all be documented and enjoyed at a later date. When developing your pictures, consider ordering an additional set so you can send pictures of your guests along with your thank you.

▶ **Bring a party to school.** Many schools allow parents to bring cupcakes or other special treats to school for a class party. If this is permitted at your child's school, be sure that you do whatever the children have come to expect from a school party. Contact the teacher to determine what to provide and how the party will be run. Some teachers allow parents to attend while others do not. If parents are not invited to join, if you send in a camera, most teachers will be happy to take some pictures for you. Never assume anything and ask your child for details. One parent we know was put to shame by her daughter for not providing a cupcake for the nursery school director. The teachers had never mentioned this custom, but her daughter was clear about the routine.

▶ **A basic birthday checklist.** Most of the birthday books and articles on birthday party planning list many suggestions for creating a successful party that you should certainly peruse. Some basics to put on your birthday checklist:

☑ Invitations. Mail invitations rather than distributing them in class. This ensures that the invitations will make it home and can prevent hurt feelings among children who are not being invited. Allow approximately three weeks advance notice for a party, because city kids tend to have very full social calendars. Include details about the party on the invitation such as: attire (sneakers, dress for a mess, outdoor gear); directions (cross streets are helpful); whether a meal will be served; whether the party is a drop-off; details about the party (skating, crafts, rock climbing). A tip for busy parents: address the invitations and thank-you cards at the same time to speed up the thank-you process.

◪ Decorations and supplies. If not being provided by the party place, you will need paper goods (cups, plates, utensils, napkins, table clothes) and other decorations (balloons, streamers, banner, etc.). Rubber balloons can be dangerous for young children, so use with caution. Pinatas can provide both decoration and an activity. You can use decorations to carry out your theme. Homemade decorations can be fun to make and build excitement for the birthday child. Remember to bring your camera, video, flash, batteries, film and large bags to bring home the gifts.

◪ Music. You can play music while the children eat or for dancing as an activity. Select the music carefully. Sometimes even young children like popular music more than a Barney sing-along. You can also use music to reflect your theme.

◪ Games and activities. Have enough supplies on hand so that all children get a turn and have a plan for how and when activities will be done. It is always a nice touch to make certain that everyone goes home a winner by having a participation prize.

◪ Favors. Be sure that the favor is age appropriate and does not pose any hazards. If the favors are not identical, they should have the same perceived value. Activities that become a favor (i.e., T-shirt painting) are always popular. It is often worth the extra time to put names on favors, or the bags they are in, to avoid fighting among the children. If you have a theme, you can buy, make or package favors in keeping with the theme.

▶ **Planning is the key to success.** It is really true. One of the reasons that birthday party places seem to execute flawless parties is because they have a formula that works for them. The party flows from start to finish and the children are kept moving throughout. You do not need to be a party professional to achieve the same results. A good plan does not have to be perfect or action packed. The bottom line is to keep the kids busy and engaged. In your planning, have ideas on what to do with children who arrive early or late and the amount of time to dedicate to the show, various activities and refreshments, how and when to distribute favors and some games or activities if there is a lull or while you wait for the children to be picked up.

▶ **There are many ways to make children feel special on their birthdays, and a party is just one of them.** Each family has its own routines and traditions. The party does not have to be the only way to recognize the birthday child. You can make the day special in many ways. You can start the day off right with a birthday breakfast, complete with decorations. You can create birthday privileges such as deciding what is for dinner. You can review the videos or photos from prior birthdays, take an annual birthday portrait, display a birthday banner, or create a birthday scrapbook that is added to each year. However you choose to honor family birthdays, you will have a chance to create happy memories for your children.

▶ **Spreading birthday cheer.** For many parents, the Manhattan birthday party scene seems at times to go too far. The celebration of a child's birth among good friends somehow gets lost when parties become extravaganzas, costs get out of hand and the goal of the party turns into how much loot the birthday child can bring home. There is an alternative that, for families so inclined, creates an opportunity for parents to encourage their children to use the occasion of a birthday for helping others.

Families can, in connection with a birthday party, donate up to $100 (either by reducing the cost of the party or making a separate contribution) to the Children for Children Foundation. The Foundation will in turn use the donated funds to make donations to New York City public schools. Participating children receive materials from the Foundation to include in their party invitations and a Certificate of Appreciation. For more information, you can contact Children For Children Foundation at 985 Fifth Avenue, New York, NY 10021, 249-3482 or 794-1545.

▶ **Too much birthday.** Birthdays can be great, but sometimes too much of a good thing all at once is no fun at all. As parents, we want so much to show our children how much they are loved. In Manhattan, with the world at our fingertips, it is often tempting to take an idea one step further and perhaps one step too far. Just because we can have a tea party at the Plaza does not mean it is appropriate for a second birthday. When we try too hard to make a party more unique, more novel, we are in danger of creating an atmosphere where the event is more important than the child. So relax, take a step back from the birthday mania, and have a party that makes sense to you and the birthday boy or girl.

◢

Resources

Locations, entertainers, services and party planners

The Parents League Guide to New York and Calendar and on-site birthday files (available to members only)
Parents League of New York, Inc. (open only during the school year)
115 East 82nd Street
New York, NY 10028
Phone 737-7385

Big Apple Parent. 533-2277. Monthly. Free. Widely distributed throughout the city. Subscriptions available. Produces an annual birthday party guide. www.bigappleparents.com

City Baby by Kelly Ashton and Pamela Weinberg (City & Company, 1997)

Family Entertainment Guide. 787-3789. Five issues per year (seasonal plus holiday). Free. Available at schools, libraries and family facilities. To receive an issue, send your request for the *Family Entertainment Guide*, a self-addressed manila envelope and $4.00 to Family Publications, 37 West 72nd Street, New York, NY 10023.

Kids Birthday Party Directory. 787-3789. Free. To receive an issue, send your request for the *Kids Birthday Party Directory*, a self-addressed manila envelope and $4.00 to Family Publications, 37 West 72nd Street, New York, NY 10023.

Kids Take New York by Christine C. Moriarty (Bookhappy Books, 1997)

New York Family. 914 381-7474. Monthly. Free. Available at pediatricians' offices, schools, libraries and stores. Subscriptions available. Produces an annual birthday party guide. www.nyfamily.com

PARENTGUIDE. 213-8840. Monthly. Free. Available at pediatricians' offices, schools, libraries and stores. Subscriptions available. Produces an annual birthday party guide.

See Chapter 12 for facilities that offer birthday party services.

Party ideas, advice, themes and recipes

Birthday Parties, Best Party Tips and Ideas for Ages 1 - 8 by Vicki Lansky (Book Trade Distribution, 1995)

The Children's Party Handbook by Alison Boteler (Barron's, 1986)

The Penny Whistle Birthday Party Book by Meredith Brokaw and Annie Bilber (Simon & Schuster/Fireside, 1992)

Action Games - Interactive 30-minute video, Action Games Series: Party Games by Sharon Scherr, 6647 N. River Road, Glendale, WI 53217, 800 399-2637

Children For Children Foundation
985 Fifth Avenue
New York, NY 10021
249-3482 or 794-1545

Chapter 12

KEEPING THE KIDS BUSY AND YOURSELF SANE

T here are some children who never want to leave their homes and others champing at the bit to get up and out by dawn. While some quite literally never stop moving, others can sit quietly focused for hours. Wherever your children may fall in the spectrum, as parents, we try to direct their activity so that their seemingly endless stream of energy and their vivid imaginations have a healthy and productive outlet.

Manhattan is home to some of the world's great museums, zoos, parks and libraries as well as a thriving creative community in almost any discipline you can imagine. This affords Manhattan's youngest set the opportunity to explore almost anything their hearts desire, in many instances under the direction of some of the greatest talents of our time. However, as resourceful as most city parents are, we often find ourselves drawing a big blank when it comes to deciding on something to do. Like the child standing in front of a closet full of toys complaining that there is nothing to do, the abundance of choices at our fingertips can render even the most competent parent helpless.

Mastering the ABC's of juvenile entertainment and enrichment does not have to be the first step on the road to insanity, although we can guarantee that the number of things kids can do in Manhattan is indeed mind boggling. The first step to keeping the kids busy and yourself sane is to get a handle on what is actually out there for children to do. In this chapter, we have endeavored to do just that by providing an extensive listing of the possibilities.

Our ABC guide to children's activities includes: **A**ctivities and classes; **B**oredom Busters, which cover various drop-in activities, excursions, parks, public libraries and sporting events; and **C**ultural institutions, galleries, gardens, museums and zoos. In our **A**ctivities and **C**ultural sections, we have listed the classes, programs and workshops that are offered for children. A subject index has been created for our **A**ctivities section, but don't forget to look through our **C**ultural section for additional opportunities to explore art, music, gardening and much more. This information will, we hope, assist you in making choices for and with your children. We have omitted such specifics as operating hours, because that sort of information tends to change frequently (and sometimes seasonally). We urge you to call for and confirm details for all programs and facilities in advance.

To help you in your planning, where appropriate we have indicated whether the facility, program or activity is handicapped accessible, hosts birthday parties, has summer programming and/or school vacation programs by use of the following codes: **HA** for handicapped accessible or **HAL** for handicapped accessible/limited; **B** for birthday possibilities; **S** for summer programming (including anything from full camp to special summer workshops) and **V** for vacation programs held during breaks throughout the school year. Unfortunately it is impossible to be more specific than that because these terms mean different things to different organizations. For example, birthday parties can mean anything from space rental to a soup-to-nuts party package. Keep in mind too, even if a facility is not officially handicapped accessible, the staff may be able to offer assistance or make an alternative entrance available to individuals with disabilities in order to make possible a visit to the facility.

As you peruse the ABC's of keeping the kids busy and yourself sane, we hope that the listings in this chapter spark your imagination and provide options for how your children (and family!) can spend time in ways that prove both meaningful and fun. As for your sanity, we guarantee nothing.

Activities and Classes

Manhattan has an abundance of classes and programs to meet the needs of curious, active and accomplished children. We are fortunate to have an incredible number of talented individuals drawn here to pursue their professions, particularly in the arts. As a result, our children frequently have the opportunity to be taught by amazing teachers. As if that was not enough, there really is something for everyone. From your basic mommy and me class to learning how to garden in the asphalt jungle, you can probably find it, or find someone who will teach you privately, in Manhattan.

The fact that a class or program exists, however, does not mean that it is right for your child. For an experience to be positive, it is important to match your child's interests and abilities with age-appropriate activities. To introduce a child to something (i.e., playing an instrument) before he or she is ready (physically, socially or even emotionally) can turn him or her off to something that later on would be perfectly fine.

We must fight off the impulse to give our children too much of a head start on developing abilities or skills and make realistic determinations about their capabilities as well as what they actually enjoy.

Additionally, not all classes or facilities are the same. Each facility has both a unique philosophy, physical plant and instructors, all of which create a certain atmosphere. It is up to you to decide whether that atmosphere will suit your child. For example, some children can tolerate a gym where several classes are conducted at the same time, while others become overwhelmed by that much noise and activity. Some children love large classes, while others may find them intimidating. It is a good practice to visit the facility, meet the head of the program or even observe a class before signing up for an activity. Many facilities offer a free trial class, so by all means take advantage of this benefit if available.

Be aware, too, that what is supposedly the "best" class or program is not always for everyone. A class is only the best if your child is having a positive experience and learning what he or she is there for while having some fun.

Some of the things you may want to consider when selecting an activity:

◢ Younger children. Does your child need to be accompanied by an adult? If so, is the class mostly attended by parents or caregivers (very important to know if you are looking for play-dates too)? How does the schedule fit with your child's naps, meals, other activities, schedules of siblings, etc? If the child will attend without you, how is separation handled?

◢ Your child's interests. Make sure the activity makes sense for your child's age, skill level, physical ability and attention span. For older children in particular, be sure that your child is interested and committed to the program. There is nothing like spending several hundred dollars for a class only to find yourself forcing your child to go each week. Depending on the age of your child, it might be helpful to have him or her participate in the decision to take the class. It is hardly a guarantee that he or she will stick with it, but at least you can answer a protest by pointing out that he or she made the decision.

◪ Cost. Look at the cost per class rather than the overall cost. A program can seem like a bargain until you realize it only meets for 10 sessions as compared to another that meets 15 sessions.

◪ Program basics. Before signing up, it is worth inquiring about dropout policies, refunds, make-up classes and continuity of staff (will your child have the same instructor throughout the series), the range of ages of the children in the class and the number of children taking the class. If the program is a drop-off program or children will be bussed there directly from school, make sure to inquire about the facility's security and supervision procedures (who meets children at the bus, are they accompanied to the locker room or bathrooms, etc) and if applicable, whether an adult will wait with them until they are picked up. Visit the facility to be sure it is clean, safe and secure. If the program involves potentially dangerous physical activity (such as advanced gymnastics or hockey), inquire as to how the participating children are safeguarded against injury.

◪ Transportation. How will your child get to and from the class? In good weather, walking or taking the bus may be a breeze, but in bad weather taxis may be required. Is the facility easy or hard to get to and get home from? Some programs offer bus service (pick up from school, drop off at home), which can be a blessing. If bussing is offered, be sure to find out how long the bus trip will be. Bussing may not be so great if your child is going to have a major rush hour commute.

◪ Overscheduling. Consider the number of programs that make sense for your child. With all the interesting classes available around town, it is often hard to resist signing up for everything that sounds good. However, while a busy week may be a good thing, a too busy week can become difficult to maintain. It is all too easy for a heavy schedule of enrichment programs to become a stressing experience. Sometimes it is better to plan light with ample down time and fill in with drop-in activities, time in the park and playdates.

◪ How serious? There are classes designed to expose children to an activity and those designed to immerse them in it. The age and personality of your child can help you decide which is better for him or her. Younger children generally enjoy classes as much for the socializing as they do for the activity and may be more interested in taking a class with a friend than in what they are taking. Some children have a natural talent, genuine curiosity or focus that is best satisfied with a class that really gets into the meat of the subject.

As you embark on the ongoing process of enrolling your children in various classes and programs, we encourage you to call places for details and class schedules, ask questions, visit the locations that interest you and your child and, when appropriate, involve your child in the decision. It is up to each of us to establish our own comfort levels and to gauge what is likely to be a positive experience and what is not worth the effort. Each child deserves to find and develop a love of something, and in this city, there is certainly the opportunity to do so.

The classes and programs are listed in alphabetical order and include the location, phone number, ages served and program offerings. At the end of this section you will find an index of classes and programs by category (swimming, dance, music, sports, etc.). A geographical code follows each facility listed in the index under a particular category so that you can determine its general location and look up only those facilities most convenient to you. Because class times and seasonal schedules change frequently, we cannot list such program details. There are quite a few organizations that offer a full range of classes catering to many different interests and age levels. In those instances the indication for ages may not apply to all courses offered by a particular facility.

Finally, names can be deceiving, so be aware as you use this resource, nothing can replace your inquiry. For example, there are many programs referred to as "mommy and me" classes. The term "mommy and me" has become a generic phrase for classes, typically geared to the under-three-year-old crowd, at which the child is accompanied by an adult during class time. In many cases, the adult can be either parent (mommy or daddy) or caregiver, but in some classes will be strictly limited to parents. We recommend contacting organizations directly for specifics.

We wish you luck in organizing your children's schedules, the stamina required to keep the ball rolling, the patience to keep up with their ever-changing interests and the sense of humor you will need when they say "I don't want to do that anymore."

Activities and Classes

B   for birthday possibilities
S   for summer programming (including anything from full camp to special summer workshops)
V   for vacation programs

■ 14th Street Y   B S
Sol Goldman YM-YWHA of the Educational Alliance, Inc.
344 East 14th Street at First Avenue
780-0800
Ages: infant +
Art, dance, gymnastics, mommy and me, music, theater/creative dramatics and swimming. Programs in Jewish life and learning and a Japanese Parenting and Family Center.

■ 74th Street Magic B S
510 East 74th Street at York Avenue
737-2989
Ages: 6 months +
Art, ballet, cooking, gymnastics, hip-hop, mommy and me, music,
musical theater, rhythmic gymnastics and science. Preschool
alternative program available.

■ 92nd Street Y B S
1395 Lexington Avenue at 92nd Street
415-5453
Ages: infant +
Athletics/sports, arts and crafts, boxing/self-defense, circus arts,
cooking, dance and movement, educational enrichment,
gymnastics, martial arts, mommy and me, music, swimming, tennis
and theater arts. Programs for children with developmental
disabilities. Other programs include Park Bench, basketball leagues,
gymnastics and swim teams, ensemble performance companies,
Jewish culture.

■ ACE - IT Junior Development Tennis Program
at Fila Sports Club
44-02 Vernon Blvd., Long Island City
718 937-2381, extension 29
Ages: 6 +
Tennis instruction for all levels. Pee Wee tennis for younger kids.
Transportation available.

■ ACT Programs at Cathedral of St. John the Divine B S V
Amsterdam Avenue between 111th and 112th Streets
316-7530
Ages: K - 6th grade
After-school program.

■ Abby's Place
165 West 86th Street at Amsterdam Avenue in the West
Presbyterian Church
316-5706
Ages: 18 months - 4 .6
Mommy and me program including art, circle time, movement,
music and snack. Drop-off program for older children.

- Abizaid Arts Studio B S
107 Grand Street between Broadway and Mercer Street, 2nd Floor
941-8480
Ages: 2 - 11
"Leap'n Lizards" dance class. Yoga, flamenco and multidisciplinary/alternative/ethnic dance program.

- Actor's Workshop
757-2835 or 877-4899
Ages: 4 +
Individual coaching and teaching by appointment with Flo Salant Greenberg. Classes for teens.

- Aerobic West Fitness Club/Swim Program B S
131 West 86th Street between Columbus and Amsterdam Avenues
787-3356
Ages: 6 months +
Swimming instruction.

- After School Workshop B S
45 East 81st Street between Madison and Park Avenues (in P.S. 6 but not affiliated with the school)
734-7620
Ages: 5 - 13
Arts and crafts, ballet, computers, homework help, sports and tennis.

- Aikido of Ueshiba
142 West 18th Street between Sixth and Seventh Avenues
242-6246
Ages: 6 +
Martial arts instruction.

- Alfred E. Smith Recreation Center S
80 Catherine Street between Madison Avenue and South Street
285-0300
Ages: 7 +
Arts and crafts, breakdancing, computer room with an Internet for Kids program, gardening, co-ed sports including baseball, basketball, and soccer. Movie night, video game night and Saturday rollerblading.

■ All City Junior Tennis S
Roosevelt Island Racquet Club, 280 Main Street next to tram
Manhattan Plaza Racquet Club, 450 West 43rd Street at 10th
Avenue
Columbus Tennis Club, 795 Columbus Avenue at 98th Street
935-0250
Ages: 5 +
Tennis instruction for all levels. Transportation available.

■ Alvin Ailey American Dance Center S
211 West 61st Street between Amsterdam and West End Avenues,
3rd Floor
767-0940
Ages: 3 +
Creative movement, pre-professional track in ballet and other
dance forms by audition and a Saturday sampler multidisciplinary
dance program.

■ The American Academy of Dramatic Arts S
120 Madison Avenue between 30th and 31st Streets
686-9244
Ages: 8 +
Saturday morning acting, movement, speech/voice classes.

■ The American Youth Dance Theater
434 East 75th Street between First and York Avenues
717-5419
Ages: 2 +
Ballet, creative movement, Isadora Duncan, jazz, modern, mommy
and me movement, Spanish dance and tap.

■ Applause Musical Workshop
Multiple locations
439-9050
Ages: 7 +
Weekend musical theater workshops.

■ Art Safari, Inc. B S
2 Fifth Avenue at Washington Square
529-1484
Ages: 4 - 11
Art program including mask-making, painting, puppet-making and
sculpture.

■ Art Students League of New York S
215 West 57th Street between Broadway and Seventh Avenue
247-4510
Ages: 8 +
Saturday art program.

■ Arts Gate Center S
70 Mulberry Street between Canal and Bayard Streets, 2nd Floor
349-0126
Ages: 5 +
Weekend piano and ballet instruction.

■ Asphalt Green B S
555 East 90th Street at York Avenue
369-8890
Ages: preschool +
Art and recreation, basketball, dance and movement, fine and
graphic arts, football, gymnastics, martial arts, mommy and me,
photography, soccer, softball, swimming and tennis. Community
sports leagues. Gymnastics and swim teams.

■ Asser Levy Recreation Center S
East 23rd Street and FDR Drive
447-2020
Ages: 18 months - 12
After-school program, kids' karate and Rhythmic Tots.

■ Astros Sports Club
Multiple locations
749-7202
Ages: 4 +
Co-ed program concentrating on outdoor team sports.
Transportation available.

■ B. Muse, Inc. S
48 West 68th Street between Central Park West and Columbus Avenue
250 West 106th Street at Broadway
222-0608
Ages: 2 +
Ballet, creative movement, Isadora Duncan, jazz, mommy and me, modern dance and yoga. Young Dancers Performing Group by audition only.

■ Ballet Academy East B S
1651 Third Avenue between 92nd and 93rd Streets
410-9140
Ages: 2 +
Ballet instruction for all levels. Classes in jazz, modern, mommy and me movement and tap.

■ Ballet Hispanico S
167 West 89th Street between Columbus and Amsterdam Avenues
362-6710
Ages: 4 +
Ballet, flamenco, jazz and modern.

■ Basketball City B S
Pier 63 at West 23rd Street and 12th Avenue
924-4040
Ages: 6 +
Basketball clinics, leagues and tournaments. Open playtime.

■ Berlitz Jr. S
40 West 51st Street between Fifth and Sixth Avenues
765-1000
Ages: 5 +
Individual, semiprivate, cross-cultural and group instruction in all languages at various locations.

■ biz Kids NY S
125 Barrow Street at Washington Street
243-6638
Ages: 8 +
Professional training for commercial, film and TV. Acting workshops and conservatory classes.

- Blade Fencing
212 West 15th Street between Seventh and Eighth Avenues
620-0114
Ages: 8 +
Private fencing instruction by appointment.

- Bloomingdale School of Music S
323 West 108th Street between Broadway and Riverside Drive
663-6021
Ages: 10 months +
Classes in guitar, keyboard, music/movement and violin. Private instruction in all instruments. Suzuki piano, violin and cello. Some ensemble groups.

- Boys Choir - Church of the Transfiguration
1 East 29th Street between Fifth and Madison Avenues
684-6770
Ages: 9 - 11
Boys' choir by audition only.

- Boy Scouts of America
345 Hudson Street (office)
242-1100
Ages: 6 +
Call to locate the den closest to you or start your own.

- Bridge for Dance S
2726 Broadway between 104th and 105th Streets
749-1165
Ages: 3 +
Ballet, creative movement, hip-hop, jazz, modern, tap and yoga.

- Broadway Dance Center S
221 West 57th Street at Broadway, 5th Floor
582-9304
Ages: 3 +
Ballet, creative movement, jazz, modern, mommy and me, tap and voice.

- CYO Manhattan Youth Baseball
Multiple locations
722-6383
Ages: K +
Co-ed youth baseball program. All-girls' teams for fourth graders and older.

- The Calhoun School S
160 West 74th Street between Amsterdam and Columbus Avenues
433 West End Avenue at 81st Street
877-1700
Ages: 4 +
After-school program open to all.

- Campbell Music Studio S
305 West End Avenue at 74th Street
436 East 69th Street between First and York Avenues
496-0105
Ages: 18 months +
Preschool music includes creative movement and singing. The program is non-instrumental up to age five. Music history and theory for advanced students. Piano instruction for all levels.

- Carmine Recreation Center S V
3 Clarkson Street off Seventh Avenue South
242-5228 or 242-5418
Ages: 3 - 12
After-school program, swimming classes, drop-in recreation opportunities.

- Cavaliers Athletic Club S
Multiple locations
580-1755
Ages: K - 10
Seasonal sports program and summer sports day camp. Transportation available.

- Champs Sports Club
Multiple locations
996-7646
Ages: 4 - 10
Gymnastics, ice skating, team sports and tennis after-school programs. Transportation available.

- Chelsea Equestrian Center
23rd Street and the Hudson River
367-9090
Ages: 5 +
Membership required. Horseback riding instruction for all levels, private and group.

- Chelsea Piers B S V
23rd Street and the Hudson River
336-6666
Ages: infant +
Aggressive skating, basketball, batting, bowling, dance, figure skating, golf, gymnastics, in-line skating, ice hockey, ice skating, martial arts, micro-soccer, mommy and me, rock climbing, roller hockey and soccer.

- Chess in the Schools
353 West 46th Street between Eighth and Ninth Avenues
757-0613
Ages: K - 8th grade.
Chess instruction and games. Saturday morning drop-in program, children grouped by ability. Sunday, intermediate/advanced drop-in program offered.

- Child's Play East and West S
593 Park Avenue at 64th Street in Central Presbyterian Church
236 West 73rd Street between Broadway and West End Avenue in the Rutgers Presbyterian Church
838-1504
Ages: 9 months - 4
Parent and child program (no caregivers) organized by age, Spanish for Tots and home schoolers' groups for all ages.

- Children's Acting Academy S
East and West Side locations
860-7101
Ages: 5 +
Creative movement for young students and training in improvisation, performance technique, speech and voice for older students. TV workshops. Interview required. Summer teen program.

- The Children's Aid Society - Greenwich Village Center B S V
219 Sullivan Street between West Third and Bleecker Streets
254-3074
Ages: tots +
After-school program, arts and crafts, cooking, dance and
movement, martial arts, performing and visual arts and toddler
time.

- Children's Athletic Training Center - CATS B S
593 Park Avenue at 64th Street in Central Presbyterian Church
751-4876
236 West 73rd Street between Broadway and West End Avenue in
Rutgers Presbyterian Church
877-3154
235 East 49th Street between Second and Third Avenues
751-4876
Ages: 1 - 12
Multi-sports classes for boys and girls.

- Children's Movement Studio
536 East Fifth Street between Avenues A and B
982-5751
Ages: 1 - 11
Ballet, creative movement and modern. Run and Jump (for boys)
and Tai Chi (for girls).

- The Children's Oasis S
33 East 12th Street between University Place and Broadway at The
Village Temple
917 226-7501
Ages: 11 - 34 months
Mommy and me program including art, circle time, movement,
music and snack.

- Children's Tumbling B S
9-15 Murray Street between Broadway and Church Street,
10th Floor
233-3418
Ages: 2 - 12
Mommy and me, circus arts, creative movement and gymnastics.

- Chris Porte's After School Junior Tennis S
Multiple locations
288-4005
Ages: 5 +
Tennis instruction for all levels. Transportation available.

- Church Street School for Music & Art B S
74 Warren Street between West Broadway and Greenwich Street
571-7290
Ages: 2 +
Art Express and classes for brass ensembles, flute, folk and rock
guitar, music and movement, Dalcroze eurythmics, recorder and
visual arts. Private instruction in most instruments.

- Circus Gymnastics B S
2121 Broadway between 74th and 75th Streets
799-3755
Ages: 6 months +
Gymnastics instruction for all levels, mommy and me classes.

- City Lights Youth Theater
130 West 56th Street between Sixth and Seventh Avenues at City
Center
262-0200
Ages: 2nd grade +
Year-round workshops in acting.

- City Music Schools S
162 West 83rd Street between Columbus and Amsterdam Avenues
877-6045
Ages: 5 +
Music instruction, orchestra, band and string ensembles.

- Claremont Riding Academy S
175 West 89th Street between Columbus and Amsterdam Avenues
724-5100
Ages: 6 +
Private horseback riding instruction for all levels.

- The Collective S
541 Sixth Avenue between 14th and 15th Streets
741-0091
Ages: 10 +
Instruction in all instruments. Private lessons for all ages. Hand drumming classes available.

- Columbus Gym B S
606 Columbus Avenue at 89th Street
721-0090
Ages: 1 - 12
Arts and crafts, gymnastics, mommy and me.

- La Croisette French School for Children S
861-7723
Ages: 2 - 13
This French language center offers a program for children aged 2.9–5 and an after-school program for children aged 2–13. In-home instruction available on the Upper East Side.

- Crosstown Tennis B S
14 West 31st Street between Fifth Avenue and Broadway, 2nd Floor
947-5780
Ages: 5 +
Tennis instruction for all levels.

- Dalton Serendipity Program B S V
53 East 91st Street between Park and Madison Avenues
423-5200
Ages: 5 +
After-school program open to all.

- Dan's Cougars Sports Club B V
Multiple locations
800 914-5457
Ages: 5 +
Co-ed general sports program. Leagues in baseball, basketball and soccer. Group excursions available; e.g., Disney, Hershey Park.

- Dance Theater of Harlem School S
466 West 152nd Street between St. Nicholas and Amsterdam
Avenues
690-2800
Ages: 3 +
Instruction in ballet and tap.

- Dance Theater Workshop
219 West 19th Street between Seventh and Eighth Avenues
691-6500
Ages: 5 +
Instruction in modern dance, improvisation and composition.

- Deutsche Sprachschule New York
25th Street and FDR Drive at the UN International School
718 625-5424
Ages: 4 +
Saturday German language classes.

- Dieu Donné Papermill, Inc. B S
433 Broome Street between Broadway and Crosby Street
226-0573
Ages: K +
Papermaking classes and workshops.

- Diller-Quaile School of Music
24 East 95th Street between Fifth and Madison Avenues
369-1484
Ages: 1 +
Comprehensive music program. Individual instrumental and voice
instruction available.

- Discoveries For Twos Program
Hollingworth Center at Teachers College, Columbia University
678-3851
Ages: 2 - 2.11
Parent and child Saturday morning program.

- Discovery Programs Inc. S
251 West 100th Street between Broadway and West End Avenue
749-8717
Ages: 3 +
Art and science (Young Leonardos), ballet, gymnastics, musical
theater, tae kwon do and tap. Toddler alternative nursery program.

- Djoniba Dance & Drum Center S
37 East 18th Street between Broadway and Park Avenue, 7th Floor
477-3464
Ages: 3 +
African dance, African drums and ballet.

- Drago's Gymnastics B
50 West 57th Street between Fifth and Sixth Avenues
757-0724
Ages: 6 +
Gymnastics instruction for all levels.

- Early Ear S
48 West 68th Street between Central Park West and Columbus
Avenue
265 West 87th Street between Broadway and West End Avenue
877-7125
Ages: 4 months - 4
Early childhood music classes.

- Earthworks and Artisans B
2182 Broadway at 77th Street, 2nd Floor
873-5220
Ages: 6 +
Pottery instruction.

- East Meets West
320 West 37th Street between Eighth and Ninth Avenues, 3rd Floor
268-2045
Ages: 5 +
Instruction in Okinawan karate for all levels.

- Ellen Robbins Modern Dance
219 West 19th Street between Seventh and Eighth Avenues
254-0286
Ages: 5 +
Modern dance technique, improvisation and composition.

- Elliott's Gym & Studio for Kids B S
65 West 70th Street between Central Park West and Columbus
Avenue
595-0260
Ages: infant - 12
Classes in ballet, colors, creative art, gymnastics, pre-ballet, pre-
nursery, mommy and me, movement, tooltime, tumbling and
swimming. A class is offered for "munchkins," 0 -12 months.

- Elspeth Sladden Computer Keyboarding
500 West End Avenue between 84th and 85th Streets
874-2427
Ages: 9 +
Instruction in the use of PC and MAC computer systems.

- Empire All-Star Sports Club B S
Multiple locations
695-4869
Ages: 6 - 13; sports program for tots
Basketball, gym sports, rollerblading, roller hockey, soccer,
swimming and tennis.

- Ethics for Children
New York Society for Ethical Culture
2 West 64th Street at Central Park West
874-5210 Curtis Borg, Director
Ages: 4 - 13
A non-theistic program involving discussions, music, art and
dramatics, all of which provide the context for developing moral
reasoning.

- The Family Music Center B S
120 West 76th Street between Columbus and Amsterdam Avenues
339 East 84th Street between First and Second Avenues
864-2476
25 East 35th Street between Madison and Park Avenues
914 961-8220
Ages: 18 months - 6
Kindermusik ®, Musikgarden ®, and piano instruction for all levels
and ages.

- Fred Astaire Dance Studio
666 Broadway between Bleecker and Bond Streets
475-7776
Ages: 6 +
Ballroom dancing.

- French Conservatory of Music at Carnegie Hall
154 West 57th Street at Seventh Avenue, 13th Floor
246-7378
Ages: 4 +
Instruction for children's choir, flute, piano, string instruments and
voice for all levels.

- French Institute/Alliance Française
22 East 60th Street between Park and Madison Avenues
355-6100
Ages: 5 +
Saturday morning language classes.

- Friends Seminary B S V
222 East 16th Street off Third Avenue
979-5030
Ages: 5 +
After-school program open to all.

- Funworks B S
225 East 51st Street between Second and Third Avenues
112 East 75th Street between Park and Lexington Avenues
759-1937
Ages: 10 months - 4
Music, art and movement combination classes. Inquire about
Playtime hours.

- Futurekids S
1628 First Avenue between 84th and 85th Streets
717-0110
Ages: 3 +
Computer learning center for kids.

- German for Children
787-7543
Ages: 3 +
After-school German language classes.

- Girl Scout Council of Greater NY, Inc. S
43 West 23rd Street between Fifth and Sixth Avenues, 7th Floor
(office)
645-4000
Ages: 5 +
Call to locate the troop closest to you or start your own. Summer
camping.

- Global Enrichment & Discovery Classes
1287 Madison Avenue between 91st and 92nd Streets
410-4767
Ages: 3 .6 - 10
Hands-on activities in art history, earth science, geography,
language, literature, math, science, writing and zoology.

- Goddard-Riverside Community Center
647 Columbus Avenue between 91st and 92nd Streets
799-9400
Ages: 6 - 11
After-school program including computers, environmental
education, homework help, performing and visual arts, sports and
fitness.

- Gramercy Park School of Music S
9 East 36th Street between Fifth and Madison Avenues
683-8937
Ages: readiness-based
Private instruction for the piano, recorder, voice and other
instruments.

■ Greenwich House of Music School S
46 Barrow Street between Seventh Avenue and Bedford Street
242-4770
Ages: 2 +
Music and art for children. Private instruction for most orchestral
instruments.

■ Greenwich House Pottery B S
16 Jones Street between Bleecker and West Fourth Streets
242-4106
Ages: 2 .6 +
All levels of clay instruction, hand work and potter's wheel.

■ Greenwich Village Youth Council S
437 West 16th Street (office)
414-4742, David Kaplan
268 Mulberry Street at The Youth Center, 274-1497
213-15 Eldridge Street at The Joy Center, 979-2442
Ages: 7 +
Free arts and crafts, athletics/sports, computers, educational
enrichment, music and theater arts. Home to the Greenwich Village
Girls Basketball leagues.

■ Gym Time Gymnastics Center B S
1520 York Avenue at 80th Street
861-7732
Ages: 6 months +
Gymnastics instruction for boys and girls at all levels. Age-
appropriate developmental fitness classes including: floor hockey,
soccer, tae kwon do, tennis and tiny tot fitness. Location shared
with Rhythm and Glues allowing parents to schedule coordinating
classes.

■ Gymboree B S
401 East 84th Street at First Avenue
64 West Third Street between LaGuardia Place and Thompson Street
50 Lexington Avenue at 24th Street
210 West 91st Street between Broadway and Amsterdam Avenue
30 West 68th Street between Central Park West and Columbus
Avenue
308-6353
Ages: 3 months to 4
Gymagination and Kindermusik®.

■ HRC Tennis and Yacht Club B
Piers 13 and 14 at the South Street Seaport
422-9300
Ages: 4 - 8
Tennis instruction for all levels, including "tiny tot" tennis.

■ HRC Village Courts S
110 University Place between 12th and 13th Streets
989-2300
Ages: 5 - 12
Tennis instruction for all levels.

■ Harbor Conservancy for the Performing Arts S
1 East 104th Street between Fifth and Madison Avenues
427-2244, extension 573
Ages: 6 +
African dance, ballet, hip-hop, jazz, modern and tap dance, music
and theater arts.

■ Harlem School of the Arts S
645 St. Nicholas Avenue between 141st and 145th Streets
926-4100 extension 303
Ages: 4 +
Ballet, drama, jazz, modern, tap, theater and visual arts. Musical
instruction, chorus and voice.

■ Henry Street Settlement S
466 Grand Street at Pitt Street
598-0400
Ages: 2 +
Dance, drama, music, theater and visual arts and voice. Parent and
tot classes.

■ Herard Center of Multimedia
47 West 34th Street, Suite 1023, across from Macy's
268-0915
Ages: 3rd grade +
Computer instruction.

■ Herbert Berghof Studio S
120 Bank Street at Hudson Street
675-2370

Ages: 9 +
Acting classes.

■ Hi Art S
Midtown and Lincoln Center Studios
362-8190
Ages: 2 - 6
Parent and child workshops, which offer an introduction to "Hi Art." "Culture Bugs" offered during the summer.

■ Hot Shots of New York B S
Multiple locations
961-1733
Ages: 5 - 12
Basketball programs and clinics for boys and girls. Traveling teams for boys and girls.

■ The Ice Studio B
1034 Lexington Avenue between 73rd and 74th Streets, 2nd Floor
535-0304
Ages: 3 +
Private and group ice skating instruction. Skate rentals available.

■ The Improv Shop B S
Multiple locations
718 596-3971
Ages: 5 +
Comedy workshop series culminating in a performance.

■ Improvisational Theater for Children B
East and West Side locations
874-5054
Ages: 7 +
A program that encourages children to express themselves creatively through the language of movement and theater.

■ In Grandma's Attic B S
48 West 68th Street at Studio Maestro
726-2362
Ages: 2 - 12
A fantasy-based creative dance program, guiding students through story, dance, dress-up and pretend.

■ The InterSchool Orchestras of New York
Multiple locations
410-0370
Ages: 6 +
Five orchestras for young instrumentalists at all levels.
Opportunities to participate in The Brooklyn Wind Band,
percussion and chamber music ensembles.

■ Jack & Jill Playgroup
61 Gramercy Park between Lexington and Park Avenues
475-0855
Ages: 20 - 30 months
Mommy and me program.

■ Janet Nixon Enterprises
779-3018
Ages: young adults
Etiquette workshops, "Manners for Young Diplomats."

■ Japan Karate Association of New York
2121 Broadway at 74th Street, 4th Floor
799-5500
Ages: 6 +
Martial arts instruction.

■ Jeff Nerenberg Tennis Academy B
Manhattan Plaza Racquet Club, 450 West 43rd Street at Tenth
Avenue and other locations
718 549-9391
Ages: 7 +
Tennis instruction for all levels. Kinder Tennis, an introductory
tennis program. Grand Prix travel team, USTA national player
development program. Transportation available.

■ Jewish Community Center of The Upper West Side S
15 West 65th Street between Central Park West and Columbus
Avenue
580-0099, extension 213
Ages: infants +
Classes are currently offered at various locations on the Upper West
Side. Call for specifics. Co-ed baseball, basketball and soccer leagues.

- Jodi's Gym B S
244 East 84th Street between Second and Third Avenues
772-7633
Ages: 6 months - 12
Gymnastics instruction for all levels including pre-team and team programs, gym and gym and music.

- Joe Espinosa's Sports Club S
Multiple locations
662-8807
Ages: 1st - 8th grades
After-school co-ed baseball, basketball and hockey leagues. Transportation provided.

- Joffery Ballet School S
434 Sixth Avenue between Ninth and Tenth Streets
254-8520
Ages: 3 +
Graded classes in creative movement, pre-ballet, ballet, character and jazz.

- Judy Lasko Modern Dance
3 West 95th Street off Central Park West
864-3143
Ages: 3 +
After-school co-ed modern dance classes. Teen company.

- Juilliard Pre-College Division
60 Lincoln Center Plaza between Broadway and Amsterdam Avenue
799-5000 extension 241
Ages: 8 +
Saturday music program for gifted children.

- Jump For Joy Disco-Robics For Kids B
Multiple locations
535-8916
Ages: 6 - 11
Fitness and fun rock/disco dance routines.

■ Junior School/Neighborhood Playhouse
340 East 54th Street between First and Second Avenues
688-3770 Joan Rater, Director
Ages: 8 +
Theatrical training including acting, dance and voice. Twelve
students maximum.

■ Karen's Performing Arts After School S
331 West 25th Street between Eighth and Ninth Avenues
243-5192
Ages: 5 - 11
Multidisciplinary program includes on-camera training, dance,
drama, vocalization, sports and art. Regular performances for
children. Other classes include: African dance, musical theater,
clowning and hip-hop.

■ Keystone Dance
252 West 30th Street between Seventh and Eighth Avenues
629-3107
Ages: 2 - 13
Creative and modern dance.

■ Kid City Theater Co.
50 West 13th Street at the Thirteenth Street Theater
727-2186
Ages: 7 - 12
Musical theater group.

■ Kids Co-Motion in Soho B S
579 Broadway between Prince and Houston Streets
165 West 86th Street at Amsterdam Avenue in the West
Presbyterian Church
431-8489
Ages: 1 - 11
Beginning ballet, choreography, creative movement, dance action
fitness, dance movement, mommy and me and music and tumbling
classes.

■ Kids 'n Comedy Workshop
877-6115
Ages: 9 +
Comedy workshops.

- Kids on Wheels B S
Joel Rappelfeld's Rollerblading
744-4444
Ages: 5 +
In-line skating programs offered after school and weekends. Private and group instruction and family programs available.

- Knickerbocker Greys
643 Park Avenue at 67th Street in the Seventh Regiment Armory
683-3154
Ages: 7 +
This organization dates back to 1881 and continues to teach leadership skills in a military milieu.

- Kokushi Budo Institute of New York S
331 Riverside Drive between 105th and 106th Streets
866-6777
Ages: 6 +
Instruction in aikido, jiujitsu, judo and karate.

- Kyokushin Karate
284 Fifth Avenue at 30th Street
947-3334
Ages: 4 +
Instruction in karate.

- Language Workshop for Children S
888 Lexington Avenue between 65th and 66th Streets
369-0830
Ages: 6 months - 12
Language for tots, after-school and Saturday language classes in French, Japanese and Spanish. French and Spanish day camps.

- Lasker Rink B
Central Park at 110th Street
289-0599
Ages: 3 +
Typically, from November through March the rink is open for outdoor private and group skating and ice hockey instruction. From July 4th to Labor Day the rink is converted back into a swimming pool and is available for swimming.

■ Lee Strasberg Theater Institute S
Young People's Program
115 East 15th Street between Union Square and Irving Place
533-5500
Ages: 7 +
Acting for the camera, basic acting and technique as well as dance instruction, Young Actors & Company production.

■ Lezly Skate School S
Multiple locations
777-3232
Ages: 11 +
In-line and traditional skating instruction.

■ Life Sport Gymnastics B S
165 West 86th Street at Amsterdam Avenue at the West Presbyterian Church
769-3131
Ages: 2 +
Gymnastics instruction for all levels.

■ Little League Baseball
860 585-4730
Call this general number for referral to local administration affiliates for specific information. Teams are co-ed.

■ Loco-Motion Dance Theater for Children S
West Village Location
979-6124
Ages: 4 +
Acting and dance.

■ The Loft Kitchen B
551 West 22nd Street between Tenth and 11th Avenues
924-0177
Ages: 10 +
Form own group for cooking instruction.

■ Lotus Music & Dance Studios S
109 West 27th Street between Sixth and Seventh Avenues, 8th Floor
627-1076
Ages: 5 +
Multicultural classes, dance, music and yoga.

- Lucy Moses School for Music & Dance S
129 West 67th Street between Amsterdam Avenue and Broadway
501-3360
Ages: 18 months +
Art, chorus, Dalcroze eurythmics, dance, music and theater. Musical theater workshops.

- Madison Square Boys' and Girls' Club S
301 East 29th Street between First and Second Avenues
532-5751
Ages: 6 +
After-school program begins with the Paine Webber Power Hour for homework. Other programs include sports education, computer lab and poetry workshop. Youth Employment Program.

- Manhattan Ballet School, Inc. S
149 East 72nd Street between Lexington and Third Avenues
535-6556
Ages: 3 +
Classical training in ballet, pre-ballet through professional. Nutcracker and spring performances.

- Manhattan Chess Club
353 West 46th Street between Eighth and Ninth Avenues
333-5888
Ages: 5 +
Instruction and tournaments for all levels of chess play.

- Manners House Calls
472-1270
Ages: 7 - 12
A three- to five-week in-home program designed to encourage children to be more mannerly and more considerate citizens. Crash courses available.

- Mannes College of Music - Preparatory Division
150 West 85th Street between Columbus and Amsterdam Avenues
580-0210
Ages: 4 +
Pre-instrumental instruction. Training in chamber ensembles, chorus, orchestra and theory. Private and group instruction. Musical theater workshops.

■ Marlyn Hengst Hamlin Acting Company
115 Central Park West at 72nd Street
580-0251
Ages: 13 +
Acting classes.

■ Martha Graham School of Contemporary Dance S
316 East 63rd Street between First and Second Avenues
838-5886
Ages: 2.6 +
Creative movement and modern dance.

■ Mary Ann Hall's Music for Children S
2 East 90th Street at the Church of the Heavenly Rest
800 633-0078
Ages: 1 - 7
Children explore music through fantasy play, eurythmic
movement, singing, dancing and piano.

■ Marymount Manhattan College - Kids 'n Kin S
221 East 71st Street between Second and Third Avenues
517-0564
Ages: 5 - 12
Computers, dance, drawing, math, reading comprehension, science,
storytelling and swimming. Swimming program for children
starting at 18 months is also available.

■ McBurney YMCA B S
215 West 23rd Street between Seventh and Eighth Avenues
741-9210
Ages: Pre-school +
Pre-school dance, exercise and play classes. After-school classes in
arts and crafts, basketball, computers, dance, drawing, game sports,
karate and theater.

■ Metropolis Fencing School/Club B S
45 West 21st Street between Fifth and Sixth Avenues, 2nd Floor
463-8044
Ages: 7 +
Private and group instruction.

- Midtown Karate Dojo
465 Lexington Avenue between 45th and 46th Streets
599-1966
Ages: 6 +
Instruction in karate.

- Midtown Tennis Club B
341 Eighth Avenue at 27th Street
989-8572
Ages: 4 +
Junior development program for all levels and "munchkin" tennis for tots. October through June, Junior and Parent/Child tournaments.

- Morningside Dance Works S
525 West 120th Street, Horace Mann Building, Teacher's College
678-3298
Ages: 3 +
Dance programs.

- Mozart for Children
West Side locations
942-2743
Ages: 2.6 - 7
Classes introducing young children to classical music. In-home group instruction available.

- Music for Aardvarks and Other Mammals
440 Lafayette Street at Astor Place opposite Public Theater in Musical Theater Works
718 858-1741, David Weinstone
Ages: 6 months - 5
Parent/child music classes for city kids.

- Music, Fun, & Learning B S
East and West Side locations
717-1853
Ages: 4 months - 10
Private flute and piano instruction. Music and movement classes. Tuneful Tales story hour and an after-school World Traveler program.

■ Music Together S
Multiple locations
244-3046
Ages: 6 months - 4
Movement, songs and rhythmic rhymes.

■ My Favorite Place B S
265 West 87th Street between Broadway and West End Avenue
362-5320
Ages: 18 months - 10
Art for toddlers, after-school arts program for school-age kids.

■ N.Y. Road Runners Club
9 East 89th Street between Fifth and Madison Avenues
860-4455
Ages: 2 +
Junior Road Runner's Club Series. City Sports for Kids (914 366-4175).

■ Neubert Ballet Institute at Carnegie Hall
881 Seventh Avenue, Studio 819 at 57th Street
246-3166
Ages: 4 +
Pre-ballet through all levels of ballet instruction.

■ New Dance Group Arts Center
254 West 47th Street between Broadway and Eighth Avenue
719-2733
Ages: 5 +
Ballet instruction for all levels.

■ New Federal Theatre, Inc. S
292 Henry Street (Office)
353-1176
Ages: 13 +
Drama workshops. Program conducted out of the Henry Street Settlement.

■ New Media Repertory Company, Inc.
512 East 80th Street between East End and York Avenues
734-5195
Ages: 4 +
Theatrical classes.

■ New York Budo S
12 West 27th Street between Broadway and Sixth Avenue, 4th Floor
725-7388
Ages: 6 - 13
Saturday morning Ninja training.

■ New York Junior Tennis League S
24-16 Queens Plaza South, Long Island City
718 786-7110
Ages: 8 +
Tennis instruction for all levels.

■ New York Sailing School S
22 Pelham Road, New Rochelle
914 235-6052
Ages: 12 +
Learn to sail program.

■ New York School of Classical Dance S
944 Eighth Avenue at 56th Street
397-4852
Ages: 9.6 +
Intensive ballet training for boys and girls.

■ New York SkateOut B S
72nd Street and Fifth Avenue, in Central Park
486-1919, 935-1319
Ages: 3 +
In-line and traditional skating instruction for fun, fitness, and
safety for kids, adults and families. Scouts on Skates community
program and activities.

- New York Sports Club
151 East 86th Street between Lexington and Third Avenues
860-8630
Ages: 7 +
Fitness program for kids including junior squash classes. No membership required.

- New York Theater Ballet B S
30 East 31st Street between Madison and Park Avenues
679-0401
Ages: 3 +
Pre-ballet through advanced instruction in ballet.

- Nina Youshkevitch Ballet Workshop
27 West 72nd Street between Central Park West and Columbus Avenue
873-0455
Ages: 11 +
Co-ed ballet instruction for all levels.

- Oishi Judo Club
79 Leonard Street between Broadway and Church Street
966-6850
Ages: 5 +
Instruction in judo.

- Organized Student
Ms. Donna Goldberg
769-0026
Ages: 10 +
Training in organizational skills for academic success.

- The Origami Workshop B
645-5670
Ages: 7 +
In-home origami instruction available year-round.

- Parents' Cooperative Playgroup at St. Bartholomew Preschool
109 East 50th Street between Park and Lexington Avenues
378-0238
Ages: 10 months - 2 .6
A professionally facilitated, parent-orchestrated playgroup.

- Parsons School of Design S
2 West 13th Street at Fifth Avenue
229-8933
Ages: 3rd grade +
Art and design classes on Saturdays.

- Perichild Program B S
132 Fourth Avenue at 13th Street
505-0886
Ages: 18 months +
Ballet, creative movement, hip-hop, jazz, modern, tae kwon do and tap.

- Peter Kump's School of Culinary Arts B S
50 West 23rd Street between Fifth and Sixth Avenues
307 East 92nd Street between First and Second Avenues
410-4601 extension 228
Ages: 6 +
After-school and weekend cooking classes.

- Peter Westbrook Foundation
459-4538
Ages: 10 +
Saturday morning fencing instruction.

- Piano Partners
531 East 72nd Street off York Avenue
628-3912
Ages: 8 +
Piano and musical software instruction.

- Playspace B S
2473 Broadway at 92nd Street
769-2300
Ages: 6 months - 6
Baby games, toddler and after-school art, kinderdance and music.

- Playground Project Recreation Program S
West 91st Street, Parkhouse at Riverside Park
718 884-5928
Ages: 1 - 4
Parkhouse Toddlers project offers parent/child classes including art, creative play, music and storytelling.

■ Poppyseed Pre-Nursery S
424 West End Avenue between 80th and 81st Streets
877-7614
Ages: infants - 3
Art, arts and crafts, dance, free play, mini-gym, mommy and me
and music.

■ Prepare, Inc.
147 West 25th Street between Fifth and Sixth Avenues
255-0505, 800 442-7273
Ages: 5 +
Personal safety training offered year-round.

■ Pulse Ensemble Theatre B S
432 West 42nd Street between Ninth and Tenth Avenues
695-1596
Ages: 9 +
Acting classes.

■ Rain or Shine B S
115 East 29th Street between Park and Lexington Avenues
532-4420
Ages: 6 months - 6
Creative movement, circle time playgroup and pre-ballet.

■ Randy Mani Tennis Academy S
Sutton East Tennis Club at 60th Street and York Avenue
Crosstown Tennis on 31st Street between Fifth Avenue and
Broadway
Stadium Racket Club 11 East 162nd Street across from Yankee
Stadium
914 674-6060
Ages: 3 - 8
Tennis instruction for all levels and Pee Wee tennis. Competitive
tennis program run out of Crosstown Tennis location.
Transportation available.

■ Recreation Center 54 B S
348 East 54th Street between First and Second Avenues
397-3154
Ages: 5 +
After-school and Saturday program. Sports program including
basketball, soccer, baseball and gym games. Ballet, karate and arts
and crafts.

■ Rhinelander Children's Center S
350 East 88th Street between First and Second Avenues
876-0500
Ages: infants - 12
Art, cooking, computer, dance, martial arts, movement, music and
theater arts. Kinder Club, a full after-school program for K - second
grade with transportation from some locations. Private
instrumental and vocal instruction.

■ Rhythm and Glues B S
1520 York Avenue at 80th Street
861-7732
Ages: 1 - 8
Arts and crafts, cooking, dance, drama, music and movement and
science. Adult and child preschool format class. Location shared
with Gym Time gymnastics, allowing parents to schedule
coordinating classes.

■ Richard Chun Martial Arts School B S
220 East 86th Street between Second and Third Avenues
772-3700
Ages: 3 +
Instruction in tae kwon do.

■ The Rink at Rockefeller Plaza   B
Fifth Avenue between 49th and 50th Streets
332-7654
Ages: 3 +
Private, semiprivate and group ice skating instruction during winter
months. Skate rentals available.

- Riverdale Equestrian Center B S
West 254th Street and Broadway in Van Cortland Park, Riverdale
718 548-4848
Ages: 5 +
Private, semiprivate and group English riding instruction at all
levels.

- Robert Quackenbush's Workshops
223 East 78th Street between Second and Third Avenues
744-3822
Ages: 5 - 12
After-school art classes.

- Rodeph Sholom School S
10 West 84th Street between Central Park West and Columbus
Avenue
362-8800
Ages: 3 - 12
After-school program open to all.

- S. Henry Cho's Karate Institute B S
46 West 56th Street between Fifth and Sixth Avenues
245-4499
Ages: 5 +
Instruction in karate.

- Saturday Art School at Pratt Institute
200 Willoughby Avenue, Brooklyn
718 636-3654
Ages: 3 +
Parent and child classes for pre-schoolers and a variety of art classes
for school-age children.

- School of American Ballet S
70 Lincoln Center Plaza on 65th Street between Broadway and
Amsterdam Avenue
877-0600
Ages: 8 +
Instruction in ballet by audition only.

- School for Strings
419 West 54th Street between Ninth and Tenth Avenues
315-0915
Ages: 3 +
Suzuki cello, piano and violin. String orchestra and chamber music.

- School of Visual Arts S
209 East 23rd Street between Second and Third Avenues
592-2560
Ages: K - 9th grade
Saturday art program, explores many art forms.

- Science Development Program, Inc.
Fordham University at Lincoln Center
113 West 60th Street at Columbus Avenue
864-4897
Ages: 7 +
Saturday science program.

- Sculpture Center B
167 East 69th Street between Lexington and Third Avenues
737-9870
Ages: 7 - 12
Clay, plaster, paper, wood and stone sculpting.

- Seido Karate
61 West 23rd Street between Fifth and Sixth Avenues
924-0511
Ages: 6 +
Instruction in Japanese-style karate.

- Shuffles B
Studio Maestro on 68th Street between Central Park West and
Columbus Avenue
877-6622
Ages: 3.6 +
Tap dancing classes for all levels, musical theater program for ages
eight and older, end of program mini-musical recital.

■ Singers Forum S
39 West 19th Street between Fifth and Sixth Avenues
366-0541
Ages: 7 +
Private and group instruction in voice technique and speech,
summer musical theater workshops.

■ Skating Club of New York
West 23rd Street at Chelsea Piers
627-1976
Ages: 5 +
Second oldest membership club of the United States Figure Skating
Association. Children can join at various levels to skate in a club
atmosphere and represent the club at competitions.

■ Soho Children's Acting Studio B
345 West Broadway between Grand and Broome Streets
219-8688
Ages: 4 +
Classes in acting with opportunities to participate in a performance
group.

■ Sokol
420 East 71st Street between York and First Avenues
861-8206
Ages: toddler +
Gym and gymnastics instruction for all levels.

■ Spence School - Second Act B S
22 East 91st Street between Fifth and Madison Avenues
289-5940
Ages: K - 5th grade
After-school program open to all, co-ed.

■ Stan Bardakh
212 West 15th Street between Seventh and Eighth Avenues
620-0114
Ages: 8 +
Fencing instruction.

- Stella Adler Conservatory of Acting S
419 Lafayette Street near Astor Place, 6th Floor
260-0525
Ages: 10 +
Movement, theater and voice.

- Steps on Broadway S
2121 Broadway at West 74th Street
874-2410
Ages 4 +
Ballet, jazz, modern, pre-ballet and tap.

- The Studio
501 East 75th Street at York Avenue
737-6313
Ages: 8 +
Art classes, workshops and portfolio development.

- The Sunshine Kids' Club S
230 East 83rd Street between Second and Third Avenues
439-9876
Ages: 6 months - 3
Parent/child music and art. Hour-long classes include Play Room enrichment. Private piano and chess instruction available for children and adults.

- Supermud Pottery School B S
2744 Broadway between 105th and 106th Streets, 2nd Floor
865-9190
Ages: 5 +
Classes in pottery, hand work and potter's wheel, paint bar.

- Sutton Gymnastics and Fitness Inc. B S
20 Cooper Square between Fifth Street and Third Avenue
533-9390
Ages: 18 months +
Baby gymnastics and gymnastics instruction for all levels.

- TADA! B
120 West 28th Street between Sixth and Seventh Avenues
627-1732
Ages: 5 +
Acting and musical theater.

■ Take Me to the Water
Multiple locations
828-1756 or 888 SWIM NYC
Ages: 3 +
Private and group swimming instruction in heated pools for all levels. Swim team.

■ The Techno Team Lab provided by Radicel Education Technology Services B S
160 Columbus Avenue between 67th and 68th Streets at the Reebok Sports Club
501-1425
Ages: 4 +
Educational Technology Specialist teaches platforms, programs and academic developmental skills through individualized computer classes.

■ Telma Gama S
Multiple locations
678-0883
Ages: 1st grade +
Private and group instruction in dance improvisation, jazz, modern and tap.

■ Theater and Dance with Scarlett Antonia
Multiple locations
866-4198, 800 799-5831
Ages: 8 +
Theater and dance workshops and performance programs.

■ Theatrical Workshop for Children B S
Multiple locations
978-0079
Ages: 3 - 12
Theater games, creative dramatics, improvisation, singing, storytelling and movement activities.

- Third Street Music School Settlement S
235 East 11th Street between Second and Third Avenues
777-3240
Ages: 21 months +
Early childhood program. Suzuki program. Individual and group instruction in most instruments, ballet, creative movement, dance and visual arts, Spanish dance and tap.

- Thomas Jefferson Recreation Center S
2180 First Avenue at 112th Street
860-1383
Ages: 6 +
After-school program including arts and crafts, game room, homework help, soccer, softball and karate. Fencing on Saturdays.

- Topspin Tennis Academy B S
Multiple locations
465-2520
Ages: 2 +
Tennis instruction for all levels, competitive drills, match play and video analysis. "Tiny tots" clinics. Transportation available.

- The Training Floor
428 East 75th Street between First and York Avenues
628-6969
Ages: 10 +
Physical fitness training, boxing and kick boxing year-round.

- Trevor Day School S
11 East 89th Street between Fifth and Madison Avenues
369-8040
Ages: K - 12
Private instruction for wind instruments, guitar and piano.

- Tumble Town B S
17 Lexington Avenue at 23rd Street located in Baruch College
802-5632
Ages: 6 months - 6
Music and gym combination classes. Pre-K gymnastics.

• Turtle Bay Music School S
244 East 52nd Street between Second and Third Avenues
753-8811
Ages: 18 months +
Suzuki, Orff Schulwerk, Tuneful Tots, chamber music ensemble,
jazz, teen flute ensemble. Private traditional instruction, Suzuki
piano, violin, cello and flute.

• USA Oyama's Karate B S
350 Sixth Avenue, west of West Fourth Street, 2nd Floor.
477-2888
Ages: 6 - 12
Instruction in karate.

• USTA National Tennis Center S
Corona Park, Flushing Meadows
718 760-6200
Ages: 4 +
Tennis instruction for all levels.

• Uptown Athletic Club B S V
Multiple locations
426-2160
Ages: pre-K - 5th grade
After-school instructional sports program. Transportation from
most schools and drop-off at home.

• Vanderbilt YMCA B S V
224 East 47th Street between Second and Third Avenues
756-9600
Ages: infant +
New mom and baby class, early childhood center programs
including swimming and gym. Adventure programs including art,
dance, gymnastics and swimming. After-school programs including
basketball, street hockey and karate. Additional programs include:
teen center, leadership club, youth and government club, earth
services corps and youth theater. Scholarships available. Virtual Y -
a literacy-based after-school program.

■ Video Associates Studio
630 Ninth Avenue between 44th and 45th Streets, Suite 301
397-0018
Ages: 7 +
Workshops including work in improvisation, screen study, monologue and on-camera work for films, sitcoms, commercials and soaps for professionals and nonprofessionals.

■ Village Community School B S
272 West 10th Street between Greenwich and Washington Streets
691-5146
Ages: 5 +
After-school program open to all.

■ Virtual Reality Pictures
20 West 22nd Street between Fifth and Sixth Avenues, 11th Floor
337-0911
Ages: 13 +
One-on-one, group or in-home demonstrations using three-dimensional and other creative software programs not available in stores.

■ Weist Barron Studios S
35 West 45th Street off Fifth Avenue
840-7025
Ages: 5 +
Acting conservatory with an emphasis on film and TV. Programs include "Kids Love Acting" and "ACTEEN." Commercial, film and TV acting classes.

■ Wendy Hillird's Rhythmic Gymnastics S
166 West 92nd Street at Amsterdam Avenue
721-3256
Ages: 3 +
Specializing in rhythmic gymnastics and also offering gymnastic tumbling.

■ West Side Dance Project S
162 West 83rd Street between Columbus and Amsterdam Avenues
580-0915
Ages: 2.6 +
Ballet, jazz and tap.

■ West Side Soccer League
663-7660
Ages: 5 before August 31st of the current year and older
West Side Soccer League is a member of the American Youth Soccer Organization (AYSO). Call for registration materials. Parents are expected to volunteer and league games are played in the fall and spring.

■ West Side Tae Kwon Do B S
661 Amsterdam Avenue between 92nd and 93rd Streets
663-3998
Ages: 4 +
Instruction in martial arts.

■ West Side YMCA S
5 West 63rd Street at Central Park West
875-4112
Ages: 3 months +
Art, ballet, basketball, general sports, gymnastics, jazz, martial arts, mommy and me, music, musical production, theater arts and swimming. After-school program operates out of P.S. 166, on-site program for P.S. 87 and P.S. 199.

■ Wollman Rink
Central Park north of 59th Street at Sixth Avenue
396-1010 extension 5
Ages: 3 +
During the winter months the rink is used for ice skating, offering private and group figure skating and hockey instruction. In the late spring, summer and early fall the rink is used for in-line skating. In-line skating and hockey instruction available.

■ YWCA of the City of New York S
610 Lexington Avenue at 53rd Street
755-4500
Ages: infants +
Swimming instruction and swim team, after-school program.

■ Yorkville Youth Athletic Association
Multiple locations
570-5657
Ages: K - 8th grade
Co-ed Little league baseball program. Other sports leagues include basketball, tennis and volleyball. Call for specific age requirements.

■ The Young People's Chorus of New York
Lexington Avenue at 92nd Street in residence at The 92nd Street Y
415-5579
Ages: 8 +
An ensemble of 150 boys and girls; by audition only.

■ Zujitsu Training Center B
210 East 23rd Street between Second and Third Avenues, 4th Floor
779-4033
Ages: 6 +
Instruction in contemporary martial arts.

Subject Index

Neighborhood Locator

es   East Side, East 23rd Street through and including East 60th Street

lm   Lower Manhattan, below 23rd Street

mul multiple locations

ou   Outside the borough of Manhattan

ues Upper East Side, East 61st Street up to East 110th Street

um   Upper Manhattan, 110th Street and above

uws Upper West Side, West 61st Street up to West 110th Street

ws   West Side, West 23rd Street through and including West 60th Street

Acting, including Comedy, Drama, Musical Theater, Speech, Theater Arts and Voice

Theatrical Workshops for Children mul
Vanderbilt YMCA es
Video Associates Studio ws
Weist Barron Studios ws
West Side YMCA uws

After-School Programs

ACT Programs at Cathedral of St. John the Divine um
After School Workshop ues
Asser Levy Recreation Center es
The Calhoun School uws
Carmine Recreation Center lm
The Children's Aid Society - Greenwich Village Center lm
Dalton Serendipity Program ues
Friends Seminary lm
Goddard-Riverside Community Center uws
Madison Square Boys' and Girls' Club es
Recreation Center 54 es
Rhinelander Children's Center ues
Rodeph Sholom School uws
Spence School - Second Act ues
Thomas Jefferson Recreation Center um
Village Community School lm
West Side YMCA uws
YWCA of the City of New York es

Art, including Arts and Crafts, Ceramics, Drawing, Painting, Sculpting and Visual Arts.

14th Street Y lm
74th Street Magic ues
92nd Street Y ues
After School Workshop ues
Alfred E. Smith Recreation lm
Art Safari lm
Art Students League ws
Asphalt Green ues
The Children's Aid Society - Greenwich Village Center lm
Church Street School for Music and Art lm
Columbus Gym uws

Discovery Programs, Inc. uws
Earthworks and Artisans uws
Elliot's Gym & Studio for Kids uws
Greenwich House of Music School lm
Greenwich House Pottery lm
Greenwich Village Youth Council lm
Henry Street Settlement lm
Hi Art mul
Lucy Moses School for Music and Dance uws
Marymount Manhattan College - Kids 'n Kin ues
McBurney YMCA ws
My Favorite Place uws
Parsons School of Design lm
Playspace uws
Poppyseed Pre-Nursery uws
Recreation Center 54 es
Rhinelander Children's Center ues
Rhythm and Glues ues
Robert Quackenbush's Workshop ues
Saturday Art School at Pratt Institute out
School of Visual Arts es
Sculpture Center ues
The Studio ues
The Sunshine Kids' Club ues
Supermud Pottery School uws
Third Street Music School Settlement lm
Vanderbilt YMCA es
West Side YMCA uws

Chess

Chess in the Schools ws
Manhattan Chess Club ws
The Sunshine Kids' Club ues

Circus Arts

92nd Street Y ues
Children's Tumbling lm

Computer Classes/Training

After School Workshop ues
Alfred E. Smith Recreation Center
    lm
Elspeth Sladden Computer
    Keyboarding uws
FutureKids ues
Greenwich Village Youth Council
    lm
Herard Center of Multimedia ws
Madison Square Boys' and Girls'
    Club es
Marymount Manhattan College -
    Kids 'n Kin ues
McBurney YMCA ws
Rhinelander Children's Center ues
The Techno Team Lab uws
Virtual Reality Pictures lm

Cooking

74th Street Magic ues
92nd Street Y ues
The Children's Aid Society -
    Greenwich Village Center lm
The Loft Kitchen lm
Peter Kump's School of Culinary
    Arts mul
Rhinelander Children's Center ues
Rhythm and Glues ues

Dance, including Ballet, Ballroom, Creative Movement, Hip-Hop, Isadora Duncan, Jazz, Tap and other forms.

14th Street Y lm
74th Street Magic ues
92nd Street Y ues
Abizaid Arts Studio lm
After School Workshop ues
Alfred E. Smith Recreation Center
    lm
Alvin Ailey American Dance Center
    uws
The American Youth Dance
    Theater ues
Arts Gate Center lm
Asphalt Green ues
B. Muse, Inc. mul

Ballet Academy East ues
Ballet Hispanico uws
Bridge for Dance uws
Broadway Dance Center ws
Chelsea Piers ws
Children's Acting Academy mul
The Children's Aid Society -
    Greenwich Village Center lm
Children's Movement Studio lm
Children's Tumbling lm
Dance Theater of Harlem School
    um
Dance Theater Workshop lm
Discovery Programs, Inc. uws
Djoniba Dance and Drum Center
    lm
Ellen Robbins Modern Dance lm
Elliott's Gym and Studio for Kids
    uws
Fred Astaire Dance Studio uws
Harbor Conservancy for the
    Performing Arts ues
Harlem School of the Arts um
Henry Street Settlement lm
In Grandma's Attic uws
Joffery Ballet School lm
Judy Lasko Modern Dance uws
Jump For Joy Disco-Robics For Kids
    mul
Karen's Performing Arts After
    School ws
Keystone Dance ws
Kids Co-Motion in Soho lm
Loco-Motion Dance Theatre for
    Children lm
Lotus Music and Dance Studios ws
Lucy Moses School for Music and
    Dance uws
Manhattan Ballet School ues
Martha Graham School of
    Contemporary Dance ues
Marymount Manhattan College -
    Kids 'n Kin ues
McBurney YMCA ws
Morningside Dance Works um
Neubert Ballet Institute at Carnegie
    Hall ws
New Dance Group Arts Center ws
New York School of Classical
    Dance ws

New York Theater Ballet es
Nina Youshkevitch Ballet
   Workshop uws
Perichild Program lm
Playspace uws
Poppyseed Pre-Nursery uws
Rain or Shine es
Recreation Center 54 es
Rhinelander Children's Center ues
Rhythm and Glues ues
School of American Ballet uws
Shuffles uws
Steps on Broadway uws
Telma Gama mul
Theater and Dance with Scarlett
   Antonia mul
Third Street Music School
   Settlement lm
Vanderbilt YMCA es
West Side Dance Project uws
West Side YMCA uws

Fencing

Blade Fencing lm
Metropolis Fencing School lm
Peter Westbrook Foundation mul
Stan Bardakh lm
Thomas Jefferson Recreation
   Center um

Gymnastics, including Rhythmic and Tumbling

14th Street Y lm
74th Street Magic ues
92nd Street Y ues
Asphalt Green ues
Champs Sport Club mul
Chelsea Piers ws
Children's Tumbling lm
Circus Gymnastics uws
Columbus Gym uws
Discovery Programs, Inc. uws
Drago's Gymnastics ws
Elliot's Gym & Studio for Kids uws
Gym Time Gymnastic ues
Jodi's Gym ues
Kids Co-Motion in Soho mul
Life Sport Gymnastics uws

Sokol ues
Sutton Gymnastics and Fitness,
   Inc. lm
Tumble Town es
Vanderbilt YMCA es
Wendy Hillird's Rhythmic
   Gymnastics uws
West Side YMCA uws

Horseback Riding

Chelsea Equestrian Center ws
Claremont Riding Academy uws
Riverdale Equestrian Center um

Ice Skating, including Figure Skating and Hockey

Champs Sports Club mul
Chelsea Piers ws
The Ice Studio ues
Lasker Rink um
The Rink at Rockefeller Plaza ws
Skating Club of New York ws
Wollman Rink ws

In-Line Skating

Chelsea Piers ws
Kids on Wheels mul
Lezly Skate School mul
New York SkateOut ues
Wollman Rink ws

Languages

14th Street Y lm
Berlitz Jr. ws
Child's Play East and West ues and
   uws
La Croisette French School for
   Children ues
Deutsche Sprachschule New York
   es
French Institute/Alliance Française
   ues
German for Children
Language Workshop for Children
   ues

Martial Arts

92nd Street Y ues
Aikido of Ueshiba lm
Asphalt Green ues
Asser Levy Recreation Center es
Chelsea Piers ws
The Children's Aid Society -
    Greenwich Village Center lm
Discovery Programs, Inc. uws
East Meets West ws
Gym Time Gymnastics ues
Japan Karate Association of New
    York uws
Kokushi Budo Institute of New
    York uws
Kyokushin Karate ws
McBurney YMCA ws
Midtown Karate Dojo es
New York Budo ws
Oishi Judo Club lm
Perichild Program lm
Recreation Center 54 es
Rhinelander Children's Center ues
Richard Chun Martial Arts School
    ues
S. Henry Cho's Karate Institute ws
Seido Karate ws
USA Oyama's Karate lm
Vanderbilt YMCA es
West Side Tae Kwon Do uws
West Side YMCA uws
Zujitsu Training Center es

Music

14th Street Y lm
74th Street Magic ues
92nd Street Y ues
Arts Gate Center lm
Asser Levy Recreation Center es
Bloomingdale School of Music uws
Boy's Choir - Church of the
    Transfiguration es
Campbell Music Studio mul
Church Street School for Music and
    Art lm
City Music Schools uws
The Collective lm

Diller-Quaile School of Music ues
Djoniba Dance and Drum Center
    lm
Early Ear uws
The Family Music Center mul
French Conservatory of Music at
    Carnegie Hall ws
Gramercy Park School of Music es
Greenwich House of Music School
    lm
Greenwich Village Youth Council
    lm
Gymboree mul
Harbor Conservancy for the
    Performing Arts ues
Harlem School of the Arts um
Henry Street Settlement lm
The InterSchool Orchestras of New
    York mul
Juilliard Pre-College Division uws
Kids Co-Motion in Soho lm
Lotus Music and Dance Studio ws
Lucy Moses School for Music and
    Dance uws
Mannes College of Music -
    Preparatory Division uws
Mary Ann Hall's Music for
    Children ues
Mozart for Children ws
Music for Aardvarks and Other
    Mammals lm
Music, Fun & Learning mul
Music Together mul
Piano Partners ues
Playspace uws
Poppyseed Pre-Nursery uws
Rhinelander Children's Center ues
Rhythm and Glues ues
School for Strings ws
Singers Forum lm
The Sunshine Kids' Club ues
Third Street Music lm
Trevor Day School ues
Turtle Bay Music School es
West Side YMCA uws
The Young People's Chorus of New
    York ues

Personal Enrichment Skills

14th Street Y - Jewish life and learning Classes lm

92nd Street Y - Jewish culture programs, programs for children with developmental disabilities ues

Ethics for Children - Classes for the development of moral reasoning uws

Janet Nixon - Etiquette instruction mul

Knickerbocker Greys - Leadership training ues

Manners House Calls - Etiquette instruction mul

Organized Student - Organizational training mul

Prepare, Inc. - Personal safety training ws

Vanderbilt YMCA - Leadership Center, Youth and Government Club es

Programs for Young Children (2 and under) including Mommy and Me, Parent/child and/or Alternative nursery

Note: entries marked * include programming for children 18 months and younger.

14th Street Y* lm
74th Street Magic* ues
92nd Street Y* ues
Abby's Place uws
Abizaid Arts Studio lm
Aerobic West Fitness Club/Swim Program* uws
American Youth Dance Theater ues
Asphalt Green ues
Asser Levy Recreation Center es
B. Muse, Inc. uws
Ballet Academy East ues
Bloomingdale School of Music* uws
Broadway Dance Center ws
Campbell Music Studio uws

Chelsea Piers* ws
The Children's Aid Society - Greenwich Village Center lm
Children's Athletic Training Center - CATS* es/ues/uws
The Children's Oasis* lm
Child's Play East and West* ues/uws
Church Street School for Music & Art lm
Circus Gymnastics* uws
Columbus Gym* uws
La Croisette French School for Children ues
Diller-Quaile School of Music* ues
Discoveries for Twos Program um
Discovery Programs, Inc. ws
Early Ear* uws
Elliot's Gym & Studio for Kids* uws
The Family Music Center ues/uws
Funworks* mul
Greenwich House of Music School lm
Gym Time Gymnastics Center* ues
Gymboree* mul
Henry Street Settlement lm
Hi Art mul
In Grandma's Attic uws
Jack & Jill Playgroup lm
Jewish Community Center of the Upper West Side* uws
Jodi's Gym* ues
Kids Co-Motion in Soho* mul
Language Workshop for children* ues
LifeSport Gymnastics uws
Lucy Moses School for Music & Dance uws
Mary Ann Hall's Music for Children* ues
Marymount Manhattan College - Kids 'n Kin ues
Mc Burney YMCA ws
Music for Aardvarks and Other Mammals* lm
Music, Fun & Learning* mul
Music Together* mul
My Favorite Place uws
N.Y. Road Runners Club ues

Parent's Cooperative Playgroup at
   St. Bartholomew Preschool* es
Perichild Program lm
Playspace* uws
Playground Project Recreation
   Program uws
Poppyseed Pre-Nursery* uws
Rain or Shine* es
Rhinelander Children's Center ues
Rhythm and Glues* ues
The Sunshine Kids' Club ues
Sokol ues
Sutton Gymnastics and Fitness lm
Third Street Music School
   Settlement lm
Topspin Tennis Academy mul
Turtle Bay Music School es
Vanderbilt YMCA* es
West Side YMCA* uws
YWCA of the City of New York* es

Gym Time Gymnastics ues
Hot Shots of New York mul
Jewish Community Center on the
   Upper West Side uws
Joe Espinosa's Sports Club mul
Little League Baseball mul
Madison Square Boys' and Girls'
   Club es
McBurney YMCA ws
N. Y. Road Runners Club ues
New York Sports Club ues
Poppyseed Pre-Nursery uws
Recreation Center 54 es
The Training Floor ues
Uptown Athletic Club mul
Vanderbilt YMCA es
West Side Soccer League mul
West Side YMCA uws
Yorkville Youth Athletic
   Association mul

Science

74th Street Magic ues
Marymount Manhattan College -
   Kids 'n Kin ues
Rhythm and Glues ues
Science Development Program, Inc.
   ws

Sports and Athletics including Gym and Mini-Gyms

92nd Street Y ues
After School Workshop ues
Alfred E. Smith Recreation Center
   lm
Asphalt Green ues
Astros Sports Club ws
Basketball City ws
CYO Manhattan Youth Baseball
   mul
Cavaliers Athletic Club mul
Champs Sports Club mul
Chelsea Piers ws
Children's Athletic Training Center
   - CATS ues/uws
Dan's Cougars Sports Club mul
Empire All-Star Sports Club mul
Greenwich Village Youth Council
   lm

Swimming

14th Street Y lm
92nd Street Y ues
Aerobic West Fitness Club/Swim
   Program uws
Asphalt Green ues
Carmine Recreation Center lm
Elliot's Gym & Studio for Kids uws
Empire All-Star Sports Club mul
Marymount Manhattan College -
   Kids 'n Kin ues
Take Me to the Water mul
Vanderbilt YMCA es
West Side YMCA uws
YWCA of the City of New York es

Tennis

92nd Street Y ues
ACE-IT Junior Development Tennis
   Program out
After School Workshop ues
All City Junior Tennis mul
Asphalt Green ues
Chris Porte's After School Junior
   Tennis mul
Crosstown Tennis ws
Empire All-Star Sports Club mul
Gym Time Gymnastics Center ues

HRC Tennis and Yacht Club lm
HRC Village Courts lm
Jeff Nerenberg Tennis Academy
    mul
Midtown Tennis Club ws
New York Junior Tennis League
    out
Randy Mani Tennis Academy mul
Topspin Tennis Academy mul
USTA National Tennis Center out

Yoga

Abizaid Arts Studio lm
B. Muse, Inc. mul
Bridge for Dance uws
Lotus Music & Dance Studios ws

Other

92nd Street Y - Boxing/self defense
    ues
Alfred E. Smith Recreation Center -
    Gardening lm
Asphalt Green - Photography ues
Boy Scouts - Scouting mul
Chelsea Piers - Bowling, golf, rock
    climbing ws

Child's Play East and West - Home
    schoolers' groups ues/uws
Dieu Donné Papermill, Inc. -
    Papermaking lm
Elliott's Gym & Studio for Kids -
    Tooltime uws
Funworks - Free playtime mul
Girl Scout Council of Greater NY,
    Inc. - Scouting mul
Global Enrichment & Discovery
    Classes - Multidisciplinary pro-
    gram ues
Greenwich Village Youth Council
    lm
Madison Square Boys' and Girls'
    Club - Poetry workshop and
    youth employment service es
Marymount Manhattan College -
    Kids 'n Kin - Math and reading
    program ues
New York Sailing School - Sailing
    out
The Origami Workshop - Origami
    mul
The Training Gym - Boxing ues
Vanderbilt YMCA - Teen center,
    earth service corp., Virtual Y
    (literacy program)

Boredom Busters

Boredom Busters consist of a wide range of everyday drop-in activities and in and around town adventures. So whether you are looking to provide some cabin fever relief or trying to plan something for that upcoming day off from school, Boredom Busters will provide just the inspiration needed to help you keep them busy.

Entries are listed in alphabetical order and include the activity, location, phone number, ages best served and a brief description. For some entries, such as the one for Central Park, we follow a different format to better provide you with the full range of possibilities. We recommend calling for detailed information and, when appropriate, making reservations.

B   for birthday possibilities
HA   for handicapped accessible or **HAL** for handicapped accessible/limited

■ Arts Connection HA
120 West 46th Street between Sixth and Seventh Avenues
302-7433
Ages best served: 5 +
"Saturday Alive" family workshops followed by a performance.

■ Asphalt Green HA B
555 East 90th Street between York Avenue and 91st Street
369-8890
Ages best served: 6 months + , with adult
Open swimming sessions in Olympic and Delacorte (smaller and warmer) pools. Call for hours and rates.

- Bowlmor Lanes HA B
110 University Place between 12th and 13th Streets
255-8188
Ages best served: 4 +
Bumper bowling for beginners, regular bowling for older children
and adults.

- Bryant Park
42nd Street and Sixth Avenue
922-9393
During the summer months there are various activities for kids. Call
for details.

- Carl Schurz Park
86th Street and East End Avenue
A beautiful park overlooking the East River that has a playground,
doggie playground and areas for biking and rollerblading.

- Carnegie Hall Individual Tours HA
57th Street at Seventh Avenue
247-7800
Ages best served: 5 +
Weekday tours available to find out what goes on behind the scenes
at Carnegie Hall.

- Central Park
From 59th Street (or Central Park South) to 110th Street and from
Central Park West to Fifth Avenue.
360-3444
840 acres in total and with many playgrounds and special spots
within it, the park is available to visitors for most activities with the
exception of barbecuing. To find out more about the park, you can
get a quarterly publication, "Central Park Views," produced by the
Central Park Conservancy. It provides lots of valuable information
about the park and upcoming programs and events. You can pick
up a copy free at any of the visitors' centers: The Charles A. Dana
Discovery Center, The Dairy, Belvedere Castle and The North
Meadow Recreation Center (locations listed below). Copies of
"Central Park Views" are mailed to Central Park Conservancy
members free. For membership information call
310-6641.

Listed below are some of the special spots in Central Park of particular interest to children.

Alice in Wonderland Sculpture. Near Fifth Avenue at 75th Street.

Balto the Sled Dog Statue. East side of the park at 67th Street.

Carriage Rides. Located on 59th Street between Fifth and Sixth Avenues or at Tavern on the Green.

The Carousel. Mid-park at 64th Street, 879-0244; 396-1010, extension 14, for birthday party reservations.

Cleopatra's Needle. Behind the Metropolitan Museum at 81st Street.

Conservatory Garden. At 105th Street and Fifth Avenue.

Conservatory Water. Enter the park at 72nd and head north along Fifth Avenue.

The Charles A. Dana Discovery Center. At 110th Street between Fifth and Lenox Avenues, 860-1370. Nature classes, arts and crafts, family workshops and fishing (photo ID required for fishing).

The Dairy. Mid-park at 65th Street, 794-6564. Displays, interactive computer programs and models provide visitors with information on the design, architecture and history of Central Park.

Delacorte Clock. North of the Central Park Zoo at 65th Street.

Hans Christian Anderson Statue. On the east side of the park at 72nd Street.

Henry Luce Nature Observatory. Located in Belvedere Castle at 79th Street south of Turtle Pond, 772-0210. Learn about the nature all around us, even in Manhattan. Identify bugs, birds and much more.

Loeb Boathouse. East Drive at 74th Street, 517-2233 for dining reservations. Rent boats with lifejackets; available mid-March through October. ID required.

North Meadow Recreation Center. Mid-park at 97th Street, 348-4867. Youth center offering a variety of outdoor activities, some available on a drop-in basis, others requiring registration.

Strawberry Fields. On the west side of Central Park at 72nd Street.

Wollman Rink. South of the 65th Street transverse in the center of the park, 396-1010. During the winter months the rink is prepped for ice skating. In warmer weather, Wollman transforms into a rollerblading rink with a special area dedicated to a basketball challenge course.

Trolley Tours of Central Park Grand Army Plaza at Fifth Avenue and 60th Street. Call 360-2727, 397-3809 for reservations.
Zoo/Central Park Wildlife Center/Tisch Children's Zoo. 64th Street near Fifth Avenue, 861-6030.

Some helpful hints:
When in Central Park it is easy to forget you are in the center of one of the world's largest and busiest cities. Use the same safety rules for your family as you would elsewhere in the city, such as staying away from isolated areas and being aware of your surroundings. The park is well patrolled but an ounce of prevention is worth a pound of cure.

Becoming geographically disoriented in the park is not an uncommon problem. One helpful tip is that on some lamp posts the cross street is painted to help identify your location.

Listed below are some important park numbers:
Information 360-3444
Emergencies 570-4820
Urban Park Rangers 988-4952

Playgrounds within Central Park:
East Side
Fifth Avenue between 67th and 68th Streets
Fifth Avenue between 71st and 72nd Streets
Fifth Avenue between 75th and 76th Streets
Fifth Avenue between 79th and 80th Streets
Fifth Avenue between 84th and 85th Streets
Fifth Avenue between 98th and 99th Streets
108th and 109th Streets; enter on 110th Street and walk south
110th Street between Fifth and Lenox Avenues
West Side
Heckscher Playground. Central Park South and 62nd Street; enter at Seventh Avenue and Central Park South and walk north.
Central Park West and 67th Street
Central Park West between 76th and 77th Streets
Diana Ross Playground - Central Park West and 81st Street
Central Park West between 84th and 85th Streets

Central Park West between 85th and 86th Streets
Central Park West between 90th and 91st Streets
Central Park West between 93rd and 94th Streets
Central Park West between 96th and 97th Streets
Central Park West between 99th and 100th Streets

■ Chelsea Piers Sports and Entertainment Complex B
Piers 59-62 at 23rd Street on the Hudson River
336-6666
Ages best served: varies depending on activity and skill level
Batting cages, ice skating, rollerblading, golf, and bowling available
on a drop-in basis during scheduled times.

■ Circle Line HA
Pier 83 at West 42nd Street
Pier 16 at the South Street Seaport
563-3200
Ages best served: toddlers +
The Circle Line cruise leaving from Pier 83 (West 42nd Street) takes
you on a three-hour cruise around the island of Manhattan.
Toddlers and very active children might find this too long an
adventure. Bring lap activities to provide additional entertainment.
The Pier 16 cruise is approximately one hour in length and tours
lower Manhattan.

■ The Craft Studio HA B
1657 Third Avenue between 92nd and 93rd Streets
831-6626
Ages best served: 3 +
Drop-in projects including painting plaster molds, flower pots,
watering cans and decorating chocolate with edible paints.

■ Dieu Donné Papermill HAL B
433 Broome Street between Crosby Street and Broadway
226-0573
Ages best served: 5 +
Tour a genuine papermill and see how paper is made.

■ Empire State Building Observatory HA
350 Fifth Avenue between 33rd and 34th Streets
736-3100
Ages best served: parental discretion

■ Extra Vertical Climbing Center B
61 West 62nd Street in the Harmony Atrium
586-5718
Ages best served: 5 +
Climb the walls, literally.

■ Fulton Fish Market Tour
165 John Street near the South Street Seaport
748-8590
Ages best served: 10 +
Tour the country's oldest wholesale fish market. Tours are offered
through the South Street Seaport Museum and require a minimum
of eight or tour is canceled. Call for scheduled dates, reservations
required.

■ Gracie Mansion HA
East End Avenue at 88th Street
570-4751
Ages best served: 11 +
Weekday tours of the official residence of the Mayor of New York
are available by reservation only.

■ Hackers, Hitters & Hoops HA B
123 West 18th Street between Sixth and Seventh Avenues
929-7482
Ages best served: 7 +
An indoor game park for sports enthusiasts.

■ Ice Rink at Rockefeller Plaza B
49th and 50th Streets between Fifth and Sixth Avenues
332-7654
Ages best served: 3 +
Experience the magic of skating in one of the most recognized spots
in the world. Skate rentals available. Call for public skating hours.

■ Ice Studio B
1034 Lexington Avenue between 73rd and 74th Streets, 2nd Floor
535-0304
Ages best served: 3 +
This intimate setting allows those testing the ice a perfect
opportunity. Skate rentals available. Call for public skating hours.
Closed August.

■ Kid Mazeum B
80 East End Avenue at 83rd Street
327-4800
Ages best served: toddler - 6
An indoor playground with opportunity for imaginative play,
climbing and music exploration.

■ Lazer Park B
163 West 46th Street between Broadway and Sixth Avenue
398-3060
Ages best served: 7 +
Lazer tag for the intrepid.

■ Leisure Time Bowling HA B
625 Eighth Avenue and 40th Street in the Port Authority Bus
Terminal
268-6909
Ages best served: 4 +
Bumper bowling for beginners, regular bowling for older children
and adults.

■ Liberty Helicopters
West 30th Street Heliport
967-4550
Ages best served: parental discretion
Aerial tours of the Hudson, lower Manhattan and up to Central
Park.

■ Libraries
The New York Public Library system contains a wealth of literary
works for even the youngest of readers. Children can get their own
library cards as soon as they can copy the letters of their names
(parents must supply proof of residency with three forms of
identification, such as a driver's license, cable bill, etc.). The library

branches listed below have children's areas and sometimes even entire children's floors. Programs offered vary but can include: films, story hours, workshops, computer games and instruction and, best of all, the opportunity to borrow some books. The Donnell Library, on West 53rd Street, has the honor of being the permanent residence of Winnie-the-Pooh and his friends. Call the branch you wish to visit for specific hours. A monthly calendar of citywide activities and events can be obtained at any branch.

New York Public Libraries' Office of Children's Services 340-0904
58th Street Branch 127 East 58th Street 759-7358
67th Street Branch 328 East 67th Street 734-1717
96th Street Branch 112 East 96th Street 289-0908
115th Street Branch 203 West 115th Street 666-9393
Chatham Square Branch 33 East Broadway 964-6598
Columbia Branch 514 West 113th Street 864-2530
Donnell Library Center 20 West 53rd Street 621-0615
Early Childhood Resource and Information Center 66 Leroy Street 929-0815
Epiphany Branch 228 East 23rd Street 679-2645
Harlem Branch 9 West 124th Street 348-5620
Jefferson Market Branch 425 Sixth Avenue 243-4334
Kips Bay Branch 446 Third Avenue 683-2520
Lincoln Center 127 Amsterdam Avenue 870-1633
Muhlenberg Branch 209 West 23rd Street 924-1585
Ottendorfer 135 Second Avenue 674-0947
Riverside Branch 127 Amsterdam Avenue 870-1810
St. Agnes 444 Amsterdam Avenue 877-4380
Tompkins Square 331 East 10th Street 228-4747
Webster Branch 1465 York Avenue 288-5049
Yorkville Branch 222 East 79th Street 744-5824

■ Lincoln Center Tours HA
Broadway and 64th Street
546-2656, 875-5350 tour desk information
Ages best served: 5 + according to interest
Behind the scenes look at New York City's most famous cultural center. Rehearsals viewed weekdays. Meet at the Metropolitan Opera House, the Concourse level next to gift shop. Call for weekly schedules.

- Little Shop of Plaster B
106 West 90th Street between Columbus and Amsterdam Avenues, 877-9771
431 East 73rd Street between First and York Avenues, 717-6636
Ages best served: 4 +
Paint plaster molds of your choice.

- Madison Square Garden Tour
Seventh Avenue between 31st and 33rd Streets
465-5800
Ages best served: 9 +
See what's behind the bleachers, visit a corporate box, check out the locker rooms and more. Tickets available at the box office.

- My Favorite Place B
265 West 87th Street between Broadway and West End Avenue
362-5320
Ages best served: 6 months - 4; classes are age-specific
An indoor playroom and toy store offering toddler and after-school drop-in programs at scheduled times.

- NBC Studio Tour
GE Building 30 Rockefeller Plaza between 49th and 50th Streets
664-4000
Ages best served: children under 6 not permitted
See what happens on television from the other side of the screen. Tickets are sold on a first come, first served basis.

- Nelson A. Rockefeller Park, formerly the Hudson River Park
Battery Park City
267-9700
Enter at the end of Chambers or Vesey Streets or at the World Financial Center, and walk north along the river. This site offers a fabulous playground with breathtaking views. Special events are organized for all ages including: recreational and arts programs, music and storytelling, after-school programs, drawing classes, fishing and walking tours. May through October.

- New York Skyride HA B
350 Fifth Avenue in Empire State Building at 34th Street
800 975-9743
Ages best served: 3 +
Big-screen flight simulator takes you for a ride over Manhattan.

- New York Stock Exchange HA
Interactive Education Center
20 Broad Street between Wall Street and Exchange Place
656-5165
Ages best served: 8 +
Self-guided tours weekdays at no charge. See what makes the ticker
tape tick.

- New York Waterway Cruises HAL
Pier 78 at 38th Street and 12th Avenue
800 533-3779
Ages best served: toddler +
A number of cruise opportunities available for various lengths of
time. Toddlers and very active children might find some excursions
too long an adventure. Bring lap activities to provide additional
entertainment.

- Our Name Is Mud HA B
1566 Second Avenue between 81st and 82nd Streets, 570-6868
506 Amsterdam Avenue between 84th and 85th Streets, 579-5575
59 Greenwich Avenue at Seventh Avenue, 647-7899
Ages best served: 4 +
Glaze the clay piece of your choice on a drop-in basis.

- Parades, street festivals and other happenings
The Mayor's Street Activity Office
788-7439
Calendar of Community Events delivered by automated voice
system.

- Parks
Special Events Hotline
888 NY PARKS

■ Playspace HA B
2473 Broadway at 92nd Street
769-2300
Ages best served: 6 months - 6
An indoor playground.

■ Post Office Tour - The Morgan Mail Facility HA
341 Ninth Avenue between 29th and 30th Streets
330-2300
Ages best served: for children 7 + only
Tours on weekdays of the Post Office's automated mail processing.
Generally a two-week advanced reservation is required.

■ Pull Cart HA
31 West 21st Street between Fifth and Sixth Avenues, 7th Floor
727-7089
Ages best served: all, with parental assistance
Drop-in craft wonderland.

■ Radio City Music Hall Tours HA
1260 Sixth Avenue between 50th and 51st Streets
632-4041
Ages best served: 10 +
Backstage tours of this world-famous theater.

■ Rain or Shine HA B
115 East 29th Street between Park and Lexington Avenues
532-4420
Ages best served: 6 months - 6
An indoor playground.

■ The Sony IMAX Theater HA B
Broadway at 68th Street in the Sony Lincoln Square Theater
336-5000
Ages best served: generally 4 + , but varies depending upon movie
content and parental discretion
Feature films especially produced for the Sony IMAX theaters.
Images larger than life put the viewer in the middle of the action.

- Sports Events
    Madison Square Garden
    Seventh Avenue between 31st and 33rd Streets
    465-6741
    The Garden hosts more events than you can imagine.
    Everything from basketball to hockey, from wrestling to the
    circus, from dog and cat shows to horse shows, concerts, tennis
    matches and more. For upcoming events call the Garden. The
    teams that call the Garden home include the New York Knicks
    and the New York Rangers.

    New York Giants
    Giants Stadium
    The Meadowlands, East Rutherford, New Jersey
    201 935-8222

    New York Islanders
    Nassau Coliseum
    Uniondale, New York
    516 794-4100

    New York Jets
    Giants Stadium
    The Meadowlands, East Rutherford, New Jersey
    516 560-8200

    New York Mets
    Shea Stadium
    Flushing, New York
    718 507-6387, 718 507-8499 for automated ticket and
    schedule information

    New York Yankees
    Yankee Stadium
    Bronx, New York
    718 293-6000

- Tin Pan Alley Studios
1 East 28th Street between Fifth and Madison Avenues, 3rd Floor
545-1344
Ages: 5 - 13
Make your own CD. Studio musicians accompany child's
performance of a collection of songs and/or instrumental selections.

- The Toddler Playground HA B
131 West 86th Street, 5th Floor
787-3356
Ages best served: 10 months - 4
Indoor playground September through April.

- United Nations Buildings & Gardens HA
First Avenue between 42nd and 48th Streets.
963-7713
Ages best served: children under 5 not permitted on tours
Visitors' entrance at 46th Street. 45-minute tours given daily.

- Web sites for happenings around town:
www.citysearch.com
www.newyork.sidewalk.com

- World Financial Center HA
Battery Park City between Vesey and Liberty Streets
945-2600
Ages best served: varies depending upon program
The Winter Garden located in the World Financial Center is a most
amazing indoor public space. Shows, concerts, dance programs,
family activities.

- World Trade Center Observation Deck HA
2 World Trade Center
323-2340
Ages best served: parental discretion
See Manhattan and beyond from way up high.

- XS New York HA B
1457 Broadway with entrances on Broadway and Seventh Avenue
in Times Square
398-5467
Ages best served: 6 +
Virtual game arena, Lazer tag.

Cultural Institutions, Galleries, Gardens, Museums and Zoos

Cultivating culture is serious fun in the Big Apple. The city's museums offer a variety of classes, workshops, lectures, seminars and other programs geared to inspire a child's natural creativity and curiosity. New York City's Wildlife Conservation Society, which has for over a hundred years encouraged visitors to care about our natural resources and heritage, is also responsible for one of the nation's largest urban wildlife parks. In addition, there are dozens of galleries and gardens to explore. Many of the locations listed below will be familiar to you. You may have even spent time wandering their corridors and paths as a child. You will likely be surprised however at the breadth of programming that is available for children and families at those same places today.

We also remind you that it is worth considering becoming a member of some of the institutions listed in this section, and not only because they are eminently worthy causes. If you plan on visiting a place several times over the course of the year, you may well find that the cost of membership beats the price of admission for multiple visits. Additionally, membership typically comes with privileges such as priority registration for programs, discounts and special members-only events.

You may notice that the entries in this section sometimes take you off the island of Manhattan. The ones we have included outside of Manhattan are, in our view, big enough, special enough or unique enough that we felt they deserved mention.

Entries are listed in alphabetical order and include the name of the facility, address, phone number, a brief description and the ages best served. Please keep in mind that in this section the indication for "ages best served" will sometimes apply specifically to the family programming that is offered. Many organizations provide an incredible number of opportunities for children of all ages to explore what they have to offer in special programs geared to particular ages. We recommend calling for detailed information and when appropriate, to register in advance.

B for birthday possibilities
HA for handicapped accessible or **HAL** for handicapped accessible/limited
S for summer programming (including anything from full camp to special summer workshops)
V for vacation programs

■ Abigail Adams Smith Museum
421 East 61st Street between First and York Avenues
838-6878
Experience New York City as it once was in this restored 18th century house. Evening and weekend programs for families. Special annual events for children. Ages best served: 7 + , programs for specific ages.

■ African-American Wax Museum
316 West 115th Street between Manhattan Avenue and Frederick Douglas Blvd.
678-7818
Museum honoring great African-Americans. By appointment only. Ages best served: for all ages

■ Alice Austen House HA B
2 Hylan Boulevard
Rosebank, Staten Island
718 816-4506
Alice Austen was famous for her contribution to early photography. This one-room farmhouse originally built in 1690 was home to the Austen family. Ages best served: 7 + , programs for 5 +

■ Alley Pond Environmental Center HA B S
228-06 Northern Blvd. Queens
718 229-4000
A 700-acre park is the setting for this center's many learning
opportunities. The indoor facility, wetlands and many exploration
trails allow visitors to study environmental history and science. An
extensive educational department offers many programs including
weekend, summer and special clubs. Ages best served: pre-K +

■ American Craft Museum HA B S
40 West 53rd Street between Fifth and Sixth Avenues
956-3535
This was the first museum dedicated to the work of fine craft artists.
Exhibitions include works from both established and emerging
artists. Ages best served: 7 + , programs for younger children

■ American Museum of Natural History HA B
Central Park West between 77th and 81st Streets
769-5100, 769-5200 for reservations and program information
The museum houses an extensive range of exhibits that cover the
history of human life and natural evolution. There is a Discovery
Room for children that requires tickets but is free of charge. The
Natural Science Center is also open to children for exploration at
specified times. Ages best served: for all ages, programs age-specific

■ American Museum of Natural History - Hayden Planetarium
81st Street between Central Park West and Columbus Avenue
769-5100
The Hayden Planetarium is being renovated. A new center for Earth
and Space is being constructed and will include a new Hayden
Planetarium. The opening is scheduled for the year 2000.

■ American Museum of the Moving Image HA B
36-01 35th Avenue, Astoria
718 784-0077
Near the Kaufman Astoria Studios complex at 36th Street. This
museum houses a wonderful collection of films and all kinds of
artifacts from the industry. Hands-on exhibits allow first-hand
testing of the principles and techniques used by filmmakers. Ages
best served: 5 +

■ American Numismatic Society
Broadway at 155th Street in Audubon Terrace Museum Complex
234-3130
The exhibition galleries have extensive collections of coins, medals
and paper money. An appointment can be scheduled for a tour
with a curator. Ages best served: 8 +

■ Anne Frank Center, USA HA
584 Broadway between Houston and Prince Streets
431-7993
An exhibit that explores the life of Anne Frank, her family and
other Jewish families during WWII in Europe.
Ages best served: 10 +

■ The Aquarium for Wildlife Conservation HA B
West Eighth Street and Surf Avenue next to Coney Island
718-265-FISH (3474), 718 265-3448 for program information
Observe an abundance of sea life. Daily performances. Programs for
children and families throughout the year plus summer and holiday
programs. Ages best served: for all ages, programs age-specific

■ The Asia Society HA
725 Park Avenue at 70th Street
288-6400
Permanent and changing exhibitions create an awareness and
understanding of Asian cultures. Ages best served: 10 +

■ The Bard Graduate Center for Studies in the Decorative Arts HAL
18 West 86th Street between Central Park West and Columbus
Avenue
501-3000
Interactive programs including gallery tours, artisan
demonstrations, theatrical role playing, book readings and arts and
crafts projects. Ages best served: 6 +

■ Bronx Museum of the Arts HAL
1040 Grand Concourse at 165th Street
718 681-6000
The museum's exhibits focus on modern and contemporary art.
There is a Sunday program for the whole family.
Ages best served: 5 +

▪ The Bronx Zoo/Wildlife Conservation Park HA S
Bronx River Parkway at Fordham Road, Bronx
718 367-1010 general information, 718 220-6854 program
information
Habitats house hundreds of species. Rides, shows, feedings and a
special Children's Zoo. Seasonal exhibits, programs, lectures and
workshops. Ages best served: for all ages, programs age-specific

▪ Brooklyn Botanic Garden HAL
1000 Washington Avenue, Brooklyn
718 622-4544
Situated on 59 acres; offering a variety of programs and activities.
Ages best served: for all ages, programs age-specific

▪ Brooklyn Children's Museum HA B S
145 Brooklyn Avenue at St Mark's Avenue, Brooklyn
718 735-4432
The exhibitions and many hands-on activities here provide the
materials for children to learn about the world and different
cultures around them. Many different kinds of programs are
offered for children. Ages best served: toddlers - 13

▪ The Brooklyn Historical Society
128 Pierrepont Street at Clinton, Brooklyn Heights
718 624-0890
Exhibitions on Brooklyn history with permanent exhibits on the
Brooklyn Bridge, Coney Island, the Dodgers, The Navy Yard and
Brooklynites. Note: The Brooklyn Historical Society building will be
closed for renovation during a portion of 1998/9. Call for details.
Ages best served: 5 +

▪ The Brooklyn Museum of Art HAL
200 Eastern Parkway, Brooklyn
718 638-5000
Some of the museum's permanent exhibits include traditional art of
Africa, the South Pacific and the Americas. Paintings, sculptures,
costumes, decorative arts and period rooms are on display. There
are collections of Egyptian, Classical, Middle Eastern and Asian art.
"Arty Facts" is a weekly series of workshops and gallery visits for
families. The museum offers many programs for all different ages
and interests. Ages best served: 4 + , programs age-specific.

■ Central Park Wildlife Center, Wildlife Gallery and The Tisch
Children's Zoo HAL B
Fifth Avenue at 64th Street behind the Arsenal Building in Central
Park
861-6030
A collection of habitats within various climate zones. Shows,
activities, workshops and special events. Adjacent to the Central
Park Wildlife Center is the Children's Zoo. This facility is filled
with opportunities to "walk with the animals." Ages best served: all
ages, programs age-specific

■ The Children's Interactive Jewish Museum B
14th Street Y, Sol Golman YM-YWHA of the Educational Alliance
344 East 14th Street at First Avenue
780-0800, extension 254
A museum set up for families to learn about Jewish feasts,. fasts,
celebrations and holidays in an interactive and educational way.
Ages best served: 4 +

■ Children's Museum of the Arts HA B S
182 Lafayette Street between Broome and Grand Streets
274-0986
Newly relocated and renovated, the Museum offers many types of
programs for children and families including dance and theater
workshops. Ages best served: toddlers - 10

■ Children's Museum of Manhattan HA B S
212 West 83rd Street between Amsterdam Avenue and Broadway
721-1223
Interactive exhibits provide a unique setting for children and adults
to learn about art, science and the world around them. The
museum offers classes, workshops and many programs for children.
Ages best served: toddlers +

■ China House Gallery/China Institute in America
125 East 65th Street between Park and Lexington Avenues
744-8181
Hosts special exhibits of Chinese art and other cultural items. The
Gallery offers workshops developed to enhance special exhibits and
can range from exploring the Chinese language to instruction in
calligraphy. Ages best served: 12 + , programs for younger children

- City Hall/Governor's Room HA
City Hall
788-6865
A self-guided tour of City Hall and the Governor's room for parties of ten or less. Larger groups led by a sergeant. Provides a lesson in local government. Requires a two-week advance reservation.
Ages best served: 9 +

- The Cloisters HAL
Fort Tryon Park, upper Manhattan
650-2280
The Cloisters, on a hilltop overlooking the Hudson River, a branch of the Metropolitan Museum of Art, is devoted to the art and architecture of medieval Europe. Special workshops are offered for families, typically on Saturdays. Ages best served: 4 +

- Cooper-Hewitt National Design Museum HA
Two East 91st Street at Fifth Avenue
849-8300
The Smithsonian Institution's National Museum of Design offers changing exhibits focusing on various aspects of contemporary and historical design. Ages best served: varies depending on exhibit

- The Dyckman Farm House
4881 Broadway at 204th Street
304-9422
The last remaining Dutch Colonial farmhouse in Manhattan. Demonstrations can be scheduled in advance. Ages best served: 7 +

- Edgar Allan Poe Cottage
Grand Concourse and East Kingsbridge Road, Bronx
881-8900
The cottage where Edgar Allan Poe settled in 1846. Built in 1812, the house has been restored and now stands in dedication to one of America's greatest literary masters. Ages best served: 10 +

- Eldridge Street Project
12 Eldridge Street near Canal and Allen Streets
219-0888
Tours available of this historic landmark synagogue. Ages best served: 5 +

- Ellis Island Immigration Museum HA
Ellis Island by way of the Statue of Liberty Ferry
363-7622, for ferry schedule 269-5755
The Ellis Island immigration station, which operated from 1892 to 1954, has been restored as a museum. Among the many exhibits, the museum displays countless artifacts donated from the individuals who passed through years ago. Ages best served: all ages will enjoy the boat ride, otherwise 6 +

- The Equitable Gallery HA
787 Seventh Avenue, the Equitable Atrium
554-4731
Offers tours of art exhibitions. Ages best served: varies depending upon exhibit

- The Forbes Magazine Gallery HA
62 Fifth Avenue between 13th and 12th Streets.
620-2389
The galleries display 300 pieces of Fabergé, 12,000 toy soldiers, 500 toy boats and an assortment of historical documents and other memorabilia as well as paintings from the permanent collection. Ages best served: 7 +

- Fraunces Tavern Museum
54 Pearl Street
425-1778
Tucked in the historical Fraunces Tavern, the Tavern Museum has a permanent collection of artifacts, decorative arts, paintings and prints from 18th century America. One weekend each month, the museum conducts programs for families and children. Ages best served: 3 +

- The Frick Collection HA
1 East 70th Street at Fifth Avenue
288-0700
Formerly a single family residence, now a museum. The collection illuminates the grandeur of turn of the century high society. Ages best served: children under 10 not admitted

- Guggenheim Museum (Solomon R. Guggenheim Museum) HA
1071 Fifth Avenue between 88th and 89th Streets
Guggenheim Museum SoHo HA
575 Broadway at Prince Street
423-3500
Both locations are home to a diverse collection of contemporary art. The Museum offers programs for children and conducts family workshops at scheduled times throughout the year. Generally reservations are required. A family activity guide is available free and relates to current exhibitions. Soho Tots: A program for parents and preschoolers (ages 3 - 5) includes a gallery tour followed by a story and simple activity; call 423-3587 for reservations. Ages best served: activity guide geared for 7 and under, programs age-specific

- Hispanic Society of America
613 West 155th Street on Broadway
690-0743
The diverse collection of work housed at this reference library and museum represents the arts, literature, and culture of Spain. Ages best served: 10 +

- Historic Richmond Town HAL S
441 Clark Avenue, Staten Island
718 351-1611
This authentic village of historic buildings, including a museum, takes you back in time. Ages best served: 10 + , summer programs for younger children

- International Center of Photography HA
1130 Fifth Avenue at 94th Street
860-1777
ICP is Manhattan's only museum dedicated to photography. Great photographic works are restored and on permanent display. Changing exhibits as well. Educational opportunities, lectures and other events take place year round. Ages best served: 11 +

- Intrepid Sea, Air and Space Museum HAL
Intrepid Square, Pier 86, West 46th Street and 12th Avenue
245-2533
A decommissioned aircraft carrier houses a museum of naval
history. In addition to the aircraft carrier, other vessels are available
to tour including a submarine. Talks and workshops are offered
occasionally. Ages best served: 4 +

- Jacques Marchais Museum of Tibetan Art
338 Lighthouse Avenue, Staten Island
718-987-3500
Tibetan and Asian works of art are housed in a building designed by
Jacques Marchais to look like a Buddhist mountain temple.
Surrounded by gardens, this museum seeks to promote a better
understanding of Tibetan culture, art, philosophy and history.
Weekend workshops, family programs, concerts, dance,
performances and storytelling are scheduled. Ages best served: 6 +

- The Jewish Museum HA
1109 Fifth Avenue at 92nd Street
423-3200
This museum houses the largest collection of Judaica in America.
Contemporary and folk art exhibits depict Jewish culture
throughout history. Sunday drop-in programs for children, story
time and gallery talks. Ages best served: 4 +

- The Liberty Science Center HA B
251 Phillips Street, Liberty State Park, Jersey City
201 200-1000
This science-oriented museum features an Omni Max Theater,
interactive activities, demonstrations, hands-on exhibits, classes,
workshops, special events and more. You can get to the Liberty
Science Center by car or by taking a ferry from the World Financial
Center to the Colgate Center in Jersey City, call 800 53 FERRY, and
then a short shuttle bus to the museum.
Ages best served: toddlers +

- Lower East Side Tenement Museum B
90 Orchard Street at Broome Street
431-0233
The museum draws the visitor to America's urban immigrant roots
through tours of its 1863 tenement building, neighborhood
walking tours, exhibits, performances and media presentation. The
Confino family apartment is open on weekends for viewing and
provides an interactive experience for families with children. Ages
best served: 6 +

- Metropolitan Museum of Art HA S
Fifth Avenue at 82nd Street
879-5500
One of the premier museums in the United States. Permanent and
special exhibits are devoted to representing 5,000 years of human
expression. Special museum guides are available for children to
facilitate interaction between adult and child(ren) during a self-
guided tour. Programs for children, families and teens are run
through the membership and education departments. Ages best
served: 6 + , programs age-specific

- Morris-Jumel Mansion
65 Jumel Terrace at 160th Street in Washington Heights
923-8008
This restored building was built in 1765 as a summer house and in
1776 established by George Washington as the headquarters for the
Continental army. Summer and after-school programs are
occasionally arranged. Annual Washington's Birthday Celebration.
Ages best served: K +

- Museum For African Art HA B
593 Broadway between Houston and Prince Streets
966-1313
A celebration of history and culture. Concerts, exhibitions,
lectures, workshops, films, family and weekend programs bring to
life African art. Ages best served: K + , occasional programs
scheduled for younger children

■ Museum of American Financial History
28 Broadway across from Bowling Green Park
908-4519
This very small museum contains a "wealth" of information and is
a neat place to visit perhaps before or after a look around the Stock
Exchange. Ages best served: 10 +

■ Museum of American Folk Art   HA
2 Lincoln Square on Columbus Avenue between 65th and 66th
Streets
595-9533
Changing exhibitions explore the treasury of American folk art.
Sunday workshops for families are scheduled periodically, generally
requiring reservations. Ages best served: 5 +

■ El Museo del Barrio HA
1230 Fifth Avenue at 104th Street
831-7272
Through paintings, sculpture, graphics, photography, archaeology,
films, music and theater, the museum highlights Hispanic culture.
El Museo del Barrio is one of the the city's foremost Hispanic
cultural institutes, offering music concerts, workshops and other
programs, some of which are appropriate for children. Ages best
served: K +

■ Museum of American Illustrators
128 East 63rd Street between Park and Lexington Avenues
838-2560
Changing exhibitions feature illustrators from around the world.
Ages best served: varies depending on exhibit

■ Museum of Bronx History/Valentine-Varian House HAL
3266 Bainbridge Avenue, Bronx
881-8900
The Museum of Bronx History is contained within the Valentine-
Varian House, which is a restored farmhouse built in 1758. Well-
known Bronx residents are featured in displays. Ages best served:
10 +

■ Museum of Chinese in the Americas
70 Mulberry Street at Bayard Street, 2nd Floor
619-4785
Housed in a century-old school building, P.S. 23, the museum
features exhibits, children's book readings, walking tours of
Chinatown. Specially scheduled family programs. Ages best served:
4 +

■ The Museum of the City of New York HA
1220 Fifth Avenue at 103rd Street
534-1672
The museum collects, preserves and features original artifacts,
documents, prints, maps and other items relating to the history of
Manhattan. One of the permanent exhibits features 18th century
toys and dolls. The museum offers various programs for children
and hosts several annual events. Ages best served: 4 +

■ The Museum of Modern Art HA
11 West 53rd Street between Fifth and Sixth Avenues
708-9480
The museum houses one of the world's largest collections of 19th
and 20th century painting, sculpture, photography and design.
Workshops, lectures, films, performances and special events are
offered for children and their families. "Art Safari," a guide created
especially for children, is available for sale at the gift shop. Ages
best served: 5 +

■ The Museum of Television and Radio HA
25 West 52nd Street between Fifth and Sixth Avenues
621-6600
The museum's collection of over 90,000 radio and television
programs offers everything from news, public affairs programming
and documentaries to the performing arts, children's programming,
sports, comedy shows and advertising. There are special events for
children during the International Children's Festival, typically in
fall and spring. Ages best served: varies depending on exhibit

■ National Academy of Design HA B S
1083 Fifth Avenue at 89th Street
369-4880
Offers after-school programs, seminars, weekend and family
programs, workshops, lectures, art classes and concerts. Ages best
served: 5 +

■ National Museum of the American Indian HAL
One Bowling Green, across from Battery Park
514-3700, 514-3888 for program information.
Past and present Native American cultures are celebrated. The
museum represents cultures from the Arctic to the Antarctic. One
Saturday each month the museum features a Traditional Native
American Performance Program. Ages best served: K +

■ The New York Botanical Garden HA B S
200th Street and Southern Boulevard near the Bronx Zoo
718 817-8700
Located on 250 acres in the Bronx, The New York Botanical Garden
offers educational programs and seasonal displays to assist visitors
in understanding the plant world. Ages best served: 5 + , although
at any age a stroll through the garden can be enjoyable

■ The New York City Fire Museum HA B S
278 Spring Street near Houston
691-1303
This renovated 1904 firehouse displays equipment used to battle
fires throughout history. Programs for children and their families.
Ages best served: 2 + , programs age-specific

■ The New York City Police Museum HA
235 East 20th Street between Second and Third Avenues
477-9753
Open weekdays by appointment only. This museum is located in
the Police Academy Training School and offers the opportunity to
view badges, counterfeit money, fingerprinting equipment, firearms
and uniforms. Ages best served: 7 +

■ New York Hall of Science HA B S
47-01 111th Street, Flushing Meadows
718-699-0005
Designed to improve the public understanding of science and
technology through exhibits, programs and media and ranked as
one of the 10 top science museums, the hall features the largest
collection of interactive exhibits in New York City. A variety of
programs for children including sleepovers are offered. The
Discover Room and Bubble Area are designed for preschoolers. Ages
best served: 6 +

■ New York Historical Society HAL
2 West 77th Street at Central Park West
873-3400
The permanent collection includes everything from American
paintings to sleighs. Changing exhibits highlight the history of the
city and state. Ages best served: 10 +

■ The New York Transit Museum HA B
Boerum Place and Schermerhorn Street, Brooklyn Heights
718 243-8601
The Transit Museum is located in a decommissioned 1930s subway
station. Learn about the history of our rapid transit system. The
museum offers weekend family workshops. Ages best served: 4 +

■ North Wind Undersea Institute
610 City Island Avenue, Bronx
718-885-0701
An environmental museum with many ongoing and hands-on
exhibits. Weekend guided tours given on the hour. Ages best
served: 6 +

■ The Old Merchant's House
29 East Fourth Street between Lafayette Street and Broadway
777-1089
This restored Greek Revival row house, built in 1832, was once
owned by Samuel Treadwell, a merchant, and provides an example
of living in 19th century New York. Ages best served: 12 +

- The Paine Webber Art Gallery
1285 Sixth Avenue between 51st and 52nd Streets
713-2885
Closed on weekends. This gallery features changing exhibits. Ages best served: varies depending upon exhibit

- The Pierpont Morgan Library HA
29 East 36th Street at Madison Avenue
685-0008
Each year the library hosts annual family days in the spring and winter with readings, events, performances and activities. Ages best served: 4 +

- Queens Botanical Garden HAL
43-50 Main Street, Flushing, Queens
718-886-3800
39 acres of gardens, including a Victorian wedding garden. Workshops for families are conducted. Ages best served: 4 +

- Queens County Farm Museum B S
73-50 Little Neck Parkway, Floral Park
718-347-FARM (3276)
This unique museum is an historical full-size working farm. Special events for families are offered on weekends. Note that this is primarily an outdoor experience. Ages best served: pre-K +

- The Queens Museum of Art HA
New York City Building, Flushing Meadow - Corona Park
592-2405
The museum has fine arts exhibitions, and the "Panorama of New York," an exact scale model of the five boroughs that was designed originally for the 1964 World's Fair, is on permanent display. Weekend drop-in programs are held year round. Ages best served: 4 +

- Sony Wonder Technology Lab HA B S
550 Madison Avenue between 55th and 56th Streets in Sony Plaza
833-8100
A one-of-a-kind, interactive science and technology center designed to showcase the latest in communication technology. After-school, weekend and family programs. Ages best served: 8 +

- The South Street Seaport Museum HA B
207 Front Street and the 11-square block historic district including
Fulton Street, South Street and 17 State Street
748-8600
Exhibits explore the workings of the waterfront district from
colonial times to present. Family and children's programs as well as
workshops are offered. "NY Unearthed," a satellite exhibit of the
South Street Seaport Museum, is located at 17 State Street. Ages best
served: 5 +

- The Spanish Institute
684 Park Avenue between 69th and 70th Streets
628-0420
Changing exhibits and language classes for children. Ages best
served: language classes for 2 +

- Staten Island Botanical Garden HA
1000 Richmond Terrace, Snug Harbor Cultural Center, Staten Island
718 273-8200
15 acres of wetlands, 13 acres of various gardens. Junior Green
Team and family programming. Ages best served: all ages

- Staten Island Children's Museum HA B S
1000 Richmond Terrace, Snug Harbor Cultural Center, Staten Island
718 273-2060
The museum offers many different opportunities for children to
explore and learn by doing and an outdoor area for picnics.
Weekend workshops and activities are offered for parents and
children, including performances, storytelling, films, concerts and
craft projects. After school and summer programs too. No strollers
in the museum. Ages best served: pre-K to 12

- The Staten Island Institute of Arts & Science
75 Stuyvesant Place, Staten Island
718 727-1135
A two-block walk from the ferry terminus. Changing and
permanent exhibits. The Staten Island Ferry Collection is located
within the Institute and provides the history of the Ferry Line
including large scale models. Ages best served: 7 +

■ The Statue of Liberty National Museum
Liberty Island
363-3200
Reached by boat from Battery Park North (for ferry information call 269-5755). View New York from the crown or visit the museum in the base, which features the history and development of the famous statue. Ages best served: 6 + , due to the 22-story climb to the crown.

■ The Studio Museum in Harlem HA
144 West 125th Street between Lenox and Seventh Avenues
864-4500
This museum contains works of African-American artists. Exhibits are installed each year featuring a diversity of work produced by new and established talent. Classes, workshops, concerts and various programs are conducted on a regular and special events basis. Ages best served: K +

■ Theodore Roosevelt Birthplace, National Historic Site
28 East 20th Street off Broadway
260-1616
The boyhood home of Theodore Roosevelt features artifacts from Roosevelt's life and presidency. Tours given. Ages best served: 8 +

■ Trinity Church Museum HAL
74 Trinity Place located in Trinity Church at Broadway and Wall Street
602-0872
Exhibits highlight the Church's history and the history of the city and nation throughout the Dutch, British and American eras. Ages best served: 10+

■ The Ukrainian Museum HA
203 Second Avenue between 12th and 13th Streets
228-0110
Family workshops are typically conducted around major holidays such as Christmas and Easter. Ages best served: family program 5 +

- Wave Hill HA
West 249th Street and Independence Avenue in Riverdale
718 549-3200
28 acres of public gardens feature an incredible number of plants from around the world. The Kerlin Learning Center offers workshops for visitors to gain a better understanding of the natural history of Wave Hill, the Bronx and the world we live in. Ages best served: 3 +

- Whitney Museum of American Art HA
945 Madison Avenue at 75th Street
570-3676
American art from colonial times to present, featured in permanent and changing exhibitions. The museum offers a Saturday gallery tour and conducts a Family Fun program once a month. Ages best served: 4 +

- Yeshiva University Museum
2520 Amsterdam Avenue at the corner of West 185th Street
960-5390
Changing exhibitions highlight Jewish life, history and culture. Throughout the year the museum offers special family workshops relating to Jewish holidays. Ages best served: varies depending upon exhibit

Index

Health, general information resources,
66-67
Health care practitioners
alternative health care, 56-57
dentists (pediatric), 57-58
doctors, 46-58
licensing requirements, 67-69
remediation-oriented professionals, 53,
68-69
special needs professionals,
210-216
Health emergencies, 87-90
caregiver preparation for, 7-8,
87-88
CPR training centers, 93-94
Emergency Medical Service (EMS), 88-
90
emergency rooms, listing of,
94-96
home resources for, 87
911 for, 88, 89-90
pediatrician vs. hospital, 88
Health screening, in-home
caregivers, 117
Historic sites, listing of, 370-387
Hockey, information resources, 351
Home safety, 71-76, 77-81
child home alone, 79-81
childproofing, 71-73
emergency phone numbers, 77-78
environmental hazards, 75-76
fire, 73-74, 91-92
home safety rules, 77-79, 80-81
information resources, 96-97
window guards, 73
Home schoolers, group for, 355
Horseback riding instruction,
information
resources, 351
Hospitals
emergencies, 87-90
emergency rooms, listing of,
94-96
faculty practices, 48
NYC hospitals, listing of, 61-62
parenting programs, 150-151
pediatrician affiliation, 50

programs for special needs children,
226, 227, 230, 231, 232
Housekeeper, -combination
caregiver, 105

I

Ice skating, information resources, 351
Independent schools
acceptance, 188
application process, 181-182,
185-188, 205
financial aid, 191-192
information resources, 14-15, 163-166,
178-181, 203
interviews, 183-184
legacy applicants/siblings, 189
and newcomers to city, 181,
190-191
parent visits, 178-180, 184-185
pre-admission testing, 182-183, 186-
187
private consultants, use of,
180-181, 190-191
researching schools, 178-181
and special needs children,
220-221
time to apply, 176-177, 186
for toddlers. *See* Preschools
transferring schools, 189-190
Individual Education Program (IEP), 217,
222-223
Individuals with Disabilities Education
Act
(IDEA), 216-217
Infants
activities/programs for, 353-354
shopping resources, 276-277
In-home caregivers, 100, 101-102, 104-
125
advertising for, 106-108
agencies for, 108-112, 138-142
au pairs, 103, 105, 112
babysitters, 100, 105-106
background/criminal record check,
114, 116-117
categories of, 104-105
changing caregivers, 123-125
-combination housekeeper, 105
cost of, 103
foreign persons, 105, 112, 118

nanny schools, 112, 141-142

placement agencies, 139-142

screening services, 109, 138-139

See also In-home caregivers

Neighborhood houses

neighborhood programs, 16

resources list, 19-21

Newspapers

advertising for caregivers, 106-108

event listings, 16

New York state, programs for special needs children, 217-219, 227-229

911

crimes, 84, 91

fires, 74, 91

medical emergencies, 88, 89-90

Nursery school. *See* Preschools

O

Option/alternative schools, 195

Orthodontics, 59-60

Outerwear, 239

shopping resources, 274

Outings in Manhattan, 4-10

balanced with quiet time, 8-9

carrying too much, 6-7

general guides for, 43

planning ahead, 5-6

and restless child, 5-6

safety factors, 7-8

transportation methods, 24-33

P

Parenting, 147-148

information resources, 149-152

publications on, 21

Parents League of New York, as information source, 14-15, 19

Parking in Manhattan, 33

Parks, listing of, 370-387

Parties

party goods, shopping resources, 277

See also Birthday parties

Pediatric care, information resources, 61

Pediatricians, 46-55

changing doctors, 60

credentials/certification, 48-50

and emergencies, 88

faculty practices, 48

vs. family physician, 46-47

finding doctor, 51

group practices, 48

hospital affiliation, 50

information resources, 61

insurance coverage, 50-51

interviewing, 52-55

licensing requirements, 67-68

national organizations, 48-49

-parent relationship, 54-55

solo practitioners, 47-48

Performances, 36-37

productions for kids, 36-37

resources list, 37, 43-44

time limits, 37

Personal enrichment, information resources, 353

Photographs, of birthday parties, 292-293

Physical handicaps

handicapped accessible activities, 356, 370

information sources on, 228-229, 232

Playdates, 39-43

blind playdate, 40-41

drop-off playdate, 39-40

making/confirming time, 39

sharing issue, 41

time limits, 42

trouble during, 40, 41

Poisons

childproofing against, 72

Poison Control Center, 97

Police

crime reporting, 84, 91-92

special units for reporting, 97

Police precincts

child safety activities, 85-86

listing of, 97-98

Preschooler activities, listing of, 353-354

Preschools, 158-174

age of child, 159-160

application process, 167-168, 204

competitive aspects, 158, 168-169

information resources, 163-166, 203

interviews, 171-172

licensing of, 169

myths/facts about, 169-174

researching schools, 162-166

time to apply, 160-162

waiting lists, 173

Presents

birthday, 291-292

thank-you notes, 292

Private schools. *See* Independent schools

Product safety, information sources for, 98

Psychologists, licensing requirements, 68

Publications

event listings, 16

resources list, 21

Public schools, 193-202

acceptance to special schools, 199-200

application process, 198-202, 205

districts, listing of, 204

evaluating school, 198-199

gifted and talented programs, 195-196

information resources, 196-197, 203-204

magnet schools, 196

option/alternative schools, 195

parent choice policy, 194

preschools, 163

special education program, 221-225, 227

time to enroll, 193-194, 198

variances, 195, 200-202

Public transportation. *See* Mass transit

Q

Qualities/competencies of, in-home caregivers, 114-115

R

Racial diversity, independent school information, 179

Reference checking, in-home caregivers, 115-117

Rehabilitation Act, Section 504, 216

Religious congregations, joining, 15

Religious groups

day care information, 133, 143

instruction/classes, 353

parenting information, 149

Resale shops, 277

Resource Room, 222-223

Restaurants, 34-36

behavior discussions with kids, 34-35

child-oriented places, 35

distracting restless kids, 35, 36

resources list, 43

time limits, 34

Restless child

at adult-oriented activities, 38-39

in car, 33

information resources for drop-in activities, 356-368

places to avoid, 6

portable playthings for, 5-6

in restaurant, 35, 36

during shopping, 38-39

S

Safe havens

firehouses/trucks as, 86

Safe Haven Program, 84-85, 98

Safety

and car services, 32

general information resources, 98

home safety, 71-76, 77-81

information resources, 93-98

on mass transit, 29-30

preparing caregivers, 7-8

street safety, 8, 76-77, 81-87

Safety belts, taxis, 27

Safety Net, 85

Sailing lessons, information resources, 355

Schools

application checklists, 204-205

evaluation areas, 155-157

independent schools, 175-193

information resources, 203-205

parent involvement in, 13-14

preschools, 158-174

public schools, 193-202

safety issues, 85, 156

Science development, information resources, 354

Telephone numbers, emergency numbers in home, 77- 78

Tennis, information resources, 354-355

Theater arts, information resources, 348-349

Theater. *See* Performances

Tipping, taxis, 25, 26

Toddlers
activities/programs for, 353-354
shopping resources, 276

Toys, 239
shopping resources, 278-279

Traffic, teaching child about, 83

Transportation
car services, 31-32
driving, 33
mass transit, 29-30
safety rules for kids alone, 83
taxis, 24-29

u

United Neighborhood Houses of New York, Inc., 17, 19

v

Vacation programs, information resources, 304, 370

Variances, public schools, 195, 200-202

Visitors at door, safety rules, 78-79

Vocal classes, information resources, 348-349

Volunteering
choosing activity for, 18
resources list, 22

Volunteer Referral Center, 18

w

Watches, store for, 279

Water quality, in home, 75-76

Wechsler Preschool and Primary Scale of Intelligence (WPPSI-R), 182-183

Wildlife centers, listing of, 370-387

Window guards, 73

World Wide Web
children-related sites, 16
parenting-related sites, 152

y

Y's
parenting programs, 149, 150
programs of, 15
resources list, 21-22
school fair, 197, 204

Yoga, information resources, 355

z

Zoos, listing of, 370-387

About the Authors

Diane Chernoff-Rosen, mother of two, is a graduate of Cornell University, Georgetown University Law Center and New York University Stern School of Business and practiced law in New York City for ten years.

Lisa Levinson, mother of two, is a graduate of Boston University and worked in advertising, marketing, and promotion for over a decade.

Today, in addition to raising their children, they are actively involved in volunteer activities and are the principals of Resource Marketing Group LLC.

To the reader: If we have not included your favorite resource or you want to make us aware of additional information to be included in subsequent editions, you can contact the publisher at:

Resource Marketing Group LLC.
1202 Lexington Avenue
Suite 341
New York, NY 10028

Addendum

Chapter 2 Hometown New York
Better Business Bureau, 257 Park Avenue South, New York NY 10016
889-6400 or 900 CALL BBB (900 225-5222)

Publications
Big Apple Parent. 889-6400

Volunteering
NY Philanthropic Advisory Service of the Better Business Bureau
www.newyork.bbb.org

Chapter 5 Home Safe Home and Beyond
Childproofing Services
Tight Security Inc., 148 West 83rd Street, New York, NY 10024
721-2121

Home Safety and Health
Environmental Defense Fund
www.scorecard.org (identifies sources of manufacturing pollution in
community)

National Lead Information Center and Clearinghouse
800 424-LEAD (800 424-5323)

National Safety Council
www.nsc.org

General
American Red Cross
Babysitter training for children aged 11 to 15, 800 514-5103

Chapter 6 In Search of Mary Poppins
Nanny Background Searches and Surveillance
Vanguard Security Inc. (B, S)
PO Box 450, Munsey, NY 10952
914 577-5729
www.vanguardsecurity.com

Peace of Mind (S)
201 387-7900

Nanny Employment and Placement Agencies
Real Kidz Care
Tuckahoe, NY
914 337-6857

The Robin Kellner Agency
2 West 45th Street, Suite 1503, New York, NY 10036
247-4141

www.4nannies.com

Chapter 7 The Enlightened Parent
Manhattan Mommy, new mothers group, 979-2720

Munch, new mothers group, 717-9922

Mothering Multiples, support group for mothers of multiples, 229-7503

Chapter 10 Shop Til You Drop
All Stars New York
175 East 91st Street between Lexington and Third Avenues, 831-6480. Unique sports gifts including cards, autographs, games, collectibles, furniture, wall coverings, photos and artwork.

Diesel Superstore $$
770 Lexington Avenue at 60th Street, 308-0055. Trendy, casual clothing for kids of all ages.

FuncoLand
901 Sixth Avenue in the Manhattan Mall at 32nd Street, 868-3156. New and previously owned game systems (e.g. Nintendo and Playstation) as well as game cartridges.

G.C. Williams
In addition to the items mentioned on page 254, this store carries a unique selection of European casual, formal (including tuxedos) and outerwear for boys.

Gimel Kids $$$
1383 Third Avenue between 78th and 79th Streets, 396-3570. Fine European high fashion clothing for boys and girls.

Little Stars NYC $$
968 Third Avenue at 58th Street, 829-1155. Furniture, equipment and clothing up to size 8 for girls and 16 for boys.

Paper House
1020 Third Avenue between 60th and 61st Streets 223-3774; 180 East 86th Street between Lexington and Third Avenues 410-7950; 269 Amsterdam at 72nd Street 724-8085; 678 Broadway at 3rd Street 388-0082. Party supplies.

Party City
38 West 14th Street between 5th and 6th Avenues, 271-7310. Party supplies.

Shanghai Tang $$$
667 Madison Avenue at 61st Street, 888-0111. Unique fine clothing for boys and girls up to size 8.

Swinging Monkey
1349 Lexington Avenue between 89th and 90th Streets, 996-5528.
Personalized toys, decorative accessories, gift items for babies and
children and unique gift baskets.

Tootsies
Note the new address: 555 Hudson Street, 242-0182

Chapter 12 Keeping the Kids Busy and Yourself Sane
Parents League Summer in New York City, a comprehensive listing
of summer activities in and around New York City for toddlers to
teens. Free to Parent League members. 737-7385.

74th Street Magic. In addition to activities listed on page 305, 74th
Street Magic also offers sports classes.

After School Art, Inc., 1520 York Avenue, 718 941-4885. Classes in
drawing, painting and sculpture for grade K+.

Applause Musical Workshop on page 307 should be Applause
Theatrical Workshop, 802-4816

Big Apple Sports Club, multiple locations, 987-9865. After school
sports programs in roller hockey, basketball, soccer, football, baseball, lacrosse and organized games, competitive sports leagues in
baseball, soccer and basketball, travel teams, homework help, summer camp and holiday.

Diamond Sokolow Dance Studio, 418 West 51st Street, 581-6365.
Creative movement classes for ages 4-8, modern dance for ages 9+.

Free to be Under Three at the All Souls Church at Lexington Avenue
and 80th Street, 253-2040. Classes for children between 4 and 34
months focusing on language acquisition and large and small motor
skills.

Kids Co-Motion. Additional locations: The Soundings, 280 Rector
Place, 2nd floor, Battery Park City and Reebok Sports Club at 68th
Street and Columbus Avenue.

Mary Beth Griffith, multiple locations, 874-7966. Irish Step
Dancing for ages 3 - 15.

Next Generation Yoga, 102 West 73rd Street, 595-9306. Private or
small group yoga instruction for infants, children and those with
special needs.

Tootsies Too! 555 Hudson Street, 242-0182. Painting, drawing, jewelry making, pottery and weaving classes for ages 6-10. Drop-in
activities for ages 2-5.

Authors note: Last but not least, a very special thank you to Joel
and Matthew.